HOW TO BEAT THOSE
CORDON BLEUS

HOW TO BEAT THOSE CORDON BLEUS

Rita Leinwand's Lessons in French and Other Great Cuisines

BY RITA LEINWAND • LOIS PEYSER

ILLUSTRATED BY FRAN RABOFF

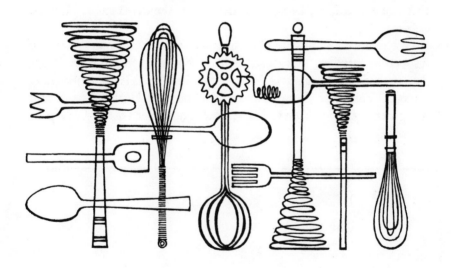

THE WARD RITCHIE PRESS • PASADENA

ACKNOWLEDGMENTS

Special thanks to Judie Robinson and Ann Shea who assisted in preparing this manuscript.

Our appreciation to all past and present assistants, particularly: Helen Beyer, Nell Benedict, and Shirley Hart for their constant and creative ideas; Anne Kupper, manager of the Williams-Sonoma Gourmet Shop in Beverly Hills, and Lynn Pennington for their early guidance; and Katie McIntyre, Shari McCloud, Helen Jacobs, Inez Korsen, Trudy Gilbert, Marge Jacobs, Sondra Stark, Mimi Grossman, Joy Chow, and Dee Shkolnik for their time and efforts.

To Florence Warner for proofreading, and to Kit Snedeker, Gemma Raso, and Nina Bauman for being helpful whenever needed.

Our gratitude to Lois Hotchkiss, Principal, University-Palisades Community Adult School, Los Angeles, for her interest and encouragement. Thanks also to her staff, particularly Chris Carlson and Rae Kinard, for being so patient with the demands of all those classes.

Our warmest thanks for their support through the years go to our respective families: Sara and Sidney Nurkin, Jo Nurkin, Mary Binder, Sylvan, Shari, and Marc Leinwand, and Irene Corona; to Arnold, Tom and Tony Peyser, Pauline and Harry Green, and Margaret Sabl; to Albert, Ellen, and Laura Raboff, and Marjorie Simon.

CONTENTS

To Three Perfect Husbands:

Sylvan Leinwand

Arnold Peyser

Albert Raboff

Introduction

I T HAS BECOME painfully obvious that the cost of food will keep going up, and the price of an elegant restaurant dinner will become more and more of a luxury. One way to have delicious meals is to cook imaginatively . . . that is the goal of *How to Beat Those Cordon Bleus*. This book emphasizes techniques that are called for again and again in cooking. Once you have mastered these techniques, the soufflé will always rise, the sauce will never curdle, and the meringue will never weep. Experienced cooks will reinforce their knowledge and novices will cease to be novices.

The recipes presented have been tested by thousands of students over the years in Rita Leinwand's classes in French and Other Great Cuisines. Each dish has been chosen to illustrate a particular technique that can be used in many other dishes.

Fast-and-easy recipes are included, along with those which require time and effort. Many enthusiastic cooks have limited time for preparing food, so we have devised shortcuts that will reproduce almost exactly the taste of the original recipe. For example, when using stocks, it is better to have homemade chicken and beef stock on hand in the freezer. Commercial stocks may be substituted, however, where needed. Fresh fruits and vegetables in season are always preferred, but there are times when they are not available or it is quicker to use the frozen ones.

As you look through the book, you will notice that there are some "Perfect" recipes such as Perfect Pâté, Perfect Quiche, Perfect Roast Chicken, and others. We've called them "Perfect" because they have withstood the test of time and thousands of students.

It is our hope that this cookbook will not only assist you in trying to "beat those cordon bleus," but that you will also thoroughly enjoy yourself in the process.

GENERAL ADVICE

READ A RECIPE all the way through before you start cooking. As a matter of fact, read it through twice. This way there will be no surprises and fewer chances that at the crucial moment you will have to look around frantically for a substitute ingredient or a makeshift utensil.

Follow a new recipe closely the first time. Once you have tried and tasted it, then modify it to suit your own taste. By all means, make notes in your cookbook regarding ideas you wish to remember about the preparation of a particular dish.

Have all ingredients at room temperature, unless otherwise noted, and assemble all the necessary equipment before starting to cook. Whenever possible, double recipes, preparing one for immediate serving and the other to go into the freezer for use at a later date. One of the joys of the age we live in is being able to keep frozen foods and ingredients on hand for easy use.

The real art of cooking is the ability to correct the seasoning and consistency of the food all through the cooking process right up until the time it is served. Cooking involves working with living materials that vary greatly in size, flavor, and amount of moisture, depending on where they are grown. This, in turn, affects a recipe and means that you may have to be the final judge of how a dish should taste. If the flavor isn't rich enough, you may have to cook down the sauce to concentrate the flavor. If too much liquid has cooked away, you may have to add more. You will also want to correct seasonings (herbs, salt, pepper, and sugar) just before serving.

Part of good cooking is planning a balanced meal. Not every course should be rich or sauced. If the entrée is rich, make the first course and dessert course light. If you've made a gloriously rich and fattening dessert, go easy on the main course.

TERMS AND METHODS

Bᴀɪɴ-Mᴀʀɪᴇ: Literally, a water-bath. A method of placing a pan with food into a larger pan which is half-filled with hot water in order to cook gently or to keep food hot without further cooking.

Bʟᴇɴᴅᴇʀ: Fill a blender no more than two-thirds full. If necessary, blend ingredients in two or three batches. A good technique when puréeing vegetables in the blender is to push them toward the blades with a stalk of celery or carrot. This prevents bits of rubber spatula or splinters from a wooden spoon from getting into the food.

Bᴏᴜǫᴜᴇᴛ Gᴀʀɴɪ (Herb Bouquet): Traditionally parsley, thyme, and bayleaf. The herbs may be wrapped in a piece of cheesecloth and tied with string, or placed in an inexpensive metal tea infuser available at most markets.

Bʀᴇᴀᴅᴄʀᴜᴍʙs: Bread of any variety that is a day or two old, or stale, can be made into breadcrumbs. Toast slices of bread in a 300-degree oven until they are lightly browned. Break the toast into pieces. Start the blender, and drop the pieces of toast through the removable center of the lid onto the whirling blades. Store in a tightly covered container.

Bᴜᴛᴛᴇʀ, Cʟᴀʀɪғɪᴇᴅ: Cut ¼ pound of butter into small pieces. Heat in a skillet until the butter melts and the milk solids go to the bottom of the pan, leaving the clear butter on top. Carefully pour through a cheesecloth-lined tea strainer, and discard the cheesecloth.

BUTTER OR MARGARINE: Always use unsalted butter or margarine.

CHEESES: Cheeses should be stored on the top shelf of the refrigerator, when possible, and turned over every few days to keep the natural oils distributed evenly throughout. Leftover cheese should not be wrapped in its old covering. Instead, use fresh plastic, foil, or waxed paper. For the best flavor, all cheeses should be allowed to come to room temperature for approximately two hours before serving. Blue cheeses, Roquefort and Danish, or domestic, should not be wrapped airtight as they need to breathe. They can be kept on a dish with a small dome. After you cut a blue cheese, smooth the cut edge with the flat of the knife to reseal it. Blue or Roquefort cheeses may be frozen in small amounts for use in salad dressing but not for table use. Freezing makes them too crumbly. Any of the hard cheeses such as Parmesan, Romano, Cheddar, and cheeses with "eyes" (Swiss-cheese types), may be grated in the blender. Start the blender, and drop cubes of cheese through the removable center of the lid onto the whirling blades. Freeze hard cheeses in one piece and grated cheese in ½-pound portions so you will not have to thaw more than you are planning to use. Cream cheese freezes well if it is first blended with a little milk (or cream) and seasonings.

CHEESE DISHES: Add a pinch of dry mustard to all cheese dishes.

CHICKEN STOCK: Homemade chicken stock is preferable for most recipes, but commercial soup concentrates can be used when stock is indicated.

CHOCOLATE: Add a pinch of salt to all chocolate dishes.

CROÛTONS: Bread of any variety that is a day or two old, or stale, can be made into croûtons. Cut the bread into ½-inch squares. Slowly heat approximately ¼ cup of olive oil (enough to cover the bottom of a skillet) with one minced garlic clove. Do not allow the oil to smoke. Toss the diced bread in the oil, stirring constantly until golden brown. Store in a tightly covered container.

DEGLAZE: A method for removing and using the fine-flavored brown bits from a pan in which meat has been sautéed or roasted, in order to give color and flavor to a sauce. You deglaze the pan, often right after the meat has been flamed, by adding a small amount of liquid, bringing it to a boil, and stirring until the small bits are dissolved.

DILL: Use fresh dill whenever possible. Fresh dill may be preserved for one year in the refrigerator. Rinse the dill and place it in a one-quart, wide-necked jar. Pour over it: 3 Tablespoons of vinegar, 1 teaspoon salt, and 1 cup of very hot water. Cover and refrigerate. To use it, remove the amount desired, rinse under running water, and pat dry with a paper towel. (If dried dill is substituted, use dill weed.)

DOUBLING A RECIPE: Double the main ingredients only; for example, double the chicken or meat, but use only one and a half times the amount of liquid. Do not double the amount of sharp spices like cayenne or pepper. More can be added to taste at the end of the cooking period if desired.

DUXELLES: Concentrated essence of mushrooms. Also known as mushroom butter.

EGGS: Use extra-large eggs for all recipes.

EGG WHITES: 1 egg white equals 1 ounce or 2 Tablespoons. Egg whites may be frozen in plastic ice cube trays, one egg white to a cube. Allow to defrost at room temperature.

EQUIVALENTS:
Butter: One stick equals ¼ pound or 8 Tablespoons or ½ cup.
Cheese: Two ounces of grated cheese equals ½ cup.
Lemon: The juice of 1 lemon equals 2 to 3 Tablespoons.
Onions: One medium onion equals approximately 3 ounces. 1 pound chopped or sliced onions equals approximately 3 ½ cups.
Rice: One cup raw rice equals 3 to 4 cups cooked rice.

FLAMING TECHNIQUE: A technique of pouring ignited liquor (preferably cognac) over browned meats and poultry, and kirsch, Grand Marnier, or cognac over fruit. For meats and poultry, flaming establishes a base for the sauce, deglazes the pan, burns off excess fat, and tenderizes. For fruits, it enhances the flavor. Flaming at the dinner table is mainly for dramatic effect. Brown the meat or poultry. Remove all but 1 Tablespoon of fat from the skillet. Heat 2 to 3 Tablespoons of cognac in an 8-ounce copper pan. Ignite, using a match, and pour the flaming liquor over the food.

NOTE: *Be sure the electric fan over the stove is turned off while flaming, so that flames are not drawn into the fan.*

FLASH-FREEZING: A method of individual freezing for quick and easy use. To flash-freeze, place the items to be frozen (such as mushrooms, crêpes, shrimp, meat balls) on a cookie sheet not touching each other. Once frozen, pack them in a freezer bag. By this method, you may remove one or more pieces as desired, rather than having to thaw them all at one time.

FLOUR: Unless otherwise called for, use all-purpose unbleached flour. It is not necessary to sift flour when measuring, unless called for in a recipe. To measure flour, drop it lightly into a metal measuring cup. Do not pack or shake it down. Wondra flour is "instantized." Use where specifically called for in recipes and for thickening sauces, making noodles, crêpes, pancakes, and pie crusts, as it does not have to "rest" before using.

GINGER: Use fresh ginger when available. It may be kept on hand for weeks by placing it in a jar and covering it with sherry. When crushed fresh ginger is called for in a recipe, place a small piece of the sherried ginger in a garlic press. A touch of fresh ginger is excellent for bringing out the flavor in chicken and chicken soup.

HEATING AND REHEATING: Unless otherwise noted, all foods should be removed from the refrigerator at least one hour before heating or reheating.

HERBES AROMATIQUES: Seasoned salt.

HERBS: Fresh herbs are preferable when available. Most herbs are easy to grow, either outside or inside, and you may find there are several that you will particularly enjoy raising. If dried herbs are substituted, use one-half the amount of fresh herbs specified. Buy dried herbs in tightly stoppered bottles (not boxes) and in the smallest amount available. Bottled herbs should be stored in a cool, dark area, never in direct sunlight. Even in sealed bottles, the shelf life of herbs is six months. Write the date of purchase on herb jars, as it is important that herbs and spices used in cooking have not lost their flavor. Whole spices, such as whole nutmeg and peppercorns, have a far longer shelf life than ground spices. To test an herb's effectiveness, crush a small amount in the palm of your hand, and sniff to see whether it retains a strong bouquet. One of the more reliable brands of herbs and spices is Wagner's, Ivyland, Pennsylvania.

JULIENNE: Food cut into long, narrow match-like strips.

LEMON: The juice of 1 lemon equals 2 to 3 Tablespoons. Lemon juice may be frozen in individual plastic ice cube trays. Once frozen, the cubes may be placed in a plastic bag. The rind may also be frozen in the lemon juice for future use. Strain to use as needed.

LIAISON AU ROUX: A term used in saucemaking for the blending of a thickening agent with butter or fat.

MEASURING INGREDIENTS: Liquid ingredients should be measured in pyrex measuring cups. (Never measure hot liquids in plastic measuring cups as the cups may melt.) Dry ingredients should be measured in metal measuring cups.

MONOSODIUM GLUTAMATE (MSG): Use when preparing foods that have been frozen in order to refresh the food. "Ajinomoto" brand is recommended as it is a natural, not a chemical, product.

MUSHROOMS: Select mushrooms that are tightly closed around the stems as they are the most tender. Do not peel mushrooms. Wash them under running water and wipe off with paper towels. To keep raw sliced mushrooms from turning black, toss with lemon juice. Mushrooms can be frozen for use in cooking, but after freezing do not use them raw. Flash-freeze unwashed mushrooms, then store them in a plastic bag. To use frozen mushrooms, rinse the frozen mushrooms under running water until they are partially defrosted and clean. (They are easiest to slice while partially frozen.) Frozen mushrooms may require more time to sauté because of the excess moisture.

NUTS: To toast nuts, spread them on a cookie sheet and roast them in a preheated 350-degree oven for about 15 minutes. Nuts may be chopped by dropping them on the whirling blades of the blender through the removable center of the lid. If your blender does not have a lid with a removable center section, cover the top of the blender with a square of foil, and cut a hole in the center of the foil. Chop the nuts ¼ cup at a time and remove quickly from the blender, or you will have nut butter. Nuts should be stored tightly covered in the refrigerator to keep them from getting stale. They may be frozen indefinitely.

ONIONS: Onions may be grated in the blender. Cut into eighths, start the blender, and drop the onions onto the whirling blades through the removable center of the lid. If necessary, add 2 to 3 Tablespoons of white wine, or stock, to help the grating process.

ONIONS, GREEN, OR SCALLIONS: When using the white part of a green onion instead of a shallot, the green part of the onion may be minced and frozen. Use whenever a recipe calls for minced green onions.

PAPRIKA: Use Hungarian paprika whenever possible. The color and flavor of paprika is released when it is heated with butter before combining with other ingredients.

PARBOIL: To cook partially by putting briefly into boiling water.

PARSLEY: Use fresh parsley whenever possible. To store, fold a paper towel into quarters, and put it on the bottom of a glass jar with a tight lid so that any moisture will be absorbed. Rinse the parsley, shake it dry, and place on top of the paper towel. The parsley should last a week or two in the refrigerator. To restore limp parsley, soak it in cold salted water. Parsley stems may be minced when you want to add parsley flavor, but not too much greens.

Parsley   Pastry Bag

PASTRY BAG: A cone-shaped bag with metal tip used for decorating either main courses (for example, with mashed potatoes) or desserts (for example, with icing or whipped cream). Buy two fourteen-inch plastic-coated pastry bags at approximately two dollars each. Do not spend more, if possible. Buy either a Number 4, 5, 6, or 7 large-star tip. Place the empty pastry bag with tip attached into a one-quart, wide-necked jar. This will enable you to use both hands to fill it. The pastry bag should be only two-thirds filled. Fold each end in, then fold over the top. You may want to practice decorating technique using instant mashed potatoes.

PEPPER: Use fresh-ground pepper whenever possible. Buy white peppercorns, as they are more fully ripened than black peppercorns and are more flavorful without being bitter.

PEPPERS: Red and green peppers may be frozen. Buy them when they are in season or on sale. Slice and seed them. Flash-freeze them, then place them in plastic bags.

PREHEATING OVEN: Preheat the oven at 25 degrees higher than the recipes indicates for 10 to 15 minutes before baking or roasting. After you set the food into the oven, reduce the heat to the required degree. (This compensates for the loss of heat when the oven door is opened.)

PREHEATING BROILER: Preheat for 10 to 15 minutes before broiling food.

REDUCTION: Method of concentrating flavors of sauces and soups by cooking rapidly, uncovered, over high heat.

ROLLING PIN: A straight rolling pin is preferable. By using a sleeve, less flour is needed to roll out the dough.

ROLLING SURFACE: Marble and formica are the best surfaces for rolling out all doughs. Rolling cloths are not recommended.

ROUX: In saucemaking, a term for the blending of a thickening agent with butter or fat.

SALT: Use coarse (kosher) salt for cooking instead of the refined, as it has more flavor. Use lesser amounts of the coarse salt.

SAUTÉEING: Use equal parts of butter and one of the following:

margarine, olive oil, or salad oil. This will add flavor while preventing the butter from burning.

SEASONING: The general rule is to add salt and pepper at the end of the cooking process. The liquid in a recipe may evaporate as it is being cooked, causing the dish to be overseasoned.

SIMMER: To cook in liquid that is maintained just below the boiling point.

SOUPS AND SAUCES: If a sauce or soup is not flavorful or it is too thin, cook it uncovered over high heat to reduce the amount of liquid and concentrate the flavor. Taste frequently to be sure it is not being reduced too much.

SOUR CREAM: Once sour cream is added to a sauce, it must be heated gently, not boiled, or it will curdle. Crème Fraîche may be substituted for sour cream without the danger of curdling on reheating.

TOMATOES: Add a pinch of sugar to all tomato dishes.

TOMATO MAGIC: A commercial product of crushed plum tomatoes. Use where Italian-style tomatoes are called for.

VANILLA SUGAR: Pour a box of confectioners' sugar into a jar with a lid. With a paring knife, split a vanilla bean lengthwise. Scrape the inside pulp into the sugar, then add the bean itself. Allow to sit for two weeks before using. Use for sprinkling on dessert omelettes, cookies, cakes, and pancakes.

WATERCRESS: May be kept in a jar of salt water and refrigerated. To use, remove the amount desired, rinse, and shake dry.

WIRE WHISK: Metal utensil extremely useful for beating eggs and sauces.

hors-d'oeuvres

CHAPTER 1

Hors-d'Oeuvres

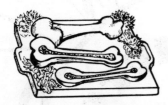

A guaranteed hit with men, women, and children and then with the dogs (when you've finished them)! The bones should be specially ordered from the butcher a week or two in advance. A good summertime hors-d'oeuvre that is probably better eaten outdoors.

CANAPÉS À LA MOELLE DE BOEUF
(Dinosaur Bones)

MEAT:

6 long beef-shin bones, split in half lengthwise (approximately 8 to 10 inches long)

BREADCRUMB FILLING:

4 to 6 large garlic cloves
2 Tablespoons paprika
1 cup breadcrumbs
½ to 1 teaspoon Herbes Aromatiques or salt and pepper to taste

Salad oil, enough to bind the filling

GARNISH:
Parsley sprigs or curly endive

UTENSILS:
Large roasting pan
Large platter

Serves 6

1. Cover the bottom of the roasting pan with crumpled foil. This will keep the bones from rolling over onto their sides. Arrange the bones in the pan.

2. Breadcrumb Filling: Mash the garlic and combine it with the paprika until it is a paste. Add the garlic-paprika mixture to the breadcrumbs. Season to taste with the Herbes Aromatiques, and add enough salad oil so that the mixture can be easily spread on the bones.

3. Spread the breadcrumb mixture over the bone marrow on each bone, pressing it firmly into the marrow.

4. Preheat the oven to 450 degrees. Bake the bones about 20 to 40 minutes, until the red color has disappeared.

Arrange the bones on a platter, and garnish with the sprigs of parsley or curly endive.

May be prepared two days ahead through Step 3, covered with plastic and then refrigerated.

May be frozen after Step 3. Preheat the oven to 350 degrees. Take the bones directly from the freezer and bake for 30 minutes; then increase the oven temperature to 450 degrees, and bake for an additional 20 to 30 minutes until the breadcrumb filling has browned, and the red color has disappeared from the bones.

A very special favorite of mine, and always a great success.

PIROZHKI À LA MOSCOVITE
(Russian Meat-Filled Pastries)

1 recipe of Cream Cheese
Pastry (see page 241)

FILLING:

3 Tablespoons butter
2 onions, chopped fine
1 pound lean ground beef
2 Tablespoons sour cream
½ teaspoon Sauce Diable
(available at local markets)
¼ cup cooked rice or ⅓ cup
toasted pine nuts
2 Tablespoons fresh dill, minced

½ teaspoon salt
¼ teaspoon pepper
2 hard-cooked eggs, chopped

EGG WASH:

1 egg
1 teaspoon water

SERVE WITH:

1 cup sour cream

*Makes 36 to 40 and
serves 10 to 12*

1. Prepare the Cream Cheese Pastry.

2. Filling: In a skillet, heat the butter and sauté the onions until golden brown. Add the ground beef and cook until it is slightly browned. Remove from the heat and drain off any excess fat. Add the sour cream, Sauce Diable, cooked rice or toasted pine nuts, dill, salt and pepper, and hard-cooked eggs.

Step 3   **Step 4**

3. To Assemble: Roll out the dough between wax paper to ⅛-inch thickness. Cut into two to three-inch rounds. Place 1 teaspoon of filling on each round.

4. Egg Wash: Beat the egg lightly and stir in the water. Paint the egg wash on the edges of the pastry rounds. Fold the dough over the filling, forming a crescent. Seal and decorate the edges with the tines of a fork. Place the pirozhki on a greased baking sheet, and brush with the remaining egg wash. Make a knife slash in the middle of each one to allow steam to escape.

5. Preheat the oven to 400 degrees. Bake until golden, about 15 to 20 minutes.

 Serve hot or cold.

 May be prepared one day ahead and refrigerated. Bring to room temperature and bake at 350 degrees 10 to 15 minutes.

 May be frozen before or after baking. Remove from freezer 30 minutes before baking or reheating.

Pâté is always elegant—and this happens to be a particularly good one. In addition to serving it as an hors-d'oeuvre, it can be used to stuff chicken breasts.

PERFECT PÂTÉ

½ pound butter
1 onion, sliced
4 Tablespoons shallots, sliced
1 green apple, peeled and chopped (⅓ cup)
1 pound chicken livers, halved
¼ cup cognac
1 teaspoon lemon juice
1 to ½ teaspoon salt
¼ teaspoon pepper

OPTIONAL:
¼ to ½ teaspoon Quatre Épices (see page 98)

½ teaspoon truffles, finely chopped or pistachio nuts
¼ pound butter, clarified

SERVE WITH:

French bread, pumpernickel, or melba toast
French cornichons (Gherkin pickles)

UTENSIL:
Terrine or 8-ounce soufflé dish

Serves 8

1. In a skillet, melt 3 Tablespoons of butter, add the onions and shallots, and sauté until they are golden brown. Add the chopped green apples, and cook for an additional 5 minutes, or until the apples are soft enough to mash with the back of a spoon. Place in a blender.

2. In the same skillet, heat 3 more Tablespoons of butter. Add the chicken livers and sauté over moderately high heat until they are browned on the outside but pink inside. Remove from the heat, and flame with cognac.

3. Put the chicken livers into the blender, and blend until smooth. Set aside the pâté and allow to cool. Refrigerate.

4. Put the remaining 10 Tablespoons of butter in a bowl, and cream it until it is smooth. Beat the pâté into the creamed butter, adding a small amount of pâté at a time. Add the lemon juice, salt, pepper, Quatre Épices, and truffles or pistachio nuts. Pack in a terrine or an 8-ounce souflé dish, and, if desired, cover with clarified butter or with plastic wrap to seal the pâté.

NOTE: *The puréed chicken livers should be cold before beating them into the creamed butter, or the butter will melt and give the pâté an oily texture.*

Before serving, remove the clarified butter, and use it for cooking. Spread a bit of butter on the bread or melba toast, then the pâté. Accompany with French cornichons.

May be prepared two days ahead and refrigerated.

Freezes perfectly for about three months. Pâté should be frozen in small quantities, so you will never have to defrost more than you will use.

Variation: Strudel à la Pâté de Fois Gras
Prepare one recipe of Perfect Pâté. Follow technique and recipe for Strudel using 6 to 8 phylo leaves (see page 254). Serve with 1 cup sour cream mixed with 2 Tablespoons dill.

These are really chicken wings—but always called drumsticks because of their shape. They can be served as an entrée, as a finger-food in a buffet, or as an hors-d'oeuvre.

SWEET AND SOUR DRUMSTICKS

12 chicken wings

COATING MIXTURE:
½ cup flour
1 teaspoon baking powder
½ cup Parmesan cheese, grated
1 teaspoon salt
⅛ teaspoon pepper
1 teaspoon paprika
½ teaspoon dried oregano
¾ cup buttermilk
Oil for frying

SWEET AND SOUR SAUCE:
1¼ cups pineapple juice
3 Tablespoons cornstarch
1 Tablespoon soy sauce
3 Tablespoons vinegar or
1½ Tablespoons
vinegar and 1½
Tablespoons lemon juice
3 Tablespoons ketchup
¼ cup brown sugar

* * *

Sesame seeds, toasted

Makes 24 sticks or serves 6

1. Chicken Wings: Cut away and discard the wing tips. Separate and disjoint the chicken wings into two pieces. With a boning knife, scrape the chicken meat away from the small end of the bone toward the opposite end, and push the meat over the end of the bone, so that it forms a ball. Discard the smaller of the two bones in the middle section of the wings.

2. Coating Mixture: Combine the flour, baking powder, Parmesan cheese, salt, pepper, paprika, and oregano. Dip the chicken sticks into a dish containing buttermilk, then into the flour mixture.

3. In a skillet, heat one inch of oil to 350 degrees. Add the chicken sticks, being careful not to crowd too many into the skillet at one time. Cook until golden brown on all sides, approximately 5 minutes. Drain them on absorbent paper.

4. Sweet and Sour Sauce: In a pan, combine the pineapple juice, cornstarch, soy sauce, vinegar (or vinegar and lemon juice), ketchup, and brown sugar, and heat until the sauce is clear.

If served as a main course, drizzle the sauce over the chicken sticks, and sprinkle with sesame seeds.
If served as hors-d'oeuvres, serve the heated sauce in a separate bowl so that the chicken sticks may be dipped in the sauce as needed.

Chicken sticks and sauce may be prepared two days ahead and refrigerated. Bring to room temperature. Bake at 350 degrees for 10 to 15 minutes.

Both chicken sticks and sauce may be frozen.

Variation: Baked Sweet and Sour Meatballs with Water Chestnuts Combine 1 pound of ground lean beef, ¼ cup tomato juice, 2 Tablespoons soy sauce, 1 beaten egg, ½ cup breadcrumbs, ⅛ teaspoon ground ginger and pepper. Drain an 8-ounce can of water chestnuts, and cut them into quarters. Shape 40 to 50 meatballs, placing a water chestnut at the center of each. Roll in toasted sesame seeds, and bake on a well-greased cookie sheet in a 300-degree oven for 20 to 25 minutes, turning several times. Heat in sweet and sour-sauce.

It's wonderful to make a double batch of these, half to freeze and half to serve.

PETITES QUICHES AUX CREVETTES
(Miniature Shrimp Tarts)

½ recipe Cream Cheese
   Pastry (see page 241)

* * *

1½ cups tiny bay shrimp,
   or 1 pound cooked shrimp
   cut into small pieces

FILLING:

1½ cups whipping cream
  3 eggs, lightly beaten
  ½ cup Gruyère or Swiss
   cheese, grated fine
  1 small clove garlic, minced

1 teaspoon dried dill weed
⅓ cup Parmesan cheese, grated
Salt and pepper

GARNISH:

Parsley or watercress

UTENSILS:

Rolling pin
2 miniature cupcake pans
Serving platter

Makes 3 dozen

1. Cream Cheese Pastry: Roll out pastry to ⅛-inch thickness; cut with a two-inch fluted biscuit cutter or the rim of a small glass. Press the rounds in the muffin tins. Divide the shrimp, spooning a small amount into each muffin tin. You may have to do this in batches to make up the three dozen.

2. Filling: In a bowl, combine the cream, eggs, grated Gruyère or Swiss cheese, garlic, dill, salt and pepper. Spoon the mixture over the shrimp, almost to the top of each muffin cup. Sprinkle with Parmesan cheese.

3. Baking: Preheat the oven to 350 degrees. Bake the tarts for 20 minutes, or until the filling is set and lightly browned.

Arrange the baked tarts on a serving platter. Garnish with sprigs of parsley or watercress.

May be prepared two days ahead through Step 3 and refrigerated. Bring to room temperature a half-hour before serving. Preheat the oven to 375 degrees, and bake for 10 to 15 minutes, or until they are heated through.

May be frozen after Step 3 in aluminum pans, and covered with foil. Remove from freezer 30 minutes before baking.

Variation: Mexican Spicy Jack Cheese Tarts—Filling
Combine 1½ cups whipping cream; 3 eggs, slightly beaten; 1½ cups Jack cheese, grated; 1 minced onion; 1 minced garlic clove; 2 to 3 ounces chopped green chiles; and 3 Tablespoons sliced black olives. Spoon into each muffin cup. See Step 3 above.

[27]

Quiche can be served hot or cold, as an hors-d'oeuvre, with the main course, or as a main course for lunch or a light supper. It's also good to take along cold on a picnic or for a box supper. Quiche can be made in a pie shell, but it is more attractive to serve if it is made in a straight-sided flan pan with a removable center.

PERFECT QUICHE

10-inch Pie Shell, prebaked
   10 minutes (see page 242)
1 egg white, lightly beaten
3 Tablespoons butter
6 leeks (white part only), split,
   washed thoroughly and sliced
½ pound smoked or boiled
   lean ham, coarsely diced
½ pound Gruyère cheese,
   coarsely grated

CUSTARD:

4 eggs at room temperature
1 egg yolk
1 cup cream, at room tem-
   perature
1 cup milk, at room tem-
   perature
1 teaspoon sugar
⅛ teaspoon nutmeg
Salt and pepper

Serves 6 to 8

1. Brush the bottom of the prebaked pie shell with the lightly beaten egg white.

2. In a skillet, melt the butter and sauté the leeks over low heat until they are almost a purée. Add the ham. Spread on the bottom of the pie shell. Sprinkle the cheese on top of it.

3. Custard: In a mixer, beat the four whole eggs and the extra yolk. Add the cream, milk, sugar, nutmeg, salt and pepper, and blend well.

4. Preheat the oven to 450 degrees. Spoon the custard gently on top of the cheese. Bake for 12 minutes, then turn the oven down to 350 degrees and bake until the custard sets, usually 30 to 40 minutes. It should be golden brown. If the custard sets before it browns, set the quiche under a hot broiler for a minute or two.

NOTE: *To test a baked custard, if it is to be served hot, insert a knife blade into the custard one inch from the center. If it comes out clean, the custard is baked sufficiently. If it is to be served cold, insert a knife blade into the custard one inch from the outside edge. If it comes out clean, the custard is baked sufficiently.*

 Serve hot or cold.

 May be prepared a day ahead through Step 3.

 Do not freeze.

Variation: Tomato, Leek and Bacon Quiche
In a skillet, melt the butter and sauté the leeks over low heat until they are almost puréed. Add the ½ lb. crumbled bacon. Spread on the bottom of the pie shell, and sprinkle the cheese on top. Slice 3 tomatoes ⅛ inch thick and arrange over the cheese.

Follow the directions above for Steps 3 and 4.

Guaranteed superb with fresh clams in the shell, and almost as good with the canned ones. If using canned clams, serve them in mushroom caps, on toast rounds, or in clam shells. (A good source for empty shells is a seafood restaurant.)

CLAMS OREGANATA
(Clams with Herbs)

USING FRESH CLAMS:

3 dozen littleneck or cherrystone clams in tightly closed shells

USING CANNED CLAMS:

4 - 7½ ounce cans minced clams
3 dozen mushroom caps, toast rounds, or clam shells

BREADCRUMB MIXTURE:

½ cup butter, melted
3 cloves garlic, minced
½ cup breadcrumbs
1 Tablespoon oregano
2 Tablespoons parsley, chopped
1 small onion, minced
¼ cup Italian white wine or dry vermouth
Salt and pepper

Serves 10 to 12

1. For Fresh Clams: Scrub and wash the clams in cold water. In a 4 to 5 quart saucepan, heat one inch of water until it comes to a boil. Add the clams, cover, and steam for about 2 to 3 minutes, or until the clams open slightly. Over a bowl, use a dull-edged spatula or flat knife and wedge it between the top and bottom clam shell to force it open. Allow the natural juices from the clams to drip into the bowl. Open the shells and leave the clams in their shells.

2. For Canned Clams: Drain the minced clams, reserving the juice in a bowl.

3. Breadcrumb Mixture: In a bowl, combine the butter, garlic, breadcrumbs, oregano, parsley, onion, wine, salt and pepper. Add enough of the clam juice to moisten the mixture.

4. Assembling: For fresh clams, spread the breadcrumb mixture over the clams in their shells, and place them on a cookie sheet. For canned clams, combine the clams with the breadcrumb mixture and spoon into mushroom caps, onto toast rounds, or into clam shells, and place on a lightly greased cookie sheet.

5. Baking: Preheat the oven to 375 degrees. Preheat the broiler as well. Bake for 10 minutes in the oven, then broil for 3 minutes.

 Arrange the clams on a platter and garnish with sprigs of parsley.

 May be prepared one day ahead through Step 3.

 Canned clam and breadcrumb mixture may be frozen.

Variation: Crab Oreganata
Combine two 7½-ounce cans of crab meat with ⅔ cup of Sauce Mornay (see page 89) or with mayonnaise, 1 Tablespoon minced parsley, and 1 teaspoon lemon juice. Spoon into mushroom caps, or onto toast rounds. Sprinkle the Breadcrumb Mixture over the crabmeat; place on a lightly greased cookie sheet. Bake as directed.

TIMBALES DE TOMATES PÂTÉ SAUMON FUMÉ
(Cherry Tomatoes Stuffed With Salmon Pâté)

40 ripe cherry tomatoes,
washed and dried

SALMON PÂTÉ:

4 ounces cream cheese at
room temperature
½ pound smoked salmon,
chopped
1 Tablespoon onion, finely
minced
2 Tablespoons lemon juice,
fresh
Heavy cream
Salt and pepper

GARNISHES:

2 teaspoons fresh dill or
1 Tablespoon dried dill weed
Capers, drained and rinsed
Watercress or parsley

UTENSIL:

Pastry bag with Number 5, 6,
or 7 large star tip, or a spoon

Serves 10 to 12

1. Tomatoes: Cut the tops off each cherry tomato from the stem end. Using the small end of a melon scoop, hollow out the seeds and pulp, leaving a quarter-inch shell. Turn upside down to drain.
2. Salmon Pâté: Into the softened cream cheese, blend the chopped salmon, onion, lemon juice and enough cream to give a creamy consistency. Add salt and pepper if needed.
3. Assembling: Turn tomatoes right side up. Using a pastry bag with a Number 5, 6, or 7 large star tip, or simply a small spoon, place the salmon pâté into each tomato. Put a caper and some dill on top of the pâté.

TO SERVE Arrange the timbales on a serving platter, and garnish with watercress or parsley.

AHEAD May be prepared one day ahead.

FREEZE Do not freeze.

This is an hors-d'oeuvre you can keep on hand for two weeks, and it gets more flavorful as the days go by.

HERRING ANTIPASTO

1 12- to 16-ounce jar herring snacks in wine
1 green pepper, diced
1 medium red onion, chopped
1 2½-ounce can ripe olives, sliced
1 12-ounce jar chile sauce
1 6-ounce jar marinated artichoke hearts, drained, and cut into small pieces

GARNISH:
¼ cup parsley, minced

SERVE WITH:
French or Italian bread or crackers

Serves 8 to 10

1. Drain the herring, reserving the juice, and cut it into julienne matchsticks. Add the onions from the jar to the herring strips.
2. Combine the herring and onions with the green pepper, red onion, olives, chile sauce and artichoke hearts. Add enough of the reserved juice from the herring to give it a piquant flavor.
3. Place in a covered bowl, and refrigerate at least twenty-four hours before serving to give the herring a chance to marinate.

Serve in a bowl, and garnish with the minced parsley.

May be prepared two weeks ahead and refrigerated.

Do not freeze.

The best and most colorful ceviche I have ever seen or eaten.

PERUVIAN CEVICHE
(Marinated Fish and Seafood)

FISH AND SHELLFISH:
- 1 pound firm, white, lean-fleshed fish (fillet of sole or halibut)
- ¼ pound small bay scallops, halved or sliced
- ¼ pound crabmeat (optional)

VEGETABLES:
- 2 green peppers, cut into julienne matchsticks
- 2 medium red onions, sliced paper thin
- 1 medium red onion, minced
- 1 to 2 small hot green chiles, chopped fine
- 3 to 4 tomatoes, peeled, and cut into cubes
- Juice of 8 to 12 limes or lemons

- 3 ears fresh corn
- 2 medium yams (or sweet potatoes), cooked (canned may be used)

* * *

- 3 to 4 Tablespoons olive oil
- Oregano, to taste
- Salt and pepper

OPTIONAL:
Cider vinegar

GARNISHES:
Cilantro or watercress, chopped
1 dozen pitted black olives
Paprika

UTENSIL:
Attractive glass or ceramic bowl

SERVE WITH:
Crisp buttered toast or tortillas

Serves 6 to 8

1. Wash the fish, and cut it into narrow strips, about ⅜-inch to 1½-inches. Put into a glass or ceramic bowl with the scallops, crabmeat, green peppers, sliced onions, chiles and tomatoes. Blend with a wooden spoon, and cover with lime (or lemon) juice. Refrigerate overnight, stirring occasionally. The marinade "cooks" the fish so that it becomes firm and opaque.

2. Boil the corn and cool. Slice the corncob into circles ½-inch thick. Cut the yams into ⅜-inch slices, and trim into decorative triangles.

3. To the fish, add the olive oil, minced onion, oregano, cider vinegar (if needed), and salt and pepper. Stir through carefully. Arrange the corn circles, yam triangles, and olives attractively on top of the fish. Sprinkle with chopped cilantro or watercress, and paprika. Refrigerate until ice cold.

Variations: The ceviche may be served in a hollowed-out tomato, or an avocado half, garnished with avocado slices and lime wedges.

Serve on individual plates with crisp buttered toast or tortillas using a slotted spoon so there will be a minimum of liquid. In Peru, you spear the corncob slice with a fork, and nibble the corn around the edges.

May be prepared five days ahead through Step 1 or one day ahead through Step 3.

Do not freeze.

A very special hors-d'oeuvre. You can keep the ingredients on hand, and make it up very quickly. Brie can be used as well as the Camembert.

CAMEMBERT EN CROÛTE
(Cheese in Pastry)

½ recipe Pie Crust (see page 242), or 2 frozen unbaked patty shells
1 4-ounce round of Camembert cheese (if domestic, remove the outer rind)

EGG WASH:
1 egg yolk
1 teaspoon water

SERVE WITH:
Cherry tomatoes

Serves 5 to 6

1. Roll out the pastry into a 9-inch circle.

2. Enclose the Camembert in the pastry. Trim away the excess dough. Set on a lightly greased pie plate, seam-side down. Paint with the egg wash. Decorate the top of the pastry with the excess dough, and brush again with the egg wash.

3. Freeze for 30 minutes.

4. Preheat the oven to 375 degrees. Take the pie plate directly from the freezer to the oven. Bake for 20 to 25 minutes or until the pastry is golden brown. Remove from the oven, and allow to remain at room temperature for 10 to 15 minutes, so the cheese is not too runny. (If the cheese is runny, it will reharden as the air hits it.)

Variation: Open Camembert Pie

1. Bake a pie crust the size of the round Camembert or Brie cheese you are using. (You may use an 8-ounce cheese.)

2. Remove the entire rind from the cheese, and set the cheese into the baked pie crust. Preheat the oven to 350 degrees. Set in the oven, and turn off the heat. Allow to remain in the oven for about 30 minutes.

3. Remove from the oven, and mark off (but do not cut) six servings. Alternate garnishes in each section, using any two or three of the following: chopped chives, chopped black olives, chopped pimiento, chopped walnuts, or chopped parsley.

Slice into five or six pie slices. Serve with cherry tomatoes.

May be prepared early in the day through Step 2 and refrigerated. Freeze for 30 minutes before baking.

Do not freeze longer than 30 minutes.

*Excellent as part of an antipasto platter or as
a relish to serve with meat or sandwiches.*

PIMIENTOS MEXICANOS
(Roasted Peppers)

2 to 3 red or green peppers
or 1 jar of whole red
peppers
2 Tablespoons capers,
rinsed and drained
2 cloves garlic, minced
8 Greek black olives,
slivered and pitted
Olive oil as needed

Parsley, minced
Fresh basil or oregano, minced

OPTIONAL:
Anchovy strips, drained and
washed

Serves 4

1. Roast whole red or green peppers on a hot barbecue or over the
   gas or heating elements on top of the stove, until they are puffy,
   turning them often. (They will then be easy to peel.) Peel, seed
   and core them, and cut into strips or dice. Allow to cool.

2. Arrange the peppers in a serving dish. Add capers, garlic, olives
   and just enough olive oil to make them glisten. Sprinkle with basil
   or oregano.

 Serve as antipasto with anchovy
strips.

 May be prepared three to four days ahead
and refrigerated.

 Fresh peppers may be frozen after they are
roasted, seeded and cored.

CHAPTER 2

Soups

INTRODUCTION TO SOUPS

No homemade food gets more acclaim from family and friends than soup. So many of us have been brainwashed by the canned soups that when we are treated to the real thing, it's like a new discovery. Homemade soup is as different from the canned variety as a fresh rose from a dried one, or garden-fresh asparagus from canned asparagus. The category is the same, but the aroma, the texture and the taste are from different planets.

Soup is the most general of all cooking terms; it covers a multitude of cooking styles and contents. In this time of high food costs and a scarcity of many foods, it is an excellent way to stretch the family budget and the meal. Soup served as a first course takes the load off the main course, and lessens the amount of meat you would otherwise buy. There are untold numbers of hearty soups that can be a dinner or lunch in themselves. They are elegant and unusual as well as filling and economical.

Good soup making is an art, and while it is not that difficult to master, it does require more than throwing any old thing into the soup pot. In France a chef is tested by the soup course, which is supposed to reveal the chef's talent and indicate the quality of the meal that is to follow.

Here are some general rules about soup-making that will help insure your success.

1. Soup recipes cannot always be exact as to the amount of liquid necessary, because the water content of vegetables varies so much from season to season, depending on the rainfall. Use the minimum quantity of liquid suggested at the beginning of each recipe. If the soup is too thick, you can add stock to thin it later on without hurt-

ing the flavor. If it is too thin, you can reduce the amount of liquid by cooking the soup uncovered over medium-high heat until it is the consistency desired.

2. When a recipe calls for a soup to be blended or puréed in the electric blender, it will be necessary to divide the soup into two or three batches. The blender container should be no more than two thirds filled or the liquid will overflow.

3. If the soup itself or any of its ingredients have been frozen, add a little Monosodium Glutamate to it while it is being reheated to freshen it. (Ajinomoto brand is recommended, because it is made from kelp not chemicals.)

4. In doubling a soup recipe, double the amount of solid ingredients, but use only one and a half times the amount of liquid called for, unless otherwise indicated. Doubling the liquid always makes the soup too thin.

5. The final touches are what make the difference between a fair and a good soup. Shortly before serving any soup, check the seasonings, add salt and pepper, and possibly herbs, if the seasonings have cooked away. Chilling food dulls the flavor, so it is particularly important to check the cold soups before serving.

6. Serve hot soups hot and cold ones cold. If possible, heat or chill the soup bowls immediately before serving. Nothing destroys the taste of marvelous soup so much as being served lukewarm when it should be hot, or at room temperature if it should be cold.

The recipes call for homemade or commercial beef and chicken stock. If homemade stocks are not available, commercial beef stock base and chicken stock base may be used, diluted according to the directions.

1. *Bouillon, broth, potage, stock, fond blanc (white or chicken stock), fond brun (brown or beef stock), and fumet de poisson (fish stock):* A clear-base extraction of meat, fowl or fish simmered for a long period of time with vegetables, herbs and spices in order to extract the maximum flavor from the ingredients. These extractions are the foundations of soups and sauces.

2. *Consommé or potage clair (clear soup):* This soup is served hot. It is bouillon or strained stock which has been clarified by the addition of beaten egg whites. It is served as a clear soup, and also with garnishes.

3. *Jellied consommé:* Served cold, this soup is consommé broth or stock which has been thickened by its own natural gelatin, or by the addition of unflavored gelatin. It is served as a hot-weather soup with garnishes.

4. *Cream Soups:* Served hot or cold, these soups are usually made with green vegetables cooked in milk and sometimes beef or chicken stock. This mixture is then puréed (mashed or pressed in a blender, food mill or sieve) and thickened with egg yolks and cream to give it a smooth consistency. It's usually cooked for short periods of time (20 to 40 minutes).

5. *Puréed Soups:* These soups are served hot or cold. Made with a meat or fowl base, they are thickened with flour, puréed (mashed or pressed in a blender, food mill or sieve), and cooked a short period of time (20 to 40 minutes).

   Exceptions to this rule are the puréed soups made with dried legumes, navy or black beans, lentils, and similar vegetables which require long, slow cooking.

6. *Velouté:* Traditionally served cold, this soup is made with a base of meat, fowl or fish stock, thickened with flour, and enriched with a mixture of egg yolks and cream.

7. *Bisque:* Served hot or cold, this is a cream soup made with a shellfish base.

This classic consommé is an excellent soup stock that is rich in taste, high in protein, and has dozens of uses. Although this is a chicken stock, the addition of beef is what gives the stock its rich and full-bodied flavor. It can be served as a broth with a variety of garnishes; it can be a meal-in-one with meat; and it is the base of many other soups, sauces, and main-course dishes. If you are going to do some serious cooking, you may want to make this stock on a regular basis, and keep it on hand in quart-sized containers in the refrigerator or freezer.

The exact amount of water is not specified because experience has shown that you get the most flavorful stock if you cover three quarters of the ingredients with water.

FOND BLANC OR CONSOMMÉ
(Chicken Stock)

MEATS:

2 pounds beef soup bones
2 pounds chicken bones, giblets and backs
3 pounds beef (stew meat, short ribs, or chuck)
3-pound fryer chicken, halved

VEGETABLES:

3 stalks celery, with leaves
3 carrots, scrubbed, unpeeled
3 leeks, white part only, split, washed thoroughly (Reserve green leek tops)
1 large onion, unpeeled, root end cut off
2 parsnips or turnips
6 sprigs parsley
5 cloves garlic, unpeeled, lightly crushed

HERBS AND SPICES:

3 sprigs fresh dill
1 teaspoon thyme
2 bay leaves
6 cloves
1 teaspoon whole allspice
3 slices fresh ginger, ⅛ inch thick
1 teaspoon peppercorns
2 teaspoons salt

* * *

Water to cover three quarters of contents

UTENSIL:

12 to 16 quart stockpot

Three or four quarts or serves 10 to 12

NOTE: *This stock should be prepared at least one day before using so that it can be chilled and the fat removed easily.*

1. Arrange the beef and chicken bones on the bottom of the stockpot. Add the beef, vegetables, herbs, salt and cold water to cover three quarters of the contents. Allow to come to a simmer slowly, or the broth will become cloudy. Simmer for 3 hours, uncovered.
2. Add the chicken halves. Cover the soup entirely with the green leek tops. Simmer for 3 hours more, or until the soup has a rich flavor. The leek tops keep the flavors from evaporating away.
3. Remove from heat. Let the meat and vegetables cool in the broth for several hours.
4. Lift out the chicken and beef and reserve for soup, sandwiches or salad. Strain the broth into large bowls or jars, and refrigerate overnight, discarding the boiled vegetables. Before using, remove and discard the solid layer of fat on top. Heat the stock until hot; add salt and pepper to taste.

Variation 1: POT-AU-FEU—The traditional French family-style boiled dinner. Reheat the chicken and beef in the chicken stock. Simmer any fresh vegetables desired until tender: carrots, celery, potatoes, turnips, green beans, leeks, or the like.

Variation 2: ALL-CHICKEN CHICKEN STOCK—Instead of the beef bones and beef, use an additional 2 pounds of chicken bones and 3 pounds of chicken.

Serve hot as a clear broth or with garnishes.

May be prepared four days ahead and kept tightly covered in the refrigerator.

May be frozen.

---

[44]

Brown stock is to soups and sauces what gold used to be to the dollar—the foundation. It's the base to the "mother sauce"—brown sauce. This is a good stock to make often, and keep on hand in quart-size containers in the refrigerator or freezer for making other soups, sauces, and main-course dishes. Served with the beef and freshly cooked vegetables, it becomes the classic boiled beef dinner.

FOND BRUN
(Beef Stock or Brown Stock)

3 Tablespoons oil

MEAT:

    3 pounds veal or beef knuckle or shin bones, cut into pieces

    2½ pounds lean stew beef

VEGETABLES:

    3 stalks celery, including leaves, cut in 2-inch pieces

    1 large onion

HERBS AND SPICES:

    4 cloves studded into onion

1 teaspoon peppercorns

2 bay leaves

4 cloves garlic, unpeeled, lightly crushed

½ teaspoon thyme

3 sprigs parsley

*   *   *

4 quarts water

*   *   *

UTENSIL:

12 to 16 quart stockpot.

Serves 6

NOTE: *This stock should be prepared at least one day before using so that it can be chilled and the fat removed easily.*

1. Preheat the oven to 400 degrees. Put the oil in a roasting or broiling pan, add the bones and the stew meat, coat them with the oil on both sides, and roast for half an hour. This gives the stock its rich brown color and hearty flavor.
2. Put the bones, meat, vegetables, herbs and spices into the stockpot. Add the 4 quarts of water. Bring it to a boil, reduce the heat and simmer for 8 to 10 hours, or until the stock reduces down to about 3 quarts. *Do not cover the pot at anytime,* or the stock will turn sour. The stock should have a rich, full-bodied taste. If it does not at the end of the 8 to 10 hours, simmer for an additional hour or two or until it does. Remove from heat.
3. Lift out the meat and reserve for soup or sandwiches. Strain the stock into large jars or bowls, discard the bones and vegetables, and refrigerate overnight. Before using, remove and discard the solid layer of fat on top. Heat the stock and meat until hot; add salt and pepper to taste.

Fresh vegetables like carrots, celery, peas, leeks, or onions may be added and simmered until tender.

May be prepared four days ahead and kept tightly covered in the refrigerator.

May be frozen.

This stock is used for poaching fish and shellfish, and is the basic stock for fish-based soups and sauces. It's good to have on hand in quart containers for easy use, and well worth the effort to make as it can be reused and refrozen many times.

FUMET DE POISSON
(Fish Stock)

Approximately 2 pounds of the head, skin and bones of any fish (except salmon)

VEGETABLES:
- 2 stalks celery with leaves, cut in 2-inch pieces
- 2 carrots, scrubbed, cut in 2-inch pieces
- ½ medium head of lettuce
- 2 leeks, white part only, split and washed thoroughly

HERBS AND SPICES:
- 2 bay leaves
- 1 teaspoon thyme
- 1 teaspoon salt
- 10 white peppercorns
- 5 sprigs fresh dill
- 3 sprigs parsley

* * *

- 2 quarts cold water
- ¼ cup tarragon vinegar

Serves 6

1. Put the fish, vegetables, herbs and spices in a large 4- to 5-quart saucepan, and cover with 2 quarts of cold water. Bring to a boil, reduce heat, and simmer uncovered for 45 minutes.

2. Strain through a colander or strainer lined with cheesecloth.

May be prepared two days ahead and kept tightly covered in the refrigerator.

May be frozen, reused and refrozen many times.

Court-bouillon is the same as fish stock, except that it contains wine and has been reduced, or cooked down. It too can be reused many times. You can prepare court-bouillon at the same time as fish stock by adding wine and lemon, and cooking for a longer period of time.

COURT-BOUILLON
(Fish Stock with Wine)

2 quarts fish stock
2 cups dry white wine
1 lemon, sliced thin, seeds
removed

¼ cup tarragon vinegar
3 sprigs fresh dill

In a 4 to 5 quart saucepan, bring the fish stock, wine, lemon, vinegar, and dill to a boil. Reduce heat, and simmer uncovered until the amount of liquid is reduced by a third to approximately 6 or 7 cups.

FAST AND EASY COURT-BOUILLON

4 8-ounce bottles of clam juice
1 quart of water
2 cups dry white wine
1 lemon, sliced thin, seeds removed
1 stalk celery, with leaves, cut
into 2-inch pieces

1 onion, halved
2 carrots, scrubbed, and
cut in 2-inch pieces
3 sprigs parsley

In a 4 to 5 quart saucepan, bring the clam juice, water, wine, lemon and vegetables to a boil. Reduce heat and simmer uncovered until the liquid has been reduced by a third, to approximately 6 or 7 cups.

May be prepared two days ahead and kept tightly covered in the refrigerator.

May be frozen, reused and refrozen many times.

This is the classic technique for clarifying consommé or stock by the addition of beaten egg whites. The result is the beautiful clear soup with the superb taste that you find in the best French restaurants.

CONSOMMÉ CLARIFIE
(Clear Consommé)

3 quarts of chicken stock recipe, with all fat removed (see page 43)

VEGETABLES:

2 stalks celery, without leaves, cut in 2-inch pieces

2 medium carrots, peeled, cut in 2-inch pieces

4 sprigs parsley

2 leeks, white part only, split and washed thoroughly

1 pound fresh tomatoes, or 1 15-ounce can of tomatoes with the juice

3 egg whites

12 ounces ground round beef, very lean

salt

Bouquet-Garni (see page 9)

GARNISH:

4 ounces dry sherry

Serves 6

1. Put all of the vegetables and egg whites in the blender and blend until the egg whites are frothy.

2. Put the consommé, vegetables and egg whites, the ground beef and the bouquet garni in a 4 to 5 quart saucepan. Stir thoroughly *once*. Do *not* stir again or the soup will be cloudy. Do not cover the pan. Slowly, allow the soup to come to a boil. Reduce the heat and simmer for 1 hour very, very slowly.

3. Strain the soup by putting a cheesecloth or a dampened dish towel over a large strainer or colander and pouring the soup through to another container. Add salt and pepper to taste. Heat thoroughly.

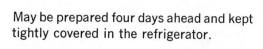

Serve hot. Float 1 tablespoon sherry in each bowl.

May be prepared four days ahead and kept tightly covered in the refrigerator.

May be frozen in a tightly covered container.

Here are the Italian and Chinese versions of the same soup, using the homemade chicken stock.

STRACIATELLA
(Threaded Egg Soup)

6 cups chicken stock
3 eggs, at room temperature
3 Tablespoons parsley, minced

3 Tablespoons Parmesan cheese, grated
Salt and pepper

Serves 6

1. In a 4 to 5 quart saucepan, bring the stock to a rolling boil.

2. In a small bowl, combine the eggs, parsley, and cheese, and beat thoroughly with a wire whisk.

3. Pour the egg-cheese-parsley mixture in a slow, steady stream into the boiling stock, while beating the soup with a wire whisk until the eggs are in long shreds. Add salt and pepper to taste. Serve immediately.

Only the chicken stock can be frozen.

DON FAH TONG
(Egg Flower Soup)

6 cups chicken stock
1 cup frozen peas, or fresh pea pods with strings removed
1½ cups fresh bean sprouts
6 dried mushrooms (or ½ cup sliced fresh or canned mushrooms), washed thoroughly and soaked in sherry

1 chicken breast, uncooked, boned and skinned, cut into cubes
1 Tablespoon soy sauce or to taste
Salt and pepper
2 eggs, at room temperature

Serves 6

1. In a 4 to 5 quart saucepan, bring the chicken stock to a simmer. Add the peas, bean sprouts, mushrooms, chicken, soy sauce, and salt and pepper to taste. Simmer until the chicken is cooked. It will turn a pale white.

2. In a small bowl, beat the eggs with a wire whisk.

3. Bring the soup to a rolling boil. Pour the eggs in a slow, steady stream, while beating the soup with a wire whisk until the eggs are in long shreds. Serve immediately.

Chicken stock may be prepared ahead.
The vegetables can be assembled, but should not be added to soup until just before serving.

CUSTARD ROYAL
(Garnish for Clear Soup)

1 egg
3 egg yolks
4 Tablespoons milk or cream
¼ teaspoon salt
Pinch white pepper
¼ teaspoon nutmeg, ground

OPTIONAL:

3½ Tablespoons tomato paste

UTENSILS:

9-inch by 5-inch loaf pan, greased
Aspic or canapé cutters, or a knife

1. In a bowl, beat the whole egg, egg yolks and milk or cream. Add salt, pepper and nutmeg. Beat until well blended.

2. Pour into loaf pan. The mixture should be ⅛ inch to ¼ inch deep. Set the loaf pan in a water bath or bain-marie. Bake in a 300 degree oven 20 to 30 minutes or until the custard is set. The custard is set when a knife, inserted into it one inch from the edge of the pan, comes out clean.

3. Allow to cool. Using small aspic or canapé cutters or a small knife, cut the custard into small diamonds, discs, or attractive shapes.

NOTE: *For clear chicken stock or consommé, add the tomato paste to the custard to give color.*

TO SERVE — Float in clear beef or chicken consommé.

AHEAD — May be prepared three days ahead, and kept tightly covered in the refrigerator.

FREEZE — Do not freeze.

Brunoise is the classic French vegetable garnish for clear soup, like the consommé clarifié, or the semiclear soups, like the beef or chicken stock. The vegetables should be cut uniformly and look attractive.

BRUNOISE
(Vegetable Garnish)

1½ Tablespoons butter
1 carrot, peeled and diced
1 small turnip, peeled and diced
1½ leeks, white part only, split, washed thoroughly and sliced
1 stalk celery, without leaves, diced
1 small onion, diced
¼ teaspoon confectioners' sugar

1 cup consommé clarifié (see page 49)
1 Tablespoon fresh peas
1 Tablespoon fresh green beans cut in ¼ inch-pieces

* * *

1 quart of consommé clarifié, or 1 quart of chicken (see page 43) or beef stock (see page 45)

1. Dice all the vegetables (except the peas) into uniform ⅛- to ½-inch squares.
2. In a small saucepan, melt the butter; add the carrot, turnip, leeks, celery, onion and sugar. Simmer, covered, over low heat until the vegetables have heightened in color. Add 1 cup of consommé clarifié, and continue cooking until the vegetables are slightly firm. They should be crisp, not overcooked.
3. In a large saucepan, heat the consommé clarifié, or the chicken or beef stock.
4. In a small saucepan, heat the brunoise, and add the peas and stringbeans. Simmer one minute or until the beans are cooked.

TO SERVE Divide the brunoise into six soup bowls, ladle hot soup over it.

AHEAD May be prepared ahead and kept tightly covered in the refrigerator for three days.

FREEZE Do not freeze.

A hearty peasant soup with delicious and colorful garnishes that has been a favorite meal over the years. It's inexpensive to make and serves so many for the money. The beans should be soaked overnight before preparing the soup.

SOPA DE FRIJOLES NEGROS
(Caribbean Black Bean Soup)

1 pound dried black beans
(turtle beans)
¼ cup olive oil
¼ pound salt pork,
cut into ½-inch cubes
¼ pound raw, cured ham
(Smithfield or a country ham)
cut into ½-inch cubes
4 large onions, chopped
4 garlic cloves, peeled, cut in half
3 stalks celery, with leaves,
chopped
12 cups chicken stock, homemade or commercial
3 Tablespoons meat glaze
(or Bovril)
¼ teaspoon cayenne

2 teaspoons cumin, ground
Salt and pepper
2 Tablespoons wine vinegar
½ cup dry sherry

GARNISH:
Serve at the table in separate bowls:
2 medium onions, chopped
2 lemons, sliced paper-thin
Cooked ham, finely chopped
3 hard-cooked eggs, sliced or
chopped, sprinkled with
paprika
1 can mild chiles, drained
and chopped
2 cups cooked rice

Serves 10 to 12

1. Rinse the beans well and remove any foreign particles. Put them in a bowl of cold water to cover, and allow them to soak overnight. (Use a large bowl as the beans expand.)

2. Heat the oil in a 4 to 5 quart saucepan. Add the salt pork, ham, onions, garlic and celery. Cook over a low heat, stirring occasionally until the fat is rendered from the salt pork (about 30 minutes).

3. Drain the soaked beans, and add them to the saucepan. Add the stock and meat glaze. Bring to a boil, reduce heat, add the cayenne and cumin. Partially cover the pot, and simmer over low heat about 4 hours, stirring occasionally. Add salt and pepper to taste.

4. Put the soup through the blender and purée. Add the vinegar and stir. Return to the saucepan and bring to a simmer over low heat.

Just before serving, remove from heat and add sherry. Serve hot.

Put garnishes in separate bowls, and serve at the table.

May be prepared four days ahead and refrigerated through Step 4.

May be frozen. Defrost overnight in the refrigerator.

This is a thick and wonderful French country soup. It is always topped with poached eggs and makes a complete and filling lunch or supper.

SOUPE AÏGO À LA MÉNAGÈRE
(French Provincial Soup)

3 slices lean bacon, cut in ½-inch strips
1 small carrot, peeled, sliced thin
1 medium onion, chopped
8 medium tomatoes, peeled and chopped (set 1 aside for garnish)
2 cloves garlic, peeled
1 bay leaf
½ teaspoon thyme
2 teaspoons salt
¼ teaspoon ground white pepper
4 cups chicken stock, homemade or commercial

¼ cup rice, uncooked

GARNISH:
4 Tablespoons butter
6 2½-inch circles of thin white bread
1 tomato, peeled and chopped
1 Tablespoon fresh dill, minced
1 Tablespoon chives, minced
6 eggs, poached

Serves 6

1. In a 4 to 5 quart saucepan, fry the bacon pieces until they are cooked, but not crisp. Drain off and discard most of the bacon fat. Sauté the carrot and onion in the remaining bacon fat until the carrot slices are tender.

2. Add seven of the chopped tomatoes (reserving one for garnish), garlic, bay leaf, thyme, salt and pepper, and sauté for 5 minutes. Add the chicken stock, cover the pan and simmer for 35 minutes.

3. Add the rice, and cook until tender, 15-20 minutes. Remove the bay leaf. Put the soup mixture into the blender, and purée for 1 minute.
4. Return to the saucepan and bring to a simmer over low heat.

Garnish:

5. In a small skillet, melt 2 Tablespoons of the butter, and brown the bread rounds on both sides. Set aside the bread, and keep warm.
6. In the same skillet, melt the remaining 2 Tablespoons of butter and sauté the chopped tomato. Add the dill and chives, and shake the pan to turn the pieces of tomato. Simmer a few minutes. Keep warm until ready to serve.

 Heat the soup. Poach one egg per person. Ladle the soup into individual bowls. Set a bread round on top, then a poached egg. Spoon tomato-dill-chive mixture over the egg.

 May be prepared three days ahead through Step 3, and refrigerated.

 May be frozen through Step 3.

The only trick with this onion soup is sautéeing the onions for a long time. You don't have to hover over them, as long as you stir them occasionally. You can use commercial concentrated chicken and beef stock bases for this recipe, so the only thing that takes time is the onions. Serve the soup in individual ovenproof bowls, or in a large earthenware French casserole.

PERFECT ONION SOUP

2 Tablespoons butter
¼ cup olive oil
12 medium onions, thinly sliced on the diagonal
½ teaspoon sugar
3 Tablespoons flour
4 Tablespoons concentrated chicken stock base dissolved in 4 cups boiling water
4 Tablespoons concentrated beef stock base dissolved in 4 cups boiling water

½ cup dry white wine
½ teaspoon Dijon mustard
Salt and pepper
8 slices toasted French bread
2 cups Gruyère cheese, grated
1 egg yolk
2 Tablespoons cognac

GARNISH:
Parmesan cheese, grated

Serves 6

1. In a large saucepan, melt the butter and oil. Add the onions, sprinkle them with sugar, and sauté over very low heat until they are a rich golden brown. This will take as long as two hours! Stir the onions occasionally.

2. When the onions are golden brown, sprinkle the flour over them, and stir until the flour is dissolved.

3. Add the boiling chicken and beef stocks and wine to the onions, and stir in the mustard. Simmer partially covered for 30 to 40 minutes. Add pepper to taste, and salt very lightly as there is salt in the cheeses. Reserve ½ cup of the soup liquid in a small pot.

4. Preheat the oven to 325 degrees. In the bottom of the individual soup dishes or the casserole, put a slice of toasted French bread per portion. Sprinkle half of the Gruyère cheese on top of each piece of bread, and very carefully ladle the soup over it allowing the bread to soak up the soup. This will keep the bread from floating to the surface. Bake 25 minutes.

    If the soup has cooked down too much, add combined chicken and beef stock for a thinner consistency, if desired.

5. In a small bowl whisk together the egg yolk and cognac. Heat the reserved ½ cup of soup broth, and slowly whisk it into the egg and cognac mixture.

Preheat the broiler. Remove the ovenproof bowls or casserole from the oven, and spoon a little of the egg-cognac-broth mixture into the soup. If necessary, lift up the bread. Stir through gently.

Top with remaining cup of Gruyère and a little Parmesan. Put under broiler until lightly browned.

May be prepared through Step 3 and refrigerated.

May be frozen after Step 2 or Step 3.

This Mexican meal-in-one soup is best made with fresh corn, but well worth making with frozen corn, too. The flavor of the corn soup, mingled with the tastes and textures of the garnishes, make it distinctive.

SOPA DE MAIZ
(Mexican Corn Soup)

3½ cups fresh corn (8 to 12 ears) cut and scraped from the cob, or 3½ cups frozen corn (not cream style), defrosted
1 cup chicken stock, homemade or commercial
4 Tablespoons butter
2 cups milk
1 clove garlic, minced
1 teaspoon oregano
Salt and pepper
1 to 2 Tablespoons canned mild green chiles, cut into cubes

GARNISH:
1 chicken breast, cooked, cut into julienne matchsticks
1 cup tomatoes, diced
1 cup Monterey Jack, Muenster, or Fontina cheese, cubed
2 Tablespoons parsley, minced
6 or more Tablespoons Tortilla Squares

Serves 6

1. For fresh corn on the cob: Using a sharp knife or corn scraper, cut off the kernels.

2. Put the corn kernels and chicken stock in the blender, and blend for about 10 seconds, only long enough to break up the kernels. Do not purée.

3. Put a fine sieve over a 4 to 5 quart saucepan, and strain the corn and stock mixture, pressing with the back of a large wooden spoon to extract as much liquid as possible. Discard the solid kernels.

4. Add the butter to the strained corn mixture and simmer slowly for 5 minutes, stirring well to keep the corn from sticking to the bottom of the pan. Add the milk, garlic, oregano, salt and pepper, and bring to a boil. Reduce the heat, add the chiles and simmer for 5 minutes.

Variation: As a first course, garnish only with tortilla squares.

Divide the chicken and tomatoes into individual soup bowls. Heat the soup slowly. Add the cheese to the hot soup. When it is melted, add the minced parsley. Ladle into each bowl, and garnish with Tortilla Squares.

May be prepared three days ahead through Step 4 and refrigerated.

May be frozen through Step 4.

TORTILLA SQUARES

6 or 8 tortillas   Shortening for deep fat frying

1. Stack the tortillas on a flat surface. Cut them into half-inch squares.

2. Drop the squares into shortening heated to 375 degrees and one inch deep. Stir with a wooden spoon until crisp and golden. Drain the tortilla squares on paper towels.

   Use on soups and salads. It can be stored for 6 weeks in covered container.

This fish soup is an incredible combination of flavors and textures that some people say is better than bouillabaisse. What makes it so good is the combination of the hot soup with the rouille (the French red garlic paste) and the melted cheese. It can be an inexpensive meal, using thick-fleshed fish, or you can dress it up with the more expensive seafood.

SOUPE AU POISSON À LA ROUILLE
(Fish Soup with Red Garlic Sauce)

4 Tablespoons olive oil
1 medium onion, chopped
1 bulb fresh fennel, chopped
(available in Italian markets)
or 1 teaspoon dried fennel
1 green pepper, chopped
4 tomatoes, peeled and chopped
2 bay leaves
10 peppercorns
1 teaspoon thyme
1 teaspoon basil
½ teaspoon saffron
1 teaspoon salt

* * *

8 cups court-bouillon (see page 48)

* * *

3 pounds thick-fleshed fish
(turbot, halibut, haddock,
snapper) or substitute 1½
pounds of seafood for 1½ pounds

of the fish (crabmeat, shrimp,
clams, mussels). If they are
already cooked, heat only.

ROUILLE:
3 egg yolks
6 cloves garlic, peeled
20 croûtons, or 2 slices bread,
toasted, broken into pieces
½ teaspoon salt
2 Tablespoons lemon juice
Pinch of cayenne
3 canned red pimientos, rinsed
and drained
1 cup olive or peanut oil

GARNISH:
6 to 8 slices French bread, toasted
2 cups (½ pound) Swiss cheese,
grated

Serves 8

1. In a 4 to 5 quart saucepan, heat the 4 Tablespoons of olive oil, add the onion, fennel, green pepper and tomatoes, and sauté until soft.

2. Add the bay leaves, peppercorns, thyme, basil, saffron, salt and court-bouillon. Stir carefully to distribute all the ingredients, and be sure the saffron is dissolved. Simmer uncovered for 1 hour.

3. Pour the soup mixture through a strainer lined with cheesecloth, and return it to the saucepan.

4. Add the fish to the soup, cover the pan with a piece of waxed paper to keep in the herb flavoring, and poach gently until the fish is no longer translucent, 10 to 15 minutes. Remove from the heat.

5. *Rouille:* In the blender, combine the egg yolks, garlic, croûtons, salt, lemon juice, cayenne and pimientos. Blend for 1 minute. The method of adding the oil is the secret of a good rouille. Pour the first half cup of the oil *drop* by *drop* into the whirling blender. Then add the remaining half cup a tablespoon at a time. The rouille should have the consistency of mayonnaise.

NOTE: *If there is broth left over but no fish, it will still be delicious served with the toasted bread, rouille and cheese.*

Gently reheat the broth and fish.
Place a slice of toasted French bread on the bottom of the individual soup bowl. Next, place a portion of poached fish on the bread. Put a spoonful of the rouille over the fish, and cover with a generous amount of grated Swiss cheese. Ladle scalding hot broth over all (to melt the cheese) and serve immediately. Pass additional bowls of rouille and grated cheese at the table. Serve with additional French bread if desired.

The fish broth and poached fish, through Step 4, may be prepared three days ahead and refrigerated.
The Rouille may be prepared one week ahead and stored, covered, in the refrigerator. You may assemble the bread, fish and rouille in individual bowls one hour ahead and allow to sit at room temperature.

The broth and the rouille may be frozen.

In France, a pistou is a delicious green herb and garlic paste that is an accompaniment to vegetable soups. It transforms a good soup into a great one.

SOUPE AU PISTOU VERT
(Zucchini Soup with Green Garlic Paste)

6 zucchini, sliced (not peeled), about 3 cups
2 medium onions, sliced (1½ cups)
4 Tablespoons olive oil or butter
6 cups chicken stock, homemade or commercial
2 cups lima beans (one 10-ounce frozen package)
1 cup peas (half of 10-ounce frozen package)
Salt and pepper
2 Tablespoons sour cream

PISTOU:

2 cloves garlic, minced

1 slice bacon, fried until crisp, drained and crumbled
2 teaspoons fresh basil, or 1 teaspoon dried basil
4 Tablespoons parsley, minced
2 egg yolks
1/3 to ½ cup Parmesan cheese, grated
1 teaspoon olive oil

GARNISH:

4 slices bacon, fried until crisp, drained and crumbled

Serves 6

1. In a 4 to 5 quart saucepan, sauté the onions and zucchini in olive oil or butter until a light brown.

2. Add the chicken stock and bring to a boil. Add the lima beans and peas, and when the mixture comes to a boil again, reduce the heat and simmer until the vegetables are soft, 20 to 25 minutes. Add salt and pepper to taste.

3. Purée the soup in the blender. Return to the saucepan.

4. *Pistou:* In the blender, put the garlic, bacon, basil, parsley and egg yolks. Blend for 1 minute. Add the Parmesan cheese, and blend again. It should now be a thick paste. If necessary, add more Parmesan. Stir in 1 teaspoon olive oil.

5. Bring the soup to a simmer over low heat. Stir in the sour cream. Do not allow the soup to boil.

NOTE: *Pistou can also be used on fish, with spaghetti, and in other vegetable soups.*

Ladle the hot soup into individual bowls. Add 1 teaspoon of pistou on top, and a little crumbled bacon. The soup should be stirred at the table.

The soup and the pistou may be prepared four days ahead through Step 4 and refrigerated separately.

The soup may be frozen after Step 3. The pistou may be frozen.

INSTANT CONSOMMÉ L'INDIENNE
(Curried Tomato Soup)

3 cups Snappy Tom Tomato Juice or tomato juice

3 cups chicken stock, homemade or commercial

2 teaspoons lemon juice

1 teaspoon sugar

4 whole cloves, tied in cheesecloth

¼ to ½ teaspoon curry powder, or more to taste

Salt to taste

GARNISH:

½ cup of jack cheese, cut into cubes

1. In a 4 to 5 quart saucepan, bring to a boil the Snappy Tom and the chicken stock. Reduce the heat and add the lemon juice, sugar and cloves. Add the curry powder, and stir with a wire whisk. Heat thoroughly for 5 to 10 minutes. Remove the cloves. Serve hot in mugs with jack cheese.

There are literally dozens of gazpachos, but so far this is the most unusual I have found. This version of gazpacho is a thick soup and should be prepared a day in advance.

GAZPACHO VASCO
(Cold Basque Vegetable Soup)

SOUP BASE:

4 cups beef stock, homemade
  or commercial, at room
  temperature
3 Tablespoons olive oil
3 Tablespoons red wine vinegar
2 Tablespoons lemon juice
1 clove garlic, minced
3 Tablespoons sugar
Salt and pepper

VEGETABLES:

1 box cherry tomatoes, halved, or
  4 medium tomatoes, chopped
1 bunch green onions, white and
  green parts, finely chopped
1 bunch radishes, sliced thin

1 large cucumber, unpeeled,
  coarsely chopped
1 medium sweet onion (red or
  Bermuda), minced
1 green pepper, seeded, finely
  chopped
8 mushrooms, sliced thin
1 bunch watercress, leaves only,
  minced

GARNISH:

1 cup sour cream or yoghurt
1 teaspoon cumin seeds, crushed

SERVE WITH:

Hot French, sour dough or
  garlic bread

Serves 6

1. Soup base: In a large bowl, combine the beef stock, oil, vinegar, lemon juice, sugar, salt and pepper, and stir well. Be sure soup is at room temperature or cool before adding the vegetables.

2. Cut or chop the vegetables as indicated, and add to the soup base. Refrigerate overnight, to allow the soup to marinate.

Serve in individual bowls. Garnish each
bowl with a dollop of sour cream or yoghurt,
and a sprinkling of cumin seeds.

May be prepared three days ahead
and kept refrigerated.

Do not freeze.

FAST AND EASY CAVIAR MADRILÈNE

3 13-ounce cans of consommé
  madrilène
2 ounces caviar, red or black

GARNISH:
6 Tablespoons sour cream
3 Tablespoons chopped chives

Serves 6

Pour madrilène into 6 soup bowls, wine goblets or individual soufflé
dishes. Stir a heaping teaspoon of caviar into each one, and refrigerate for 5 to 6 hours. Stir through several times while the madrilène
is chilling to break up the surface.

Top each bowl with a dollop of sour cream,
and sprinkle with chopped chives.

May be prepared 2 days ahead and
refrigerated.

Do not freeze.

PEKING HOT AND SOUR SOUP

2 Tablespoons (4 to 5) dried
Chinese fungi or tree ears
(Available at Chinese or Japa-
nese markets)

3 to 4 medium-size dried
Chinese mushrooms

8 dried tiger-lily buds
(golden needles)

4 cups chicken stock, homemade
or commercial

⅓ cup bamboo shoots, shredded

⅓ cup pork, lean and uncooked,
cut into julienne match-sticks

½ cake fresh bean curd, cut into
slices (1-inch by ¼-inch)

1 teaspoon soy sauce
½ teaspoon sugar
2 teaspoons wine vinegar
¼ teaspoon MSG
2 teaspoons cornstarch
3 teaspoons water
Salt and pepper

GARNISH:
1 egg, lightly beaten
1 teaspoon heated sesame oil,
4 cups rice, cooked,
(½ cup per serving)

Serves 8

1. In a bowl, soak the fungi, mushrooms and tiger-lily buds in warm water for 20 minutes. Cut fungi and mushrooms into slices.

2. Place the chicken stock, fungi, mushrooms, tiger-lily buds, bamboo shoots, pork shreds and bean curd in a 4 to 5 quart saucepan. Bring to a boil, reduce heat and simmer 10 minutes.

3. Add the soy sauce, vinegar, and monosodium glutamate (MSG).

4. In a small bowl, combine cornstarch with cold water. Mix a small amount of hot soup with the cornstarch-water mixture and return this mixture to the pan. Bring to a boil, stir, and cook 1 to 2 minutes. Add salt and pepper to taste.

Add the beaten egg to the hot soup, and stir a few times. Add sesame oil, and stir. Put ½ cup of boiled rice in each individual serving bowl. Ladle the hot soup over the rice.

May be prepared one day ahead through Step 4 and refrigerated.

Do not freeze.

This classic French soup has a subtle taste that grows on you. In texture, it should be thick and smooth. It is better to start the recipe with a minimum amount of liquid; then add a little extra stock at the end if it seems too thick.

CRÈME DuBARRY
(Cream of Cauliflower Soup)

1 medium-to-large head of cauliflower
1 teaspoon salt
1 Tablespoon lemon juice
6 Tablespoons butter
4 Tablespoons flour
4 to 6 cups chicken stock, home-made or commercial, depending on size of cauliflower
½ cup milk
¼ teaspoon nutmeg, ground
2 egg yolks

½ cup sour cream
Salt and pepper

GARNISH:
⅓ cup cauliflower flowerets, thinly sliced
2 Tablespoons parsley or chives, minced
½ cup croûtons

Serves 5 to 6

1. Wash the cauliflower and break into flowerets.

2. Blanch the cauliflower by putting it in a 4 to 5 quart saucepan, and adding enough water to cover. Add 1 teaspoon salt and 1 Table-spoon lemon juice to help whiten the cauliflower. Cook uncov-ered for 8 to 10 minutes, keeping the water at a gentle boil. Put into a colander to drain. Set aside ⅓ of a cup of flowerets for garnish.

3. In the same saucepan, melt 4 of the 6 Tablespoons of butter. Add the flour slowly, stirring constantly with a wire whisk. Cook over a low flame for 5 minutes. Be careful not to let the color go beyond the pale golden stage. Remove from heat.

[69]

4. Add the chicken stock slowly . . . 4 cups of chicken stock are usually sufficient. Stir constantly with a wire whisk to keep the mixture smooth. Add salt and pepper. Bring to a boil and add the drained cauliflower and bring to a boil again. Reduce the heat, and simmer until the cauliflower is tender and soft, about 40 minutes.

5. In the blender, purée the soup. Return it to the saucepan.

6. Add the milk to the soup, and heat to the boiling point, stirring to blend well. Simmer on very, very low heat. Add the nutmeg, and stir.

7. In a small pan, melt the other 2 Tablespoons of butter. In a bowl, beat the egg yolks, sour cream and melted butter with a wire whisk. Add ½ cup of the hot soup to this mixture, and blend well.

8. Increase the heat under the saucepan, and stir in the egg mixture for 4 to 5 minutes to bind and thicken. Do *not* let the soup boil after adding the egg yolks, or it will curdle. Reduce to low heat. Correct the thickness of the soup at this point if necessary. If it seems too thick, like a porridge, add a little hot chicken stock. Check to see if there is enough salt, pepper and nutmeg.

Sprinkle chives or parsley over the hot soup, then carefully float the thinly sliced cauliflower flowerets on the surface. (If croutons are served, pass them at the table so they do not get soggy.)

May be prepared three days ahead through Step 5 and refrigerated.

May be frozen after Step 5.

This deliciously seasoned tomato soup is a far cry from the canned variety, and takes a short time to make. It's particularly good when it's broiled—but you could serve it unbroiled as well.

SOUPE DE TOMATES GRATINÉES
(Broiled Tomato Soup)

½ cup butter
2 Tablespoons olive oil
1 large onion, sliced thin
½ teaspoon dried thyme
½ teaspoon dried basil
1 teaspoon fresh dill
8 medium, fresh tomatoes, peeled
    and cut in pieces, or 40-ounces of
    canned Italian-style tomatoes,
    drained (one 28-ounce can and
    one 15-ounce can)
3 Tablespoons tomato paste

4 Tablespoons flour
3¾ cups chicken stock, home-
    made or commercial
1 teaspoon sugar
    Salt and pepper

GARNISH:
1 cup cream, whipped
½ cup Parmesan cheese, grated

·*Serves 6*

1. In a 4 to 5 quart saucepan, heat the butter and olive oil. Add the onion, thyme, basil and dill. Cook, stirring occasionally, until the onion is soft and golden.

2. Add the tomatoes and tomato paste, and stir to blend. Simmer uncovered for 10 minutes.

3. In a small mixing bowl, blend the flour, and ½ cup of the chicken stock with a wire whisk. Add it to the tomato and onion mixture. Add the remaining chicken broth and simmer uncovered for 30

[71]

minutes. Stir frequently down to the bottom of the pan to prevent scorching.

4. Purée the soup in the blender. Return to the saucepan. Add salt and pepper to taste.

5. Reheat the soup over low heat, and add sugar. Add salt and pepper to taste.

6. Garnish: In a bowl, fold the Parmesan cheese into the whipped cream.

Variation: Instead of broiling, garnish with whipped cream, croûtons, and fresh minced dill.

Preheat the broiler. Pour the hot soup into small, individual ovenproof dishes, or into one large casserole. Float the whipped cream-Parmesan mixture on top. Sprinkle extra Parmesan over it. Broil 6 inches from heat until golden brown, about 30 seconds to 1 minute. **Do not let the cream burn.** Serve immediately.

May be prepared three days ahead through Step 4 and refrigerated.

Can be frozen after Step 4.

This is spectacular when served in one large pumpkin or in individual small pumpkins, instead of the usual soup bowls. It is equally good served hot or cold.

POTAGE PURÉE DE POTIRON
(Pumpkin Soup)

4 Tablespoons butter
1 large onion, sliced
¾ cup green onions, white part only, sliced
1 17-ounce can puréed pumpkin
4 cups chicken stock, homemade or commercial
1 bay leaf
½ teaspoon sugar
Few sprigs parsley
Pinch of nutmeg, ground
2 cups milk
Salt and pepper

* * *

1 large pumpkin, with top cut off for lid, seeds removed; or
6 small pumpkins with tops cut off for lids, seeds removed

GARNISH FOR HOT SOUP:

½ cup cream, whipped, or sour cream
½ cup chives or green onions, minced
Paprika

* * *

GARNISH FOR COLD SOUP:

½ cup cream, whipped, or sour cream
½ cup chives or green onions, minced
1 thin slice tomato per person

* * *

SERVE WITH:
Pumpernickel à la Perino's
(see page 227)

Serves 6

[73]

1. In a 4 to 5 quart saucepan, melt the butter, add the onion and green onions, and sauté until they are soft and golden.

2. Add the puréed pumpkin and stir for a few minutes. Add the chicken stock, bay leaf, sugar and parsley. Bring to a simmer, and cook over low heat for 15 minutes. Remove the bay leaf. Add the nutmeg.

3. Purée the soup in the blender. Return to the saucepan.

4. Stir the milk into the soup mixture. Add salt and pepper to taste. Simmer 5 to 10 minutes over low heat. Do not allow to boil.

5. For Cold Soup: Pour soup into large bowl (or jar), allow to cool, and refrigerate for several hours until thoroughly chilled.

To serve hot, ladle the hot soup into the hollow pumpkin(s) or soup tureen. Float a dollop of whipped or sour cream on top. Sprinkle paprika around the cream, then a large ring of chives. Accompany with Pumpernickel à la Perino's.
To serve cold, ladle the cold soup into the hollow pumpkin(s) or soup tureen. Float a thin slice of tomato on top. Cover it with dollop of whipped or sour cream, and sprinkle a circle of chives around the tomato.

May be prepared three days ahead through Step 4 and refrigerated.

May be frozen through Step 3.

In Scandinavian countries, this delightful and refreshing soup is served for breakfast. It would make a good first course for a summer brunch or lunch.

SOUPE AUX FRAISES EN MELON GLACÉ
(Chilled Strawberry Soup in Melon)

2 boxes fresh strawberries, washed thoroughly. Set aside 6 strawberries and slice
1 cup orange juice
1¼ Tablespoons instant tapioca
⅛ teaspoon allspice, ground
⅛ teaspoon cinammon
½ cup sugar
1¼ teaspoons lemon peel, grated
1 Tablespoon lemon juice

1 cup buttermilk
    *   *   *
2 chilled cantaloupes

GARNISH:

4 lemon slices, cut thin
    *   *   *
4 large fresh leaves (grapes, ivy, lemon or other)

Serves 4

1. In the blender, purée the strawberries with the orange juice. Strain the mixture into a 4 to 5 quart saucepan.

2. In a small bowl, mix the tapioca with a little of the puréed strawberries, then add to the strawberry mixture in the saucepan. Add

the allspice and cinnamon. Heat, stirring constantly, until the mixture comes to a boil. Cook 1 minute, or until thickened. Remove from heat.

3. Pour the soup into a large bowl. Add the sugar, lemon peel, lemon juice and buttermilk and blend well. Add the 6 sliced strawberries. Cover the bowl and chill at least 8 hours.

4. Cut the cantaloupes in half, making sawtooth edges. Scoop out the seeds. Turn the cantaloupe halves upside down on paper towels to drain. Cover with plastic wrap and refrigerate until ready to serve.

TO SERVE Set each cantaloupe half on a fresh leaf. Fill with strawberry soup. Top with a lemon slice.

AHEAD Soup may be prepared three days ahead and refrigerated. Cantaloupes may be cut 8 hours ahead and refrigerated.

FREEZE Soup may be frozen through Step 2.

CHAPTER 3

Sauces and Seasonings

TERMS AND TYPES OF SAUCES

In French cooking, sauces are considered the high art. There should be no mystique to sauce-making, but there are some basic sauces to learn, and general rules to follow that will guarantee success.

USES FOR SAUCES

There are three broad uses for sauces: basting, masking and pouring.

1. *Basting:* A method of keeping food moist as it bakes or roasts by spooning or painting it with sauce. Use a 2-inch white-bristle paint brush from the hardware or paint store. It's an inexpensive and effective brush for basting, and it can be washed in the dishwasher. The general rule is to baste food every 15 to 30 minutes as it cooks. Often, the sauce used for basting may be used at the table as a pouring sauce.

2. *Masking:* A method of coating already cooked hot or cold foods with a thick sauce for added flavor and appearance. An example would be using a béarnaise or a hollandaise sauce on asparagus, or a mustard dill sauce to mask poached salmon.

3. *Pouring Sauce:* A sauce used to enhance the main ingredients of a dish which is thinner than a masking sauce. Spoon a little of the pouring sauce on the individual heated dinner plate and place the serving of meat, poultry or fish on top of it; or spoon a little sauce at the side of the serving; or pour a thin ribbon on top of the serving. Do not flood the dinner plate with an excess amount of sauce.

TYPES OF THICKENING AGENTS

The general rule is to dissolve the thickening agents in a small amount of cold liquid (wine, stock, water) to make a smooth liaison, or paste, that will dissolve easily when combined with the hot ingredients.

1. *Flour:* Used for opaque sauces, like Béchamel or Velouté.

2. *Potato Starch or Potato Flour:* Used for translucent sauces, like Sauce Bordelaise. Preferred to arrowroot as overcooking has no effect. When substituting for flour, use half the amount of potato starch. It can usually be found in kosher food section of markets.

3. *Arrowroot:* Used also for translucent sauces. When substituting for flour, use half the amount of arrowroot. Do not overcook as it will cause the sauce to become too thin. Arrowroot is also used to thicken desserts.

4. *Cornstarch:* Used to thicken Oriental foods and desserts. The longer it cooks, the thicker the sauce becomes. When substituting for flour, use half the amount of cornstarch.

TECHNIQUES

1. *Roux:* A term for the blending of a thickening agent with butter or fat. It is the first step in preparing a thickened sauce.

2. *Reduction:* A crucial step in sauce-making. It is a method of concentrating the flavors by evaporating liquid. Sauces are reduced by cooking rapidly, uncovered, over high heat until the desired consistency and flavor are achieved. When a recipe calls for reducing the amount of liquid by a specific amount (like $\frac{1}{2}$ or $\frac{1}{4}$), measure the amount of sauce in a measuring cup before reducing it, and remeasure it for the correct amount before using it. If a completed sauce lacks flavor, it usually means that the sauce is not concentrated enough. Reduce it further (by $\frac{1}{4}$ to $\frac{1}{2}$), taste, and then correct for seasoning.

3. *Basic technique for all sauces:* Sauces are prepared over low heat. High heat is only used for reduction.

4. *Basic technique for white sauces such as Sauce Béchamel:* Liquids (milk or stock) must be at room temperature before using. Add the liquid to the roux while off the heat, and blend using a wire whisk or a wooden spoon. While the white sauce is cooking, it is important to use a wooden spoon to keep the mixture from accumulating on the sides of the pan. Do not use aluminum pans for making white sauces, as the aluminum will give the sauce a grayish cast.

[79]

You may want to follow a short cut of professional chefs, who keep a jar of roux and beurre manie on hand in the refrigerator. They heat the liquid ingredients for the sauce, then add roux or beurre manie to thicken at the last moment before serving.

LIAISON AU ROUX
(Cooked Thickening Paste for Brown Sauces)

2 Tablespoons solid vegetable shortening

2 Tablespoons butter
1 cup flour plus 2 Tablespoons

In an 8-inch skillet, melt the vegetable shortening and butter, and blend in the flour slowly. Cover the pan and cook over very low flame for 1½ hours, or until it is a light brown color. Stir every 10 minutes.

NOTE: *1 Tablespoon of roux thickens 1 cup of liquid.*

Add roux directly to the hot sauce, stir and cook until it is dissolved, and the sauce is thickened to the desired consistency.

May be stored covered for six months in the refrigerator.

May be frozen in Tablespoon-size foil packets.

BEURRE MANIE
(Uncooked Thickening Paste for White Sauces)

4 Tablespoons butter,   4 Tablespoons flour
  at room temperature

Cream butter and flour together, always using equal amounts.

NOTE: *One Tablespoon of Beurre Manie will thicken one cup liquid.*

Add beurre manie directly to the hot liquids and stir. Cook until it is dissolved and the sauce is thickened to the desired consistency.

May be stored covered in the refrigerator for one month.

May be frozen in tablespoon-size foil packets.

MEAT GLAZE

Place 1 cup stock in saucepan. Reduce stock over low heat until it is very thick and coats spoon heavily. Reduce to ¼ cup.

May be prepared 4 days ahead. Store in refrigerator in a small jar. It will keep for 2 months. May be frozen.

NOTE: *If homemade Meat Glaze is not available, Bovril may be substituted.*

Caramel coloring is used to darken and enrich the color of a soup or sauce.

CARAMEL COLORING

½ cup sugar
¼ cup water
2 Tablespoons boiling water

1 teaspoon vegetable oil
3 drops red food coloring

Boil the sugar and water until the sugar caramelizes and turns a very dark, burnt-brown color. Add the boiling water gradually. Add oil and red coloring. Stir and cool. Pour into a small plastic bottle with a nozzle.

Add the caramel coloring in small amounts to the soup or sauce until the desired color is reached.

May be kept at room temperature indefinitely.

This is the "mother sauce" for all the brown-base sauces, a very important part of classic cuisine.

SAUCE BRUNE
(Brown Sauce)

½ cup butter
1 pound ham or veal (or combination), diced
2 onions, sliced
2 cloves garlic
2 carrots, sliced
½ pound mushrooms, sliced (may use stems)
⅓ cup flour

2 quarts beef stock
1 bay leaf
½ cup tomato purée or Marinara Sauce (see page 93)
½ cup red wine
Salt and pepper

Makes 6 cups

1. Melt butter and sauté the meat, onions, garlic, carrots, and mushrooms until they are well browned. Add flour and blend well. Continue cooking over low heat until the flour starts to brown.

2. Slowly add stock and then the bay leaf. Mix well. Cover and simmer for one hour. Add tomato purée, wine, and salt and pepper to taste. Simmer for 30 minutes and strain.

3. If not thickened sufficiently, reduce by boiling rapidly until it is the desired consistency.

DEMI-GLACÉ SAUCE
(Shiny Dark Sauce)

1½ cups Sauce Brune
2 teaspoons beef extract or meat glaze (Bovril)

¼ cup sherry, port, or Madeira wine
Makes 1½ cups

1. Over high heat, reduce brown sauce to 1 cup. Add beef extract and the wine. Mix well and simmer for ten minutes. Do not boil.

2. Use this shiny dark sauce over tournedos, roasted duck and Rock Cornish hens.

Variation: Sauce Madère
Substitute dry Madeira for the red wine. Serve with roasts, steak, leftover meats, poultry, and sweetbreads.

[83]

SAUCE BORDELAISE
(with Sauce Brune)

2 large marrow bones, split
½ teaspoon Dijon mustard
2 Tablespoons shallots, minced
1 clove garlic, minced
¾ cup red wine
1 cup Sauce Brune (see page 83)
1 Tablespoon cognac

1 to 2 Tablespoons lemon juice
Salt and pepper

* * *

1 Tablespoon parsley, minced
2 Tablespoons butter

Makes 2 cups

1. Remove marrow from bones and place marrow in boiling water for 5 minutes. Drain. Mince the marrow and blend in the mustard.

2. In a two-quart saucepan, place shallots, garlic and wine, and cook over moderately high heat for 5 minutes. Add the Sauce Brune and cognac, and simmer over a low heat for 10 minutes.

3. Add marrow, lemon juice, and salt and pepper, to taste.

 Warm sauce over low heat. Blend in parsley and butter. Serve immediately. (Do not reheat after butter is added.)

 May be prepared four days ahead through Step 3.

 May be frozen after Step 3.

SAUCE BORDELAISE
(without Sauce Brune)

2 Tablespoons butter
2 chicken livers

SAUCE:
1 teaspoon tomato paste
1 teaspoon meat glaze or Bovril
1¼ cups chicken stock, home-
    made or commercial
2 Tablespoons sherry
2 teaspoons currant jelly
2 teaspoons potato flour
¼ cup red wine

2 Tablespoons cognac

2 marrow bones, split
1 cup red wine
1 bay leaf
¼ cup celery, minced
1 clove garlic, minced
½ teaspoon Dijon mustard
  Salt and pepper

Makes 2½ cups

1. In a two-quart saucepan, heat 1 Tablespoon of the butter, and sauté the chicken livers quickly on all sides. Flame with cognac. Remove the chicken livers and set aside. Do not wash the pan.

2. Sauce: In the same saucepan, heat the tomato paste, meat glaze, chicken stock, sherry and currant jelly. In a small bowl, dissolve the potato flour in ¼ cup wine, and add to the sauce. Allow the sauce to come to a boil and set aside.

3. In a four to five quart saucepan, heat the remaining Tablespoon of butter, and brown the marrow bones quickly. Add the cup of red wine, bay leaf, celery and garlic. Bring slowly to a boil, then add the above sauce. Simmer gently for 1 hour.

4. Cut the chicken livers into thin slices. Remove the marrow from the bones, and blend it with the Dijon mustard. Add the sliced chicken livers. Strain the sauce, and add the chicken-liver and marrow-mustard mixture to it. Season with salt and pepper.

TO SERVE   Warm sauce over low heat.

AHEAD   May be prepared two days ahead and refrigerated.

FREEZE   May be frozen.

FAST AND EASY SAUCE BORDELAISE

2 Tablespoons butter
1 shallot, minced
1 onion, sliced
2 large carrots, sliced
Meat scraps, if available
2 Tablespoons flour
1¼ cups beef stock,
    homemade or commercial
1 teaspoon meat glaze or Bovril

BOUQUET GARNI:
½ bay leaf
1 clove
4 peppercorns
3 sprigs parsley

*   *   *

Salt and pepper
¼ cup dry Madeira wine
1 Tablespoon parsley, minced

Makes 1½ cups

1. In a two-quart saucepan, heat the butter. Add the shallot, onion, carrots and meat scraps, and sauté until golden brown. Add flour and cook over low heat, stirring constantly until flour is lightly browned.

2. Add beef stock, meat glaze and bouquet garni; blend carefully. Simmer until slightly thickened, about 10 minutes. Strain and add salt, pepper, and wine. Refrigerate after sauce has cooled.

 Heat in double boiler 15 minutes before serving. If sauce is too thick, thin with 1 to 2 Tablespoons of Madeira. Add parsley.

 May be prepared four days ahead. Store covered in the refrigerator.

 May be frozen.

The green peppers from Madagascar have a distinctive taste that makes this sauce unusual. You should be able to find them in gourmet or specialty food shops. The sauce can be served with beef and roast duck.

SAUCE POIVRE VERT
(Green Pepper Sauce)

1 Tablespoon drained green peppercorns
2 Tablespoons butter
2 Tablespoons shallots, minced
5 ounces dry white wine
½ cup Sauce Brune (see page 83)
½ to 1 cup heavy cream
½ teaspoon Dijon mustard

1 teaspoon potato starch, if needed
2 Tablespoons cognac

OPTIONAL:

2 Tablespoons butter

Makes 1½ cups

1. With a mortar and pestle, coarsely crush the peppercorns.

2. In a skillet, heat the butter. When it is foaming, add the shallots and sauté for 3 to 4 minutes. Add the green peppercorns and stir. Add the wine, and cook over high heat, uncovered, until the amount of wine is reduced to about 2 ounces. Strain, and discard peppercorns. Lower heat and stir in the Sauce Brune, blending it carefully.

3. Blend in the cream and the mustard. If the sauce does not seem thick enough, dissolve 1 teaspoon of potato starch in a Tablespoon of white wine. Add it to the sauce, and bring to a simmer again until it is slightly thickened.

 TO SERVE

Heat. Add cognac and butter, if desired, just before serving.

 AHEAD

May be prepared early in the day through Step 2.

 FREEZE

Do not freeze.

*A basic white sauce is the foundation of
many other sauces, as well as the one used for
soufflés and cream soups. Take the trouble to
cook Sauce Béchamel for the full 30 minutes,
and your reward will be excellent sauces,
soufflés, and soups. It takes that much time
for the flour to be thoroughly assimilated.*

SAUCE BÉCHAMEL
(Cream Base White Sauce)

2 Tablespoons butter
4 Tablespoons onion, finely
  chopped
4 Tablespoons flour
3 cups milk, at room
  temperature
¼ teaspoon salt

3 white peppercorns
1 sprig parsley
¼ teaspoon celery seed
Pinch ground nutmeg

Makes 2 cups

1. Melt the butter in a two-quart saucepan over low heat. Sauté the onion until soft, but not brown. Stir in the flour to make a roux (paste). Cook slowly, stirring constantly with a whisk until it is lump-free and frothy, approximately 2 minutes.

2. Remove the saucepan from the heat, gradually pour in the milk. Stir constantly with a whisk until the sauce is smooth. Return to the stove and add the seasonings. Cook the sauce uncovered, stirring frequently for 30 minutes or until it is reduced by one-third. Strain the sauce.

SAUCE VELOUTÉ

Sauce Velouté is the same as Sauce Béchamel, except that stock is used instead of milk or cream.

  Follow the recipe for Sauce Béchamel, substituting 3 cups boiling white stock for the 3 cups of milk. For poultry, use chicken stock; for fish, use fish stock (fumet de poisson). For flavor enrichment, ½ cup to 1 cup of cream may be substituted in place of the same amount of white stock. Makes 2 cups.

Restaurants use Mornay Sauce to glamorize leftovers. So can you!

SAUCE MORNAY

2 cups Sauce Béchamel or
Sauce Velouté
(see page 88)
¼ to ½ cup grated Gruyère
or Swiss cheese

¼ cup grated Parmesan cheese
¼ teaspoon grated nutmeg
2 egg yolks

Makes 2¼ cups

1. Over low heat, add the Gruyère and Parmesan cheeses and nutmeg to either the Sauce Béchamel or Velouté.

2. Beat the yolks in a small bowl. Add a small amount of the hot sauce to the yolks while beating constantly.

3. Return the yolk mixture to the sauce, and blend thoroughly with a whisk. This is called liaison enrichment, and prevents curdling of the egg yolks. Stir over low heat for one minute.

Warm over low heat, stirring constantly.

May be prepared four days ahead and refrigerated.

May be frozen in styrofoam cups. When defrosting, it may look curdled. Reheat **slowly** to the boiling point, stirring with a wire whisk, to restore the sauce to its normal consistency.

SAUCE AUX CHAMPIGNONS
(Mushroom Sauce)

2 Tablespoons butter
¼ pound mushrooms, sliced thinly
1 Tablespoon shallots, minced
½ cup dry white wine
1½ cups Sauce Béchamel (see page 88)

¾ cup whipping cream, milk or sour cream (at room temperature)
2 Tablespoons parsley, minced
Salt and pepper

Makes 2½ cups

In a small skillet, heat the butter. Add the mushrooms and shallots, and sauté until lightly browned. Add wine and simmer over medium heat until it is almost evaporated. Stir in the Sauce Béchamel. Simmer for 5 minutes. Blend in cream carefully, and continue to simmer for an additional 5 minutes. (If sour cream is used, warm over low heat. Do not allow to simmer.) Add salt and pepper to taste.

Add the parsley and warm over low heat, stirring constantly.

May be prepared four days ahead and refrigerated.

May be frozen in styrofoam cups. When defrosting it may appear curdled. Reheat slowly to the boiling point, stirring with a wire whisk to restore the sauce to its normal consistency.

You'll know the butter is hot enough to make Sauce Hollandaise and Sauce Béarnaise when you hear it sizzle. Your investment in a one-pint, wide-necked thermos jar will take all the last-minute pressure off you, as it will keep the sauce hot for an hour before serving. Serve with eggs, vegetables, crêpes, and chicken.

SAUCE HOLLANDAISE

3 egg yolks
2 Tablespoons fresh lemon juice
¼ teaspoon salt
⅛ teaspoon cayenne pepper
½ cup butter

OPTIONAL:
  1 Tablespoon parsley, minced

UTENSIL:
1-pint, wide-necked thermos jar

Makes ¾ cup

1. Pour boiling water into the thermos jar to heat it.

2. Blend the egg yolks, lemon juice, salt, cayenne (and parsley) for 5 seconds.

3. In a skillet, heat the butter until it is sizzling.

4. Pour the hot sizzling butter in a steady stream into the running blender. If the butter cools at all, the sauce will not thicken properly. When all of the sizzling butter has been added (which should take about 15 seconds), turn off the blender.

5. Drain and dry the thermos jar, and immediately pour the hot sauce into it.

SAUCE BÉARNAISE

2 Tablespoons tarragon vinegar	⅛ teaspoon meat glaze (Bovril)
2 teaspoons fresh tarragon, or 1 teaspoon dried tarragon	⅛ teaspoon Sauce Robert (available at markets)
6 shallots, or the white section of 6 green onions, minced	1 cup butter
2 Tablespoons dry white wine	UTENSIL:
4 egg yolks	1-pint wide-necked thermos jar
¼ teaspoon salt	
¼ teaspoon dry mustard	*Makes 1½ cups*

1. Pour boiling water into the thermos jar to preheat it. In a skillet, heat the tarragon vinegar, tarragon, shallots and wine, and simmer until almost all of the liquid is absorbed.

2. Place the shallot mixture in the blender, add the egg yolks, salt, mustard, meat glaze, and Sauce Robert, and blend for 15 seconds.

3. In the same pan, heat the butter until it is sizzling hot.

4. Pour the hot sizzling butter in a steady stream into the running blender. If the butter cools at all, the sauce will not thicken properly. When all of the sizzling butter has been added (which should take about 15 seconds), turn off the blender.

5. Drain and dry the thermos jar, and immediately pour the hot sauce into it.

Leftover sauce may be frozen for use only for basting, not as a pouring sauce.

For better flavor, use this sauce wherever tomato paste is called for in a recipe as well as in Marinara dishes. It's good to keep on hand in small amounts frozen in ice cubes or styrofoam cups.

SAUCE MARINARA

2 Tablespoons olive oil
2 cloves garlic, minced
1 28-ounce can tomato purée
1 Tablespoon sugar
1 teaspoon oregano
1 teaspoon basil

1 Tablespoon fresh parsley, minced
1 teaspoon salt
¼ teaspoon pepper

Makes 3 cups

In a three-quart saucepan, heat the olive oil and sauté the garlic until it is golden brown. Add the tomato purée, sugar, oregano, basil, parsley, salt and pepper, and simmer for 15 minutes with the lid only partially covering the pan so that it does not splatter.

May be refrigerated for two weeks.

May be frozen for six months.

San Rufillo is a trattoria in Italy famous for its marvelous red meat sauce. Use it as a spaghetti sauce or whenever an Italian red meat sauce is called for in a recipe.

SAUCE CARNE SAN RUFILLO

2 Tablespoons olive oil
2 cloves garlic, minced
1 cup of onion, diced
2 carrots, peeled and grated
1 pound lean ground beef
½ cup green pepper, diced
½ pound mushrooms, thinly sliced
1 Tablespoon parsley, chopped
1 28-ounce can Tomato Magic or Italian plum tomatoes (available at Italian markets)
8 ounces of Marinara Sauce (see page 93)

1 6-ounce can tomato paste
1 teaspoon salt
½ teaspoon white pepper
⅛ teaspoon crushed red pepper
½ teaspoon ground allspice
1 teaspoon oregano
1 teaspoon basil
1 bay leaf
½ cup red wine

Makes 8 cups

1. In a four to five quart saucepan, heat the olive oil, and sauté the garlic, onions, and grated carrot until lightly browned.

2. Add meat and brown well. Increase the heat and cook until any liquid is evaporated.

3. Add the green pepper, mushrooms, parsley, tomatoes, Marinara Sauce, tomato paste, salt, pepper, crushed red pepper, allspice, oregano, basil and bay leaf. Simmer over low heat uncovered for 1 ½ hours.

4. Add the red wine and simmer for half an hour more. Add salt and pepper to taste.

May be prepared two weeks ahead, and refrigerated.

May be frozen.

Serve with Truites En Chemise (see page 132), sand dabs, broiled fish, cold poached salmon, or shellfish.

SAUCE AMANDINE
(Almond Sauce)

½ cup butter	3 Tablespoons dry white wine
¼ cup margarine	½ teaspoon salt
1 cup blanched almonds	⅛ teaspoon pepper
¼ teaspoon garlic, minced	
1½ Tablespoons fresh lemon juice	*Approximately 1½ cups*

1. In a skillet, melt the butter and margarine. Add the almonds and sauté until lightly browned. Stir in the garlic, lemon juice, wine, salt and pepper.
2. Heat until the sauce bubbles, stirring with a wooden spoon. Keep loosening the glaze at the bottom of the pan.

May be prepared a day ahead and refrigerated. May be frozen.

Serve with cold poached salmon, and shell-fish. It will keep in the refrigerator for one year.

MUSTARD DILL SAUCE

½ cup sugar	½ cup mayonnaise
1 cup fresh dill	2 Tablespoons oil
1 cup Dijon mustard	
⅓ cup wine vinegar	*Makes 2 cups*

In a small bowl, mix the sugar and dill together. Blend in the mustard, vinegar and mayonnaise. Add the oil slowly, and mix well.

Do not freeze.

SAUCE AUX CONCOMBRES
(Cucumber Sauce)

1 cucumber peeled, grated, and drained

SAUCE:
½ cup sour cream
¼ cup mayonnaise
1 Tablespoon lemon juice
1 teaspoon pickle relish

2 Tablespoons onion, grated
1 to 2 Tablespoons fresh dill, minced
2 Tablespoons parsley, minced
Salt and pepper to taste

Makes 1 cup

1. Sauce: In a small bowl, combine the sour cream, mayonnaise, lemon juice, pickle relish, grated onion, dill, parsley, salt and pepper.

2. Add the cucumber just before serving. If the sauce is too thin, thicken by adding more sour cream.

Sauce may be prepared 1 day ahead and refrigerated.

A classic sauce that may be served hot or cold to accompany fowl, game birds, ham or tongue.

CUMBERLAND SAUCE

¾ cup red currant jelly
¼ cup ruby port wine
Juice and rind of 1 orange
1 Tablespoon lemon juice
1 Tablespoon prepared mustard

1 teaspoon paprika
1 teaspoon fresh ginger, grated, or ½ teaspoon dried ginger

Makes 1 cup

Melt the jelly over low heat in a one-quart saucepan. Add the wine, orange and lemon juice, mustard, paprika and ginger. Simmer for a few minutes, stirring well. Add the orange rind and cook 1 minute more.

May be prepared two weeks ahead and refrigerated.

It's a great convenience to have a good seasoning salt on hand for hamburgers, broiled chicken, baked potatoes with sour cream, or dozens of other uses. Make a double batch, and give half away as a small hostess gift.

HERBES AROMATIQUES

2 cups coarse salt
1 large head of garlic, (approximately 30 cloves) peeled and cut in half
2 Tablespoons ground white pepper
1 scant Tablespoon ground ginger
1½ Tablespoons Poultry Seasoning
3 Tablespoons paprika (Hungarian, if possible)
1 Tablespoon dry mustard
3 Tablespoons chile powder
1 Tablespoon celery seed

1 Tablespoon onion powder
1 Tablespoon dried dill weed

OPTIONAL:
1 Tablespoon oregano or basil (May use fresh herbs from the garden)

UTENSIL:
Blender

*   *   *

1 stalk celery or a carrot

Makes 2½ cups

1. Put sufficient salt in the blender to cover the blades. Turn the motor on high, and drop in the cut cloves of garlic. Use a carrot, or a stalk of celery to push the garlic towards the blades. More salt may have to be added depending on the number of cloves in the head of garlic.

2. Remove the salt and minced garlic to a bowl, add the rest of the herbs and spices. Mix thoroughly. Place in a covered jar with a sprinkler top, so you can shake it easily onto foods. It does not have to be refrigerated.

A unique combination of eight spices (despite its name) that you can buy in Paris or Vienna—or make yourself. Use it with pâtés, meat loaves, sausage, or any other ground meat mixture.

QUATRE ÉPICES
(The Four Spices)

1 teaspoon ground cinnamon
2 teaspoons ground allspice
⅛ teaspoon ground cloves
½ teaspoon ground cardamom
1 teaspoon grated nutmeg
2 teaspoons ground coriander

2 teaspoons dry tarragon, finely crushed
½ teaspoon dried marjoram, finely crushed

Makes ½ cup

Combine all the spices. Store in a covered jar. It does not have to be refrigerated.

CHAPTER 4

Eggs, Omelettes, Soufflés, and Crêpes

EGGS

There is nothing like an egg! It is probably the most versatile food and ingredient in all of cooking. Eggs can be served in an incredible variety of ways: baked, boiled, coddled, fried, poached, scrambled, and shirred. Omelettes are as infinite as the imagination. Eggs can be combined into other dishes like eggs benedict, eggs en gelée, ham and eggs.

They are the magic ingredients in soufflés and meringues and in many cakes and desserts. They are used as thickening agents, binding agents, and for egg wash to paint pastry before baking. Egg dishes are served hot or cold, morning, noon, and night.

The most general rule about eggs is to cook them quickly, and gently. The fresher the eggs, the better, except in the case of hard-cooking them. All recipes in this book are based on using extra-large eggs.

1. *How to Tell a Fresh Egg:* Break the egg into a bowl. One-half of the shell will contain a membrane which should be no larger than the size of a dime. As the egg ages, the membrane enlarges to about the size of a quarter. Obviously, the egg with the smallest membrane is the freshest.

2. *Technique for Hard-Cooking Eggs:* Use the oldest eggs in the refrigerator to hard-cook, as the shells are more easily removed from older eggs. Place eggs which are at room temperature in an enamel pan, and cover with cold water. Bring the water to a

simmer, cover, and cook for 12 minutes. Remove from the heat, and allow the pan to sit covered for 5 minutes, allowing them to cool. Drain and use.

3. *Technique for Separating Eggs:* Separate eggs while they are cold. Have three bowls available. Crack each egg with the blunt edge of a knife, and pour the white into a small bowl. If it is clear of egg yolk, then add it to other egg whites. Save the yolks in the third bowl. Do not crack eggs over the bowl containing egg whites, as any small amount of egg yolk will prevent the whites from beating properly.

4. *Technique for Beating Egg Whites:* Beaten egg whites are used in soufflés, meringues, spongecakes, and many other cakes and desserts. Egg whites should be at room temperature before beating in order to get the greatest volume. For every 3 egg whites, use ⅛ teaspoon of cream of tartar, and ⅛ teaspoon of salt. (This is not necessary if you use a steel whisk to beat eggs in an unlined copper bowl, which has the same chemical effect.) Start beating the egg whites on the lowest speed of the electric mixer. When they are foamy, add the cream of tartar and salt. Keep increasing the speed until soft peaks form. (If sugar is required, it is at this point it should be added, 1 Tablespoon at a time.) Continue beating until the peaks are stiff and shiny and hold their shape. As a general rule, it is better to underbeat egg whites. If you overbeat eggs that are being used in a soufflé, the soufflé will not rise.

5. *Leftover Yolks:* May be used in sauces and for egg wash. Cover with plastic and refrigerate. Also, yolks may be poached until hard-cooked, minced, and used as a garnish.

6. *Leftover Egg Whites:* Flash-freeze in individual ice cube tray (1 egg white to each cube). Store the egg white cubes in a plastic bag for easy use. Defrost as needed at room temperature. One egg white equals 1 ounce.

FRENCH METHOD FOR POACHING EGGS

Eggs at room temperature
   (1 per serving)
2 Tablespoons vinegar

UTENSILS:
10- to 12-inch skillet (not black
   cast iron)
Slotted spoon
Bowl of cold water

1. Put the uncooked eggs in their shells into a pot of boiling water for 10 seconds. Remove them from the pot immediately.

2. In a large skillet, put 2 inches of water and 2 Tablespoons of vinegar, and bring to a simmer. Break the eggs gently into the water, and poach for 3 minutes. If an egg is not holding its shape, mold it with two large spoons. Remove each egg with a slotted spoon, and place in the bowl of cold water to stop the cooking, and to wash off any taste of vinegar.

NOTE: *If you are poaching 6 to 8 eggs, it is easy to keep track of which ones you have cooked first by arranging them in the skillet clockwise.*

TO SERVE Serve hot. If the ends of the eggs are ragged, trim with kitchen shears.

AHEAD Eggs may be poached two days in advance and refrigerated in a bowl of ice water. To reheat, place the poached eggs in a strainer and heat for 30 seconds to 1 minute in a pan of boiling water. Set the strainer on a towel to drain. Use as directed.

OMELETTES

There are two basic kinds of omelettes: savory and dessert. Any filling for crêpes may also be used for omelettes.

The omelette pan should be a curved (not straight-sided) 10-inch seasoned, aluminum pan. To season a new omelette pan, fill with coarse salt, and set over the lowest heat possible on an electric stove, or in the lowest oven temperature in a gas oven for 48 hours continuously. (If you have a friend with a new omelette pan, season hers or his at the same time!) Use the omelette pan for omelettes only. Do not wash it with water. Wipe with a paper towel, and if an abrasive is necessary, use coarse salt. For persistent spots, wipe with plain steel wool and coarse salt, never with soap. Store the omelette pan in a plastic bag so dust does not accumulate in it.

TECHNIQUE FOR OMELETTES

Classic Omelette ingredients (see page 105)
Prepared filling.
10-inch seasoned omelette pan.

1. Place the butter in the omelette pan and melt over high heat until the butter sizzles, but has not started to brown. Pour in the egg mixture all at once.

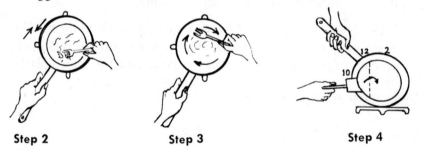

Step 2   Step 3   Step 4

2. The important thing is to start shaking the pan *immediately* with the left hand and *simultaneously* with the right hand hold the fork flat-side down rapidly and stir the eggs until they begin to set. (Something like patting your head and rubbing your stomach, but it gets easier with practice.)

3. Once the eggs have begun to set, use the fork to spread the top of the egg mixture toward the edges to allow the surface to cook. Add the filling.

4. Folding the omelette: Consider the omelette pan as a clock, with the handle as 12:00 o'clock. Tilt the handle slightly. Place the pancake turner under the omelette at 10:00 o'clock. Lift the omelette, and fold over toward the center.

Step 5   **Step 6**   **Step 7**

5. Repeat, placing the pancake turner under the omelette at 2:00 o'clock, and fold over.

6. With the pan tilted, use the pancake turner to loosen the omelette at 12:00 o'clock and fold it towards the center.

7. Turning out the omelette: Change your grip and hold the handle in the palm of your left hand. Hold a warm plate in the other hand at a right angle, and roll the omelette onto the heated plate.

NOTE: *It takes 30 to 60 seconds to make an omelette.*

The classic omelette can be filled in literally dozens of ways. After the eggs have begun to set, add the filling. It can be simply 1 to 2 Tablespoons of grated cheese, or sautéed chicken livers, duxelle, cooked shrimp and mushrooms, asparagus, cooked oysters with strips of fried bacon, tomatoes and eggplant or whatever you like. All fillings for crêpes can be interchanged for omelettes.

CLASSIC OMELETTE

3 eggs
½ teaspoon salt
⅛ teaspoon white pepper
1 teaspoon water

* * *

1 Tablespoon sweet butter

GARNISH:

1 teaspoon sweet butter

⅛ teaspoon white pepper
1 teaspoon parsley, minced

UTENSILS:

Wire whisk
10-inch omelette pan
Table fork
Pancake turner

Serves 1

1. In a small bowl, combine the eggs, salt, pepper, and water, and beat with a wire whisk.

2. Follow the directions for cooking omelettes on page 103.

Variation: Omelette Aux Fines Herbes

2 Tablespoons fresh parsley, minced
1 teaspoon thyme or tarragon

2 teaspoons shallots, chopped
⅛ teaspoon garlic, minced

Add the herbs to the egg mixture of the Classic Omelette.

TO SERVE

Spread a teaspoon of butter on top of omelette, sprinkle with white pepper and parsley.

AHEAD

May be prepared 15 minutes ahead, tented with foil, and kept warm in a preheated 200 degree oven.

*This omelette is incredibly good using all of
the ingredients, or selecting a few of them.*

OMELETTE VALENCIA

Classic Omelette (see page 105)
½ cup avocado, chopped fine
1 small tomato, peeled and
  diced
3 strips bacon, fried until crisp,
  drained, and crumbled
½ to 1 teaspoon green chiles,
  chopped fine
¼ cup Jack cheese, grated
1 Tablespoon watercress,
  minced

1 small clove garlic, minced
½ to 1 teaspoon oregano
⅛ teaspoon cumin
Salt and pepper
Sour cream

GARNISH:
Sour cream

Serves 2

1. In a bowl, combine the avocado, tomato, bacon, chiles, cheese, watercress, garlic, oregano, cumin, salt, and pepper. Add enough sour cream to bind the mixture together.

2. Preheat the broiler and follow the omelette directions on page 103. When the eggs have begun to set, place a few spoonfuls of the filling on top of the eggs before folding.

3. Fold the omelette, and spread with the remainder of the filling. Dot with sour cream.

4. Place under the broiler for a few seconds.

TO SERVE

Serve with additional sour cream
at the table.

AHEAD

May be prepared 15 minutes ahead through
Step 3 and kept warm in a preheated
200 degree oven.

Dessert omelettes differ from the savory omelettes in several ways. First, the egg whites are beaten into a meringue. Second, the omelette is baked in the oven and it is fluffy, somewhat like a soufflé. (To make a savory omelette, add a vegetable, cheese, meat, or seafood filling; eliminate the sugar and lemon rind.) If used for a lunch or dinner omelette, it serves 2.

CLASSIC OMELETTE AU SUCRE
(Dessert Omelette)

3 eggs, separated
1½ Tablespoons flour
1 teaspoon lemon rind, grated fine
⅛ teaspoon cream of tartar
⅛ teaspoon salt
1½ Tablespoons sugar
1 Tablespoon butter

CURRANT GLAZE:

2 Tablespoons currant jelly
1½ Tablespoons Galliano or Grand Marnier

GARNISH:

Confectioners' sugar
Lemon or orange slices

UTENSILS:

10-inch omelette pan
Pancake turner
Serving platter
Skewer

Serves 4

1. In a mixer, beat the yolks until lemon-colored. Add the flour and lemon rind, and blend thoroughly.

2. In a separate bowl, beat the egg whites until foamy, and add the cream of tartar and salt. Continue beating until soft peaks form. Add the sugar gradually and continue beating until the peaks are stiff and shiny. Fold into the yolk mixture.

3. Melt the butter in the omelette pan. Spread the egg mixture over the bottom and up the sides of the pan.

4. Preheat the oven to 375 degrees. Bake for 11 minutes on the middle shelf.

5. Currant Glaze: In a small pan, heat the currant jelly until it liquefies. Remove from heat, and stir in 2 teaspoons of liqueur.

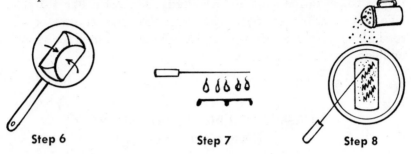

Step 6   Step 7   Step 8

6. Remove the omelette from the oven, and spread with the currant glaze. With a pancake turner, fold it into thirds lengthwise. Turn it onto a heated platter.

7. Heat the skewer until it is red hot.

8. Dust the omelette with confectioners' sugar. Sear it in three diagonal lines with the hot skewer.

Drizzle with remaining liqueur. Garnish with lemon or orange slices.

Step 1 may be done a few hours ahead.
Currant glaze and liqueur will keep
for 1 year refrigerated.
Omelette may be made 15 minutes ahead
through Step 6, tented with foil, and
kept warm in a preheated 200 degree oven.

The Viennese have always been masters of desserts. This is one of their simpler classics from the Hotel Sacher in Vienna.

OMELETTE JOHANN STRAUSS
(Omelette with Lemon Custard Filling)

2 recipes for Classic Omelette au Sucre (see page 107)

LEMON CUSTARD FILLING:

5 egg yolks
2 teaspoons grated lemon rind
4 Tablespoons lemon juice
½ cup sugar

       *   *   *

1 cup cream, whipped

GARNISHES:

Confectioners' sugar
Lemon slices

UTENSILS:
8- or 10-inch omelette pan

Serves 4

1. Lemon Custard Filling: Put the egg yolks in the top of a double boiler, and beat until lemon-colored and thick. Add the lemon rind, lemon juice, and sugar. Set the top of the double boiler in the lower pan containing simmering water (do not let the water touch the bottom of the pan), and place over low heat. Stir constantly until the mixture is thick, approximately 10 minutes.

2. Prepare the dessert omelettes. Spread half of the whipped cream on top of each omelette. Cover with lemon custard filling. Top with the remaining half of the whipped cream. Fold over each omelette.

Variation: Strawberry Cream Filling.
Combine 1 cup of strawberries with 1 Tablespoon kirsch and ½ cup sour cream.

TO SERVE

Sprinkle with powdered sugar, and garnish with twisted lemon slices.

There has always been a mystique to soufflés. Basically, a soufflé is a combination of a Sauce Béchamel, a main flavor ingredient, and beaten egg whites. Once you think of soufflés in those terms, you will never feel intimidated by them.

There are savory soufflés and dessert soufflés, with dozens of variations for each. As a matter of fact, delicious soufflés can be made from practically anything.

A soufflé must be served the moment it is removed from the oven or it will fall. The old saw is that the guests wait for the soufflé, the soufflé never waits for the guests. If you follow a few basic rules, you will turn out a perfect soufflé every time.

THE SOUFFLÉ DISH

Use a 1½-quart soufflé dish. It is the correct size to ensure proper baking and rising and will serve six to eight people. To serve more, use two 1½-quart soufflé dishes, not a larger one.

To prepare a soufflé dish for savory soufflés, grease the dish with butter, and coat with equal parts of grated Parmesan cheese and breadcrumbs. To prepare a soufflé dish for dessert soufflés, grease the dish with butter and coat with sugar.

To prepare a collar for a soufflé dish, cut a piece of waxed paper to encircle the dish, allowing two inches extra for overlapping. Fold the waxed paper in half lengthwise. Grease the upper half of the wax paper with butter or margarine. Coat it with grated Parmesan and breadcrumbs or sugar. With a string, tie the waxed paper securely around the soufflé dish.

BASIC SOUFFLÉ RECIPE

The basic soufflé mixture or "panada" is a thick Sauce Béchamel.
You can make a soufflé from practically anything using this fomula:

PANADA:
  1 Tablespoon buttter
  4 Tablespoons flour
  1 cup liquid (milk, cream,
    stock, etc.)

    *   *   *

  4 to 5 egg yolks
  5 to 8 egg whites

⅛ teaspoon cream of tartar
⅛ teaspoon salt

SAVORY SOUFFLÉS:
  1 cup of main flavor ingredient
    (cheese, fish, seafood, meat, or
    vegetable) well-drained and
    finely chopped.

Serves 6 to 8

NOTE: *Always use 1 or 2 more egg whites than yolks in all soufflés.*

1. In a saucepan, melt the butter and stir in the flour. Add the
   liquid slowly, stirring constantly. Add the main flavoring ingredient called for in the recipe and blend well.

2. In a small bowl, stir a little of the panada mixture into the yolks,
   blending carefully. Stir the yolk mixture into the panada mixture
   in the saucepan. Beat with a whisk over low heat for 1 minute.
   Remove from heat and allow to cool. The soufflé mixture should
   be warm, not hot, when the beaten egg whites are folded in.

3. Beating Egg Whites: Egg whites should be at room temperature.
   Beat the egg whites until foamy, and add cream of tartar and salt.
   For savory soufflés continue beating until egg whites are stiff but
   not dry. For dessert soufflés continue beating until soft peaks
   form. Add the sugar, 1 Tablespoon at a time, and continue beating until the peaks are smooth and shiny.

4. Folding Beaten Egg Whites into Soufflé Mixture: With a rubber
   spatula, take a quarter of the stiffly beaten egg whites and stir
   gently into the soufflé mixture to lighten it. Spread the remaining
   beaten egg whites on top of the soufflé mixture. Fold in the egg

whites by moving the spatula downward through the center of the soufflé mixture, along the bottom and up the side of the bowl near you. Rotate the bowl a quarter turn at a time, and repeat the procedure rapidly several times until the soufflé mixture is incorporated into the egg whites. Do not overblend the egg whites. Streaks of the whites should be visible.

Carefully spoon the mixture into the prepared soufflé dish. If folded properly, the soufflé mixture should come almost to the top of the dish. Just before placing the soufflé in the oven, run the dull edge of a knife around the outer edge to separate the mixture from the dish. This will help the soufflé rise more evenly.

5. Baking: Preheat the oven to 375 degrees. Bake for approximately 30 to 35 minutes, in the lower third of the oven. For individual 8-ounce soufflé dishes, bake 15 to 20 minutes.

6. Testing Soufflés: Once the soufflé is golden brown on top, and it is within a few minutes of the suggested baking time, insert a long trussing needle or skewer into the center. If it comes out clean, it means the soufflé is ready to serve. If the needle comes out with soufflé mixture on it, reduce the oven temperature to 325 degrees so that the top will not become too brown, but the soufflé will completely cook. Bake until the needle comes out clean when tested.

Bring the soufflé to the table with the collar on. Remove the string and waxed paper. Using two serving spoons, scoop the soufflé into the center and upward.

May be made early in the day through Step 2.

Do not freeze.

You'll think of sweet potatoes with a whole new respect after you taste this soufflé.

SWEET POTATO SOUFFLÉ

2/3 cup light cream
½ cup orange juice concentrate
¼ cup butter, melted
1 Tablespoon lemon juice
2½ cups mashed sweet potatoes
3 egg yolks

* * *

¾ teaspoon salt
¼ teaspoon ground allspice
¼ teaspoon ground cardamom
⅛ teaspoon ground pepper
⅛ teaspoon ground nutmeg
6 Tablespoons sugar
2 teaspoons grated orange rind
1 teaspoon grated lemon rind
15 gingersnaps, finely rolled
(about 1 cup)

5 egg whites
¼ teaspoon salt
¼ teaspoon cream of tartar

* * *

½ cup nuts, chopped
¼ cup brown sugar, packed
firm

UTENSILS:
1½-quart soufflé dish or
2-quart casserole, lightly
greased and collared

Serves 12

1. In a mixer, combine the cream, orange juice concentrate, melted butter, and lemon juice. Add the potatoes and beat until blended. Add egg yolks one at a time, beating well.

   Combine salt, allspice, cardamom, pepper, and nutmeg with 4 Tablespoons of sugar and add to potato mixture. Add the orange and lemon rinds and all but 2 Tablespoons of gingersnaps. Sprinkle the remaining 2 Tablespoons of gingersnap crumbs on the sides and bottom of the greased soufflé dish.

2. Beat the egg whites until foamy. Add the cream of tartar and salt. Continue beating until soft peaks form. Add 2 Tablespoons of sugar, 1 Tablespoon at a time, and continue beating until the peaks are stiff and shiny. Fold into potato mixture, and pour into the soufflé dish. Sprinkle chopped nuts and brown sugar on top.

3. Preheat the oven to 350 degrees. Bake for 1 hour and 15 minutes, or until done and top is brown.

Serve piping hot. Remove the collar at the table.

May be prepared early in the day through Step 1.

Do not freeze.

An absolutely elegant dessert.

PERFECT SOUFFLÉ GRAND MARNIER

2 large sugar cubes
1 orange
3 Tablespoons butter
3 Tablespoons flour
½ cup milk
¼ cup orange juice
4 egg yolks
3 Tablespoons orange marmalade
¼ cup Grand Marnier
6 egg whites
⅛ teaspoon cream of tartar
⅛ teaspoon salt

* * *

Confectioners' sugar

SERVE WITH:
1 orange, sliced thin
Crème Chantilly (see page 265)

UTENSILS:
1½ quart soufflé dish with collar

Serves 6 to 8

1. Rub the two sugar cubes over the skin of the orange to remove the zest or outer skin. Set them aside.

2. In a saucepan, melt the butter, and stir in the flour. Remove from heat. Add the milk, orange juice, and two sugar cubes with orange zest. Beat with a whisk until smooth. Return to heat until the mixture thickens.

3. In a small bowl, beat the egg yolks, marmalade, and Grand Marnier. Stir a little of the milk and orange juice mixture into the yolk mixture. Return to the saucepan. Beat with a whisk over low heat for 1 minute. Remove from heat and allow to cool.

4. In a mixer, beat the egg whites until foamy, and add the cream of tartar and salt. Continue beating until the peaks are stiff and shiny.

5. Fold the egg whites into the soufflé mixture. Pour into the prepared soufflé dish.

6. Bake for 25 minutes. Sprinkle with confectioners' sugar, and bake until puffed and golden brown, approximately 5 to 15 minutes more. (Total baking time is 30 to 45 minutes.)

Serve hot. Garnish with thin slices of orange and Crème Chantilly.

May be prepared early in the day through Step 3.

Do not freeze.

CRÊPES

*A crêpe is no more than a thin pancake,
filled and covered with a sauce and served
as an hors-d'oeuvre, main course or dessert.
It can be a creative way to use leftovers. Any
filling for crêpes may also be used for omelettes.*

TECHNIQUES FOR CRÊPES

If sweet crêpes are to be used as a cold dessert, brown them on both
sides. Otherwise, it is not necessary, as they will brown in the final
heating.

Butter for frying
Crêpes batter (see page 120).

UTENSILS:
  8-inch Teflon omelette pan
  ¼ cup size measuring cup
  Dish towel

1. Heat the pan. Melt about 1 teaspoon of butter over moderately
   high heat until the butter sizzles, but has not started to brown.
   Pour off any excess butter.

Step 2   **Step 3**   **Step 4**

2. Hold the pan off the heat with one hand; with the other, pour in
   ¼ cup of the batter.

3. Rapidly tilt the pan back and forth to distribute the batter evenly
   on the bottom and part way up the sides.

4. Pour the excess batter back into the bowl. The timing is crucial in making crêpes; the batter must be poured and swirled in a few seconds and the excess poured off. This is what makes paper-thin crêpes.

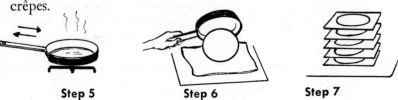

Step 5   **Step 6**   **Step 7**

5. Return the pan to the heat, shaking rapidly so the crêpe does not stick to the bottom.

6. When the top of the crêpe looks dry, and the edges are lightly browned, remove from heat, and flip onto a towel. If the crêpe is to be filled, it is not necessary to cook it on both sides.

   Allow the crêpe to cool on the towel before handling it. Repeat procedure, until all the batter is used, adding butter before each crêpe is made.

7. If crêpes are to be used immediately, fill and serve. If crêpes are made ahead, smooth out each crêpe, and stack between pieces of waxed paper or foil. Wrap the entire stack in plastic or foil.

TECHNIQUES FOR FOLDING CRÊPES, BLINTZES, AND EGG ROLLS

1. *Cigar Fold:* Place filling on browned side of crêpe. Roll up like a cigar. Place seam side down in a greased baking pan.

2. *Handkerchief Fold:* Place filling on browned side of crêpe. Fold crêpe in half. Then fold into quarters.

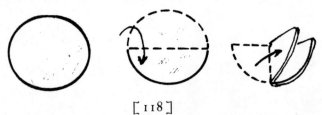

3. *Envelope Fold:* Place filling on browned side of crêpe. Fold front edge over filling. Fold sides in toward center, keeping sides straight. Roll away from you into a neat package and place seam side down in a greased baking pan.

 Crêpes (and blintzes or eggroll skins) may be prepared two days ahead through Step 7 and refrigerated.

 May be frozen through Step 7. Allow to defrost overnight in the refrigerator.

The ingredients are slightly different, but the technique is the same for both savory and sweet crêpes.

BATTER FOR SAVORY AND SWEET CRÊPES

ENTRÉE CRÊPES
(Savory Crêpes)

 4 eggs
 1 cup milk
 1 cup water
 2 cups flour, Wondra preferred
 ½ teaspoon salt
 ¼ cup butter, melted

Makes 12

CRÊPES SUCRE
(Dessert Crêpes)

 3 eggs
 1 egg yolk
 1½ Tablespoons sugar
 1¼ cups milk
 ¾ cup water
 ¼ cup Galliano, Grand
  Marnier, rum or cognac
 1¾ cups flour, Wondra preferred
 ¼ cup nuts, finely ground
 ¼ cup butter, melted

Makes 12

NOTE: *For Dessert Crêpes: Add the nuts at the same time as the flour. Do not add salt.*

1. In a small bowl, beat the eggs with a wire whisk. Add the liquids, a little at a time, beating after each addition. Add the flour and salt, and beat until smooth. Stir in the melted butter. Cover, and refrigerate for 2 to 3 hours to allow the flour to expand so that the crêpes will be light. (If Wondra flour is used, this is not necessary.)

2. To cook, follow directions for Technique for Crêpes on page 117.

Batter may be prepared three to four days ahead and refrigerated. If the batter becomes too thick, thin with milk or water to the consistency of cream.

In France, it's a crêpe; in the United States, a pancake; in the Far East, it's an egg roll, and in many European countries, it's a blintze. They are all related and are served in similar ways.

BATTER FOR BLINTZES AND EGG ROLL SKINS

8 eggs
½ teaspoon salt
⅓ cup oil or melted butter
1¼ cups water

1½ cups flour, Wondra preferred

Makes 16

1. In a small bowl, beat the eggs with a whisk. Add the salt, oil, water, and flour; mix well. Cover and refrigerate for 1 to 2 hours to allow the flour to expand so the "skins" will be light. (If Wondra is used, this is not necessary.)

2. To cook, follow directions for Technique for Crêpes on page 117.

Batter may be prepared three to four days ahead and refrigerated. If the batter becomes too thick, thin with milk or water to the consistency of cream.

I don't know who Theodora was, but the crêpe filling named in her honor is superb. Serve it for lunch, or with a main course as the pasta and vegetables.

CRÊPES THEODORA
(Crêpes with Broccoli Filling)

12 to 16 8-inch Savory Crêpes
(see page 120)

     *   *   *

¾ cup chicken stock, homemade or commercial
2 medium onions, cut into ⅛ths
2 Tablespoons butter
2 Tablespoons flour
4 ounces sour cream or cream cheese at room temperature
2 to 3 Tablespoons Parmesan cheese, grated
4 10-ounce packages frozen chopped broccoli, thawed and drained well, or 5 cups fresh broccoli, cooked and chopped
½ pound mushrooms, sliced thin
2 8-ounce cans water chestnuts, diced coarsely

Salt and pepper
2 Tablespoons lemon juice

     *   *   *

2 cups Sauce Mornay
(see page 89)

GARNISH:
2 Tablespoons Parmesan cheese, grated
4 Tablespoons Gruyère cheese, grated
1 teaspoon fresh dill, minced
4 Tablespoons parsley, minced

UTENSILS:
Au gratin dish, three-quart baking dish, or eight individual au gratin dishes, lightly greased.

Serves 12 to 16

1. In a blender, combine the chicken stock and onions until smooth. Set aside.

2. In a saucepan, melt the butter and stir in the flour. Remove from heat. Add the chicken stock-onion mixture. Beat with a whisk until smooth. Return to heat and stir until the mixture simmers. Simmer an additional 3 minutes. Add the sour cream or cream cheese, and mix well. Add 2 to 3 Tablespoons Parmesan cheese. Remove from heat and allow to cool slightly. Add the broccoli, mushrooms, water chestnuts, salt, pepper, and lemon juice; blend thoroughly.

3. To assemble: Spoon 1 to 2 Tablespoons of the broccoli filling into the end of each crêpe, and roll into a cigar shape (see page 118). Place seam-side down in the au gratin or baking dish. Pour Sauce Mornay over the crêpes, sprinkle with grated cheeses, minced dill, and 1 Tablespoon parsley.

4. Baking: Preheat the oven to 375 degrees. Bake 30 to 45 minutes, or until lightly browned.

Sprinkle with remaining parsley.
Serve hot.

May be prepared one day ahead through Step 3.

May be frozen after Step 3 for 2 to 4 weeks.

A crowd-pleaser that can be prepared in advance for a brunch, lunch, supper, or midnight snack.

CRÊPES AU FROMAGE
(Cheese Crêpes)

16 8-inch Crêpes (see page 120) or
   Blintzes (see page 121)

3 eggs
1 teaspoon baking powder

* * *

CHEESE FILLING:

½ pound Swiss cheese, grated fine
½ pound Jack cheese, grated fine
¼ cup green onions, minced
¼ cup fresh parsley, minced
1 Tablespoon fresh dill, minced

½ cup butter, melted

UTENSILS:

Cookie sheet, lightly greased
Pastry brush

Serves 8

1. Cheese Filling: In a bowl, combine the grated cheeses. Add the onions, parsley, and dill. Beat in the eggs, one at a time. Add the baking powder, and blend well.

2. Spoon 1 Tablespoon of the cheese filling onto the browned side of each crêpe. Fold into an envelope, or cigar-shape (see page 118 or 119), and set on the cookie sheet seam-side down.

3. Preheat the oven to 350 degrees. Brush crêpes with melted butter. Bake for 20 to 30 minutes, until lightly browned.

Serve hot.

May be prepared two days ahead through Step 2 and refrigerated.

Filled crêpes may be flash-frozen. Pack in freezer-proof bags.

CHAPTER 5

Seafood

If you haven't seen it swimming, it is likely that you are buying frozen fish. In the old days, fishing boats went out and returned the same day with their catch. Nowadays, the boats often stay out for a period of weeks and flash-freeze their catch on board. Fresh fish has the best flavor. Whenever possible, depending on where you live, eat fish that is fresh and in season. Catch it yourself or go to the docks and buy it from local fishermen. (Fresh salmon is usually available from the end of March through September, and its flavor is far superior to the frozen.)

The best way to keep fresh or unfrozen fish in the refrigerator is to fill a roasting pan with ice cubes, wrap the fish in plastic, and embed it in the ice. It may be held this way for several days, if the ice is replaced daily.

If fish is frozen, defrost it overnight in the refrigerator before cooking.

POACHING FISH STEAKS OR SMALL FILLETS

Fish are submerged in simmering liquids to sear their outsides and trap the flavor within. If they were cooked in cold liquids to start, the flavor would be lost.

1. Rinse the fish in either salted water (1 Tablespoon salt to 2 quarts water), or acidulated water (1 Tablespoon lemon juice to 1 quart water). Do not rinse the fish under running water or the valuable enzymes will wash away.

2. Submerge the fish in a poacher or skillet of simmering court-bouillon (see page 48). Butter a waxed paper circle and place it, buttered side down, on the surface of the fish. This will keep the fish from drying out in the poaching and will enable you to see and control the simmering.

3. Poach until the fish loses its translucency, and the flesh looks milky white and feels firm to the touch. If you cannot tell by the appearance, test the fish; if it can be flaked easily with a fork, it is done. *Do not overcook* or it will be dry and tasteless.

4. To serve fish hot, allow it to remain in the court-bouillon for 10 minutes after cooking, covered with the wax paper.
   To serve it cold, allow it to remain in the court-bouillon until it is completely cooled.

5. Lift the fish from the pan with one or two large spatulas, allowing liquid to drip back into the pan. Place the fish on a platter, and blot up excess liquid with paper towels.

Poaching a Whole Fish

1. Follow same procedure as Step 1 in poaching fish steaks and small fillets.

2. Filleting: Cut the fish in half lengthwise.
   With a boning knife, scrape carefully along the backbone, pushing away the flesh. Try to lift out the entire backbone in one piece. Feel along the length of the fish with your fingers to be sure there are no small bones left. Add the bones to the court-bouillon (see page 48).

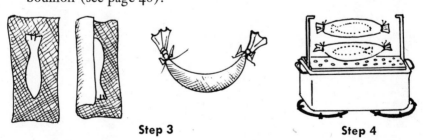

Step 3   **Step 4**

3. Making a hammock: Wrap each fillet in cheesecloth or a linen towel. Twist the ends of the fabric, and tie with string. This will keep the original shape of the fish and make it easy to handle.

4. Whole fish can be cooked in a fish poacher (poissonnière) or a roasting pan with a rack placed in it. Arrange the two wrapped fillets facing in opposite ways so the thickness of the fish is evenly distributed. Cover with cold court-bouillon and place over two burners.

   Large pieces of fish will cook from the inside out, and their exteriors will not be overcooked by the time the center is done.

5. Poaching: Bring the court-bouillon to a boil, cover with lid or foil, and reduce the heat to a simmer. Poach approximately 5 to 8 minutes per pound, depending upon the thickness of the fish. It is difficult to be exact about the length of cooking time for fish. The important thing is to poach fish until it loses its translucency, the flesh is opaque, and it flakes easily.

6. To serve fish hot, allow it to remain in the court-bouillon for 10 minutes after cooking, covered with a circle of waxed paper. To serve fish cold, allow it to remain in the court-bouillon until completely cooled.

7. Using the ends of the twisted cheesecloth hammock as handles, lift the fish out of the court-bouillon and allow the liquid to drip back into the pan. Turn each fish half onto a platter or cookie sheet covered with foil. Remove the skin. Blot up excess liquid with paper towels. Strain the court-bouillon and freeze for later use.

NOTE: *If salmon is poached in court-bouillon, the court-bouillon CANNOT be reused.*

Almost all the shellfish we buy these days has been frozen. Before using it, always defrost frozen shellfish in the refrigerator.

1. Bring the court-bouillon to a boil. Add the thawed shellfish, preferably in the shell. Allow it to cook 1 minute or until the shells turn red or pink, according to the type of shellfish.

2. Cool in the court-bouillon. Drain and refrigerate the shellfish, or use it as called for in the recipe.

TO SERVE — Serve poached fish hot or cold with these sauces: Sauce Verte (see page 238), Sauce Concombre (see page 96) or with Mustard-Dill Sauce (see page 95).

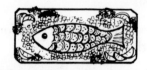

Whenever you can buy fresh salmon, you have a magnificent fish course, entrée, or part of a buffet that can be completely made, decorated and refrigerated a day ahead. I always cut the salmon in half lengthwise and decorate the two halves differently. I serve the first one on a platter, and when it begins to look a little messy, I whisk it out to the kitchen and replace it with the second platter.

SAUMON FROID GARNI
(Chilled Poached Salmon in Aspic)

4 to 6 pound salmon, without head, cut in half lengthwise
2 quarts court-bouillon (see page 48)

FOR CLARIFYING COURT-BOUILLON:

2 egg whites
Shells of 2 eggs

ASPIC:

1½ envelopes unflavored gelatin
1½ cups mayonnaise
4 Tablespoons parsley, minced
4 Tablespoons chives, minced
4 Tablespoons fresh dill, minced

GARNISH:

4 pickling cucumbers, or

2 cucumbers, unpeeled, sliced thin
1 jar or can of sliced pimientos
1 black olive
Sprigs of parsley
Lemon wedges

UTENSILS:

Fish poacher or large pan with rack
Cheesecloth
String

FOR FISH PLATTERS:

Two large platters, or one large platter and one cookie sheet covered with foil, or two cookie sheets or boards covered with foil.

1. Poach the salmon halves in the court-bouillon for approximately 5 to 8 minutes per pound, depending on the thickness of the salmon, until it loses its translucency and flakes easily. (Loosen one end of the cheesecloth hammock after salmon has poached 5 minutes per pound, and check to see if it's done.) Do not overcook, or the salmon will dry out and be tasteless. (See page 127). Allow to cool in the court-bouillon for about an hour.

2. Remove the cheesecloth hammock from the court-bouillon. Turn one salmon half out on a long serving platter skin-side up, and the other half onto a cookie sheet covered with foil. Remove the skin and bones. Save the court-bouillon to make the aspic.

3. Add 1½ envelopes of gelatin to the court bouillon, and cook over low heat until it is dissolved. Measure out 1½ cups of the court-bouillon-gelatin mixture and place it in the refrigerator until it begins to thicken. Put the remaining aspic in a shallow dish and refrigerate it until it is set so that it can be cubed or chopped for garnish later. Add 1½ cups of mayonnaise to the 1½ cups of the slightly thickened aspic, and combine thoroughly. Chill until it thickens a second time. Do not let it get too firm.

4. Coating the Salmon with Aspic: Set each salmon half on a large platter. Make a "fish head" for each salmon half out of small pieces of salmon or cucumber slices and set it where the salmon head would be. Spread the aspic entirely over each salmon half, including the "head", one layer at a time. Chill the salmon until each layer of aspic is set. Continue until all of the aspic is used. (Allow about 15 minutes for each layer of aspic to set.)

5. Decorating: With a vegetable peeler, shave the unpeeled cucumbers into round paper-thin slices. When the last layer of aspic is set, decorate one half with over-lapping slices of cucumber to represent fish scales. Arrange pimiento strips on the tail. Use the black olive for the fish's eye. Garnish with parsley and lemon wedges.

Decorate the other half with flowers made of pimiento.

Cube or chop the jellied aspic, and arrange it in small mounds around each platter.

 TO SERVE

Serve with Sauce aux Concombre (see page 96), Sauce Verte (see page 238), or Mustard-Dill Sauce (see page 95) and Hot Blue Cheese Bread (see page 139) or French bread.

 AHEAD

May be prepared one day ahead through Step 5, covered with plastic and refrigerated. Salmon may be poached two days ahead.

Do not freeze.

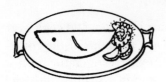

If you have a batch of crêpes on hand in the freezer, this is a quick way to serve trout. A few easy decorating touches will make each crêpe look like a fish.

TRUITES EN CHEMISE
(Stuffed Trout in Crêpes)

4 large brook trout, boned
  and halved lengthwise
2 Tablespoons lemon juice

COATING MIXTURE:

1 cup cornmeal
2 cloves garlic, minced
1 teaspoon salt
¼ teaspoon pepper

* * *

1 cup of Duxelles (see page 212)
  or 1 pound mushrooms chopped
  and sautéed with 1 chopped
  onion
⅓ cup light or heavy cream
8 8-inch crêpes (see page 120)

6 to 8 Tablespoons butter
6 to 8 Tablespoons oil

* * *

LEMON-PARSLEY BUTTER:

½ cup melted butter
2 Tablespoons parsley, minced
3 Tablespoons lemon juice
Sauce Amandine (see page 95)

GARNISH:

Parsley sprigs
Lemon wedges
Tomato or pimiento strips
8 cloves

Serves 8

1. Rinse the trout, and pat dry with paper towels. Sprinkle lemon juice in the cavity.

2. Coating Mixture: Combine the cornmeal, garlic, salt and pepper. Dredge the fish in coating and set aside.

3. Add the cream to the duxelles or sautéed mushrooms. Set aside.

4. Set out the eight crêpes.

[132]

5. In a large skillet, heat half of the butter and oil. Sauté the trout halves quickly over medium high heat, four at a time, until they are browned on the outside, but not cooked completely. Use more butter and oil if necessary.

6. Place a trout half on the front part of each crêpe. Spoon an equal amount of the mushroom mixture on top of each piece of trout. Bring the other half of the crêpe over to cover. Place on a greased baking pan.

7. Preheat the oven to 350 degrees. In a small pan, melt the butter, add the parsley and lemon juice and baste the crêpes frequently with this mixture. Bake the crêpes for 20 minutes, or until they are lightly browned.

Stud one end of the crêpe with a clove for an eye. Make a gill out of a strip of pimiento. Place a small bunch of parsley as a fish tail. Garnish with lemon wedges. Accompany with Sauce Amandine (see page 95).

May be prepared one day ahead through Step 6 and refrigerated.

Only the crêpes and the duxelles (or sautéed mushrooms) can be frozen.

Variation: Truites Amandine: Follow Steps 1 and 2 of Truites En Chemise. Sauté over medium heat until browned on both sides and the fish can be flaked easily with a fork. Do not overcook. Mask fish by spooning Sauce Amandine over it.

An absolutely delicious and exquisite-looking ring mold of fillet of sole, salmon and spinach mousse, with a mushroom and shrimp filling, and an elegant sauce spooned over and around. One of my cooking class assistants has become famous by serving this to the Hollywood movie colony.

SOLE LAURENTIEN-SAUCE JOINVILLE
(Turban of Sole with Two Mousses)

ENRICHED BÉCHAMEL SAUCE:

- 3 Tablespoons butter
- 2 shallots, minced
- 5 Tablespoons flour
- 1 cup milk, at room temperature
- 4 egg yolks (reserve egg whites)
- Salt and pepper

GROUND SALMON MOUSSE:

- 1 pound fresh salmon, uncooked, ground
- 1 teaspoon lemon juice
- 1 Tablespoon fresh dill, minced
- 1 teaspoon paprika
- Salt and pepper

SPINACH MOUSSE:

- 1 10-ounce package chopped, frozen spinach, thawed, well drained
- 1 Tablespoon green onion tops, minced
- ½ teaspoon nutmeg
- Salt and pepper

* * *

- 4 egg whites
- ⅛ teaspoon cream of tartar
- ⅛ teaspoon salt

* * *

FISH:

- 8 to 9 slices of fillet of sole, skinned

SHRIMP-MUSHROOM FILL-ING FOR CENTER OF MOLD:

- 2 Tablespoons butter
- ¾ pound mushrooms, sliced (reserve 8 to 9 slices for garnish after sautéeing)
- 2 teaspoons lemon juice
- ½ pound bay shrimp, cooked
- 2 teaspoons parsley, minced
- 2 Tablespoons dry sherry
- Salt and pepper

SAUCE JOINVILLE:

- 4 Tablespoons butter
- 4 Tablespoons flour
- 1 cup Court–Bouillon (see page 48) at room temperature
- ⅓ cup half-and-half cream, at room temperature
- 2 egg yolks
- 2 Tablespoons dry sherry
- 2 Tablespoons heavy cream
- ½ teaspoon tomato paste
- Salt and pepper

GARNISH:

- 8 to 9 slices of sautéed mushrooms, reserved from above

UTENSILS:

Two-quart or 8-inch ring mold
Large roasting pan into which the ring mold will fit
10- to 12-inch round serving platter

Serves 6

1. Enriched Béchamel Sauce: In a saucepan, melt the butter and sauté the shallots until golden brown. Blend in the flour, stirring well. Remove from heat and gradually add the milk. Cook over low heat stirring frequently until the sauce thickens. Remove from heat.

   In a small bowl, beat the four egg yolks with a whisk. Blend in a small amount of the enriched Béchamel Sauce, then add the entire mixture to the saucepan and heat for 1 minute, stirring constantly. Add salt and pepper. Set aside.

2. Ground Salmon Mousse and Spinach Mousse: Take 2 mixing bowls. In one, place the ground salmon, lemon juice, dill and paprika, and stir thoroughly. Add salt and pepper. In the second bowl, place the well-drained spinach, green onions, and nutmeg, and stir thoroughly. Add salt and pepper. Put half of the enriched Béchamel Sauce into each bowl and stir through.

3. Beat the egg whites until foamy then add ⅛ teaspoon of cream of tartar, ⅛ teaspoon salt, and continue beating until stiff, but not dry. Fold one half of the egg whites into the salmon mousse, and the other half into the spinach mousse.

Step 4   **Step 5**   **Step 6**

4. Assembling the Ring Mold: Flatten the fillets of sole slightly with a moistened mallet or rolling pin.

   In a well-greased ring mold, arrange the fillets, with the brown-streaked side up. Allow the small end of each fillet to hang over the center of the mold, the wide end over the outside edge.

5. Spread the spinach mousse carefully on top of the fillets. Over this, spread the salmon mousse.

6. Fold both ends of each fillet over the salmon mousse.

7. Preheat the oven to 350 degrees. Set the ring mold in the bain-marie (a roasting pan half-filled with boiling water) and bake for 40 to 45 minutes.

8. Shrimp-Mushroom Filling: (This may be made while ring mold is baking.) In a saucepan, melt the butter and when it is foaming, sauté the mushrooms. Stir to coat them, and add lemon juice. Shake them over a low fire for 2 minutes. Add the shrimp, parsley, dry sherry, and salt and pepper. Taste and correct seasoning if needed.

9. Sauce Joinville: (This may be made while ring mold is baking.) Melt the butter. Off the heat, stir in the flour, and cook until it foams. Add the court-bouillon, off the heat, and stir with a whisk until the mixture is smooth and slightly thickened. Add the half-and-half cream, and simmer for ten minutes.

   In a small bowl, combine the yolks, dry sherry and heavy cream. Blend in a small amount of the court-bouillon mixture, and return the entire mixture to the saucepan. Add the tomato paste, salt and pepper, stirring well. Taste and correct seasoning.

Ring Mold: Turn the ring mold upside down on a 10- to 12-inch round serving platter, and let it stand for a few minutes.
Drain off any excess liquid.
Remove the mold (it will lift off easily).
Shrimp-Mushroom Filling: Spoon the hot filling into the center of the mold.
Sauce Joinville: Spoon the hot sauce over the fish mold, allowing the extra sauce to fill the platter outside the fish mold.
Garnish: Place one mushroom slice on top of each fillet of sole.

The Spinach and Salmon mousses in Step 2 can be prepared ahead except for the addition of the beaten egg whites.

Do not freeze.

Variation: Fill the center of the mold with a mixture of white and wild rice instead of the Shrimp-Mushroom Filling.

BAKED FISH STUFFED WITH SALMON OR SPINACH MOUSSE

1 3- to 4-pound striped bass or whitefish. Ask to have it book-filleted, so the bones are removed, but the back is not cut through, and the fish can be "opened" like a book

2 Tablespoons cognac
1 Recipe Salmon Mousse (see page 134) or Spinach Mousse (see page 134)
4 Tablespoons butter, melted

Serves 6 to 8

1. Rinse the fish in acidulated water (1 Tablespoon lemon juice to 1 quart water.) Pat it dry with paper towels.

2. Open the fish like a book. Paint the insides with cognac. Spread the Salmon or Spinach Mousse on one side of the fish. Close and reshape the fish. Place it on a buttered baking dish, and brush the top with melted butter. Cover the dish with a piece of waxed paper.

3. Preheat the oven to 350 degrees. Bake the fish for 25 to 30 minutes.

Serve with Sauce Hollandaise (see page 91) or Sauce Verte (see page 238).

May be assembled 1 hour before baking.

Do not freeze.

Cioppino gets its name from the old days when fishermen and produce men would walk along the docks in San Francisco calling "Chip in" ... for any of the day's wares that had not been sold. With some wine and seasonings, the result was a magnificent fish stew (a "cousin" of bouillabaisse) that they ate with sour dough bread.

CIOPPINO
(San Francisco Fish Stew)

SOUP BASE:

½ cup olive oil
½ cup butter
1 large onion, minced
½ cup celery, minced
½ cup green pepper, minced
1 leek, minced
4 cloves garlic, minced
1 28-ounce can Tomato Magic
  (crushed tomatoes)
  or a 28-ounce can of Italian
  tomatoes
1 6-ounce can tomato paste, if
  Italian tomatoes are used
  instead of Tomato Magic
Juice of 2 large lemons

*   *   *

¼ cup parsley, minced
1 bay leaf
½ teaspoon each of oregano,
  basil, thyme, sage and
  rosemary

6 peppercorns, slightly bruised
1½ teaspoons salt
2 cups Sauce Marinara
  (see page 93)
1¾ cups dry red wine
¼ cup Marsala

SEA FOOD:

2 pounds fish cut in 2-inch pieces:
  halibut, cod, sea bass, or
  any firm-fleshed white fish
1 pound scrubbed mussels or
  clams in shells
1 pound raw shrimp, shelled
  and deveined
2 cooked crabs in shells, split
  and cleaned
12 oysters, scrubbed

GARNISH:
Lemon slices

Serves 8

1. In a large saucepan, heat the butter and olive oil. Add the minced onion, celery, green pepper, leek and garlic, and sauté for 10 minutes or until browned. Add tomatoes, tomato paste, lemon juice and seasonings. Add the Sauce Marinara. Cover and simmer for one hour, adding a little water if the mixture becomes too thick or strong to the taste. Add wine and cook 10 minutes more.

2. Bring the soup to a boil. Put the white fish and shrimp on the bottom of a deep pot. Pour the soup base over them, cover and simmer for 10 minutes. Add the clams, oysters and crabs. Cover and simmer for 3 to 5 minutes or until clams and oysters open.

With a slotted spoon, divide the fish and sea food equally into large soup dishes. Pour the hot soup over it. Garnish with lemon slices and serve with Blue Cheese Bread.

Base may be prepared three to four days ahead and refrigerated.

Soup base may be frozen.

BLUE CHEESE BREAD

1 loaf French bread, sliced diagonally down to, but not through, the bottom crust
½ pound butter, at room temperature

¼ pound blue cheese, at room temperature
6 green onions, minced
¼ cup parsley, minced

Serves 6 to 8

1. In a bowl, blend the butter, blue cheese, green onions and parsley. Spread the filling generously between the bread slices. Wrap the bread in foil.

2. Preheat the oven to 350 degrees. Heat the bread for 15 minutes, loosen the foil, and heat for 5 minutes more.

Serve hot. May be prepared two days ahead through Step 1 and refrigerated. May be frozen after Step 1. Bring to room temperature before heating.

Scampi taste glorious with this herbed butter coating. You might also want to try preparing lobster tails or any fish to be broiled or baked with it.

SCAMPI BLUE GROTTO
(Shrimp in Wine Sauce)

2 to 2½ pounds large shrimp or lobster tails (cut in 2-inch pieces)
½ cup flour
1 teaspoon paprika

      *   *   *

2 Tablespoons butter
2 Tablespoons olive oil
1 clove garlic, minced

HERBED BUTTER COATING:
½ cup crushed cornflakes
½ cup Parmesan cheese, grated
⅓ cup parsley, minced
2 cloves garlic, minced

1 teaspoon oregano
Salt and pepper
½ cup butter, softened

SAUCE:
4 Tablespoons dry vermouth or white wine
4 Tablespoons lemon juice
1 Tablespoon parsley, minced
½ teaspoon oregano

GARNISH:
Lemon wedges, dipped in paprika
Parsley sprigs

Serves 6

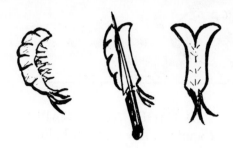

1. Partly shell the shrimp or lobster tails, leaving the tail on for additional flavor. Clean and rinse the shellfish and pat dry with paper towels. Split lengthwise to butterfly. Combine the flour and the paprika, and dust the shrimp lightly.

2. In a skillet, heat the butter and oil, and add the minced garlic. When hot, add the shrimp, and sauté until lightly browned on both sides. Remove from heat. (Do not wash skillet.)

3. Herbed Butter Coating: In a bowl, make a paste of the cornflakes, Parmesan cheese, parsley, garlic, oregano, salt and pepper, and softened butter. Cover each shrimp with this mixture, and arrange in an ovenproof baking dish.

4. Sauce: In the skillet, heat the vermouth, lemon juice, parsley and oregano over low heat for 3 minutes, stirring constantly. Keep warm until ready to serve.

5. Preheat the broiler. Broil the shrimp for a few minutes until the coating bubbles. Watch carefully so the shrimp do not burn.

 Pour the hot sauce over the broiled shrimp. Garnish with lemon wedges and parsley.

 Shrimp may be prepared early in the day through Step 3 and refrigerated.
Herbed Butter Coating may be prepared two weeks ahead and refrigerated.

 Only the Herbed Butter Coating may be frozen.

Wonderful for a brunch, lunch or light supper!

ROULADES AUX CRABES
(Soufflé Roll with Crab Filling)

1 pound crabmeat, with bony
   tissue removed
1 cup celery, chopped fine
⅓ cup green onions, chopped fine
1 cup slivered almonds, toasted
⅓ cup mayonnaise
¼ cup sour cream
1 Tablespoon lemon juice
½ teaspoon salt

GARNISH:

6 to 8 mushrooms, washed
   thoroughly
1 Tablespoon butter
6 to 8 pickled cocktail onions
Toothpicks

SOUFFLÉ ROLL:

4 Tablespoons butter
½ cup flour
2 cups milk, at room temperature
½ teaspoon salt
Dash cayenne
4 eggs, separated

UTENSILS:

11 by 16-inch jelly-roll pan
Ovenproof serving platter
Waxed paper
Two wide spatulas

Serves 8

1. Crab Filling: In a saucepan, combine the crabmeat, celery, green onions, almonds, mayonnaise, sour cream, lemon juice and salt. Heat through but do not allow to boil. Set aside.

2. Garnish: Remove mushroom stems. With a sharp paring knife, flute or notch the mushroom caps.

   In a skillet, heat the butter and sauté the mushrooms, cap side only, until golden brown. Spear each mushroom with a pickled onion, and set aside.

3. Soufflé Roll: For a Béchamel Sauce, in a saucepan, melt 4 Tablespoons butter, and blend in the flour with a wire whisk. Remove from the heat. Add milk, salt and cayenne, blending until the mixture is smooth. Return to the heat and cook until it begins to thicken and comes to a bubble—stirring constantly. Simmer for 1 minute.

   In a small bowl, beat the egg yolks with a whisk. Add some of the warm Béchamel Sauce to the yolks, blend thoroughly, and return to the saucepan. Simmer until slightly thickened, or approximately 1 minute, stirring constantly. Transfer to a large bowl.

4. Beat egg whites until stiff. Stir in ¼ cup of the beaten egg whites into the sauce to loosen it. Fold in the remainder of the egg whites.

5. Preheat the oven to 325 degrees. Grease the jelly-roll pan, and line it with waxed paper, allowing an extra inch all around the pan. Grease the waxed paper, and sprinkle lightly with flour. Spread the soufflé mixture evenly in the pan, and bake for 40 to 45 minutes until it is golden brown. When lightly pressed, the soufflé will spring back quickly.

6. Loosen the edges of the soufflé roll with a spatula, and turn it out on fresh waxed paper. Carefully peel off the cooked waxed paper.

7. To assemble: Twenty minutes before serving, heat the crab filling. With a slotted spoon, put half the crab filling on the soufflé roll, allowing the liquid to remain in the pan.
   Roll, jelly-roll fashion, using the waxed paper at the sides to steady and guide it. Lift the roll onto the heated serving platter, using the two wide spatulas, or your hands. The roll may be kept in a warm oven for only 20 to 30 minutes.

 Spoon the remaining half of the hot crab filling over the roll, and garnish with mushrooms and onions on toothpicks.

 May be prepared early in the day through Step 3.

 Do not freeze.

Variations: 1 cup of grated cheddar or Swiss cheese can be added to the soufflé roll. It will give a different flavor. The soufflé roll can be made with many other fillings, like melted cheddar cheese and fresh cooked broccoli, duxelles, or caviar and sour cream.

LOW CALORIE BAKED FISH OR SCALLOPS

HERBED COATING
MIXTURE:
(Use ⅓ cup per pound of fish or scallops)
- 4 cups breadcrumbs
- 1 Tablespoon salt
- 1 Tablespoon celery salt
- 1 Tablespoon paprika
- 1 teaspoon pepper
- ½ cup oil

OPTIONAL:
Dehydrated garlic, minced
Dehydrated onions, minced

FISH:
- 2½ pounds of fillet of sole, sand dabs, flounder, or 2½ pounds scallops sliced in half horizontally.
- ¼ cup lemon juice or white wine, or equal amounts of each

GARNISH:
Lemon wedges

Serves 6 to 8

1. Combine the breadcrumbs, salt, celery salt, paprika and pepper. Add garlic and onion, if desired. Stir in the oil.

2. Dip the fish or scallops in the lemon juice or wine so that the coating will adhere. Coat the fish or scallops with the coating mixture. Arrange them on a teflon pan, or on a pan sprayed with a commercial pan-coating so the fish will not stick.

3. Preheat the oven to 375 degrees. Bake the fish or scallops for 10 to 12 minutes.

Serve with lemon wedges.

Herbed coating mixture may be prepared in advance and stored in a cupboard in a moisture-proof container for several months. Fish or scallops may be prepared early in the day through Step 2.

Do not freeze.

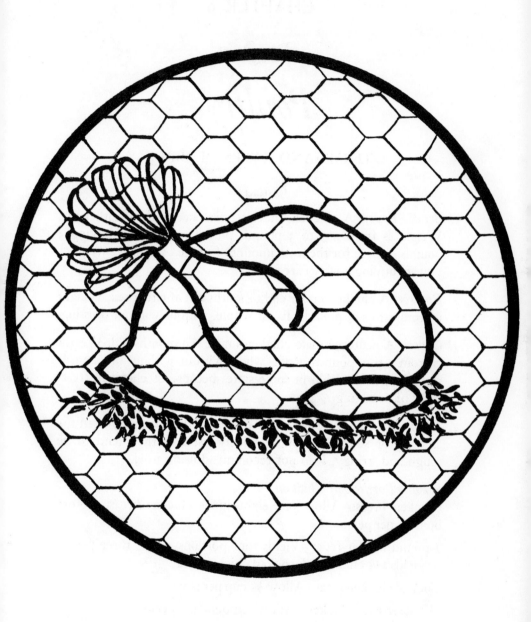

CHAPTER 6

Poultry

TERMS AND TYPES OF BIRDS

CHICKEN

1. *Broiler-Fryer:* A chicken under sixteen weeks old of either sex. Weight is from 1½ to 3 pounds plus. I recommend buying 3 pounds or over for the least amount of waste. At smaller weights, you are buying mostly carcass.

2. *Roaster:* A chicken under eight months old of either sex. Weight is from 4 to 5½ pounds. Roast whole, with or without dressing.

3. *Capon:* A neutered male chicken under ten months old. Weight is from 4 to 7 pounds. Roast whole with or without dressing. It is no longer available in some states because of chemical treatment of neutering.

4. *Fowl:* An old female bird over eight months. Formerly used for stewing or soup. No longer widely used, as they tend to be tough and stringy. I do not recommend using fowl.

5. *Serving Portions of Chicken*
Chicken breast—Allow one eight-ounce chicken breast, before boning, per person.

   3-pound broiler-fryer—Yields four portions, serves three people or yields 2½ cups diced, cooked chicken meat.

   Cooked chicken meat—Allow ½ cup per person.

   Whole roasted chicken—Allow ¾ pound per person.

6. *Freezing a Whole Chicken:* Chickens may be frozen whole. Remove neck and giblets before freezing. Place the chicken in a plastic bag, squeeze out all of the air, then tie securely. Defrost overnight in the refrigerator before using.

7. *Freezing Livers and Giblets:* When you buy a whole chicken, freeze the livers in one plastic bag, the giblets in another. You can freeze enough giblets, wing tips, and necks to prepare soup or to add to other chicken dishes, like fricassée.

   Save chicken livers until you have enough to sauté or make into pâté. To prepare pâté from chicken livers, defrost frozen chicken livers overnight in the refrigerator before using.

8. *Freezing Chicken Breasts:* Whenever possible, buy chicken breasts on sale and freeze them either whole or skinned, boned, and pounded. Defrost overnight in the refrigerator before using.

TURKEYS

1. *Hen Turkeys:* A female turkey fifteen pounds or under. Roast whole, or cut into quarters.

2. *Tom Turkey:* A male turkey sixteen pounds or more. I recommend buying a bird no larger than 22 pounds; anything heavier is too difficult to handle or fit into the oven properly.

3. *Turkey Breast:* The weight is from 8 to 14 pounds and it is white meat only. It is most economical to buy the larger size over 8 pounds, because of less waste.

ROCK CORNISH HENS

Rock Cornish Hens: They weigh from 16 to 22 ounces. Serve a 16-ounce hen per person. An 18 to 22-ounce hen can be split in half to serve two.

DUCKS AND DUCKLINGS

Duckling: I recommend a Long Island duckling, from 4 to 6 pounds, of either sex. One 4-pound duckling makes four small portions or serves three.

Trussing a chicken, turkey, or Rock Cornish hen can be easy if you have the right needle. For about sixty-five cents, buy a 6-inch trussing needle with a pointed blade. Any upholstery needle will also do. Keep a spool of thin white string, or heavy white thread on hand for trussing (not waxed).

Step 1

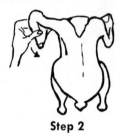
Step 2

Step 3

1. Place bird on its breast. Cut off the wing tips with a sharp knife or kitchen shears.

2. Fold the lower section of the wings down.

3. Fold the neck skin back over the backbone. Pinion the wings so they secure the neck skin. Thread the needle with a long piece of string or thread.

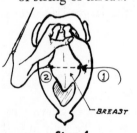
Step 4

Step 5

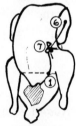
Step 6

4. Place the bird on its back. With one hand holding both chicken legs up, insert the needle into the lower part of the chicken breast (1), and pull it through the carcass and out the opposite side (2).

5. Turn the bird over onto its breast. Continuing to use the same piece of string or thread, insert the needle through the upper right wing (3), and out through the lower right wing (4). Now insert it through the upper part of the backbone. Be sure it also secures the neck skin. Next, insert the needle through the lower left wing (5), then the upper left wing (6).

6. Turn the bird onto its back. Pull the string ends at (1) and (6) firmly together, and tie in a knot at the side of the bird at (7).

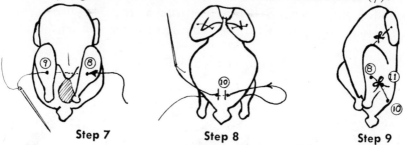

Step 7   **Step 8**   **Step 9**

7. Thread the needle with another long piece of string or thread. Turn the bird onto its back. Insert the needle at upper part of the right drumstick (8), leaving a long piece of string to tie later. Pass the needle through the bottom end of the breastbone and out the opposite drumstick (9).

8. Turn bird over on its breast. With the same piece of string, bring the needle around and insert it through the bottom of the back-bone (10).

9. Turn the bird on its side. Pull the string ends at (8) and (10) firmly together, and tie in a knot on the lower right side of the bird (11).

CHICKEN

Chicken can be prepared in an infinite number of ways. It can be baked, boiled, broiled, fried, fricasséed, poached, roasted, and sautéed; made with an endless number of marinades and sauces; encrusted in pastry; jelled in aspic; or simmered in champagne! It can look and taste like chicken or it can become a work of art. You could serve chicken seven days a week and never have it taste or look the same. It is low in calories and cholesterol, and even though the price of chicken is going up, it is still a bargain in comparison to meat. Children love it, old people digest it, and your budget approves of it.

Recipes call for chicken breasts in a variety of forms: some whole, some halved; some with skin, others skinned; some flattened or pounded; and some as is. Before preparing a recipe, be sure to read it carefully to see what form is indicated for the chicken breasts.

BONING A CHICKEN BREAST

Step 1   Step 2   Step 3

1. Take the whole chicken breast, not split, and place it on a board skin side up. Take a sharp knife and slide the blade from the rib bone at the bottom (1) up under the breast meat, toward the keel bone at the top, (2). Keep scraping the meat away from you until it is completely loosened on one side, but still attached at the keel bone. Turn the chicken breast around, and repeat the process.

2. With the point of the knife, work around the wishbone (3) to loosen the meat. Remove the wishbone.

3. With the knife blade, scrape the meat away from the length of the keel bone, trying not to cut holes in the meat. You should then be able to remove the entire bone in one piece. Save the bones for chicken stock. To remove the white tendon running along the underside of the chicken breast, hold onto the end of the tendon with one hand, take the knife in the other hand and scrape the meat away from the tendon, and pull it out. For chicken breast halves, cut lengthwise.

POUNDING A CHICKEN BREAST

Pounding a chicken is usually done with a rawhide meat mallet or the side of a cleaver. However, you can also use an unopened Number 2½ can (using the side to pound), a rolling pin, a croquet mallet, or an old iron.

Place the whole or half chicken breast between two squares of waxed paper. With a meat mallet or the side of a cleaver, pound the chicken meat with firm even strokes until it is about ¼ inch thick.

A roast chicken should be succulent and tender. Unfortunately, however, when cooked incorrectly it can be a tough old bird. Use the smallest possible roasting pan that will hold the chicken. You'll find the drippings and vegetables won't burn, and the chicken will turn out to perfection.

PERFECT ROAST CHICKEN

3 to 4 pound broiler-fryer
Herbes Aromatiques, or seasoned
   salt and pepper (see page 97)
1 small celery stalk with leaves
3 sprigs parsley
1 bay leaf
2 thin slices fresh ginger, or
   ½ teaspoon powdered ginger
1 Tablespoon peppercorns
½ teaspoon thyme
2 shallots, coarsely diced, or
   2 green onions, white portion
   only, sliced
1 clove garlic, minced

      *   *   *

4 Tablespoons butter

MIRAPOIX:
   1 medium onion, diced
   1 carrot, diced
   1 celery stalk, diced
      *   *   *
½ cup chicken stock, homemade
   or commercial
½ cup dry white wine
      *   *   *
1 Tablespoon paprika

SAUCE:
½ cup dry white wine or
   chicken stock, if necessary

UTENSIL:
Small roasting pan

Serves 3 to 4

1. Rinse the chicken inside and out, removing any veins, arteries, bits of lung, or the like, that might be hidden among the ribs. Dig out pieces of kidney usually left on either side of the lower backbone. Dry inside and out with paper towels.

    Sprinkle the inside of the chicken with Herbes Aromatiques, or seasoned salt and pepper. Place the celery, parsley, bay leaf, ginger, peppercorns, thyme, shallots, and garlic, inside the cavity.

2. Truss the chicken (see page 148).

3. Preheat the oven to 450 degrees. In a small pan, melt the butter, and brush about half of it on the outside of the chicken; then sprinkle the chicken with Herbes Aromatiques, or seasoned salt and pepper. Place in a small roasting pan, and roast for 15 minutes on each side, brushing occasionally with drippings from the pan. Remove the chicken from the pan and set it on a platter. Do not wash the pan.

[151]

4. Reduce the oven to 425 degrees. In the center of the roasting pan, arrange the mirapoix (the minced onion, carrot and celery). Arrange the chicken on its back on top of the mirapoix, which acts as a rack and creates a certain amount of steam that keeps the chicken from becoming dry. It also adds flavor to the gravy. Pour the chicken stock and wine over the chicken, and roast uncovered for an additional hour (or one hour and fifteen minutes), basting occasionally.

5. Add the paprika to the remaining melted butter. For the last 15 minutes or so of roasting, brush the chicken with this mixture. Check to see if the chicken is done. The drumstick will move easily when it is done, and when you pierce the chicken with a fork, the juices that run out will be a clear yellow with no trace of pink or red. Remove the chicken to a platter 15 minutes before carving to allow the meat to set and to be carved easily. Cover loosely with foil. Prepare the sauce at this time.

6. Sauce: Put the roasting pan on top of the stove, and heat the drippings and vegetables over medium heat for 1 minute. Add ½ cup white wine. There should be at least a half cup of sauce at this point; if there is not, add additional chicken stock. Bring to a simmer, and scrape the pan to dissolve all the brown bits on the bottom. Add salt and pepper to taste. Strain into a small saucepan and bring to a simmer again.

 Carve the chicken and arrange on a platter. Heat the sauce until it is piping hot. Spoon some of the heated sauce over the chicken. Serve the remaining sauce in a separate dish at the table.

 May be prepared several hours ahead, and arranged on an oven proof platter. Reheat in a low oven, tented with foil.

 Do not freeze.

The combination of flavors and colors of the chicken, seafood, tomatoes, and olives make this a superb entrée. You'll find the flavors are enhanced if you make it one or two days in advance, except for the seafood.

POLLO SAN SEBASTIAN
(Chicken and Seafood Casserole)

6 whole chicken breasts (¾ pound to 1 pound) split and skinned into 12 pieces

SEASONED FLOUR:

1 cup flour
Salt and pepper
1 Tablespoon paprika

* * *

2 to 4 Tablespoons butter
2 to 4 Tablespoons margarine
4 Tablespoons cognac or brandy
½ cup dry sherry

SAUCE:

2 Tablespoons butter
1 medium onion, chopped
3 cloves garlic, minced
½ pound mushrooms, sliced
2 Tablespoons Wondra flour
¼ cup cold water
1½ cups chicken stock, homemade or commercial

2 Tablespoons tomato paste
1 8-ounce bottle small pimiento-stuffed olives, drained and rinsed
2 Tablespoons chives, minced
1 bay leaf
Salt and pepper

* * *

4 tomatoes, peeled and quartered
8 3- to 4-ounce uncooked lobster tails in shells, or 8 uncooked jumbo shrimp, peeled and deveined
½ cup toasted slivered almonds
½ cup Parmesan cheese, grated

* * *

3 to 4 cups hot cooked rice

UTENSIL:

Large round baking dish

Serves 8

1. Wash the chicken breasts, and pat dry with paper towels.

2. In a brown paper bag, combine the flour, salt, pepper, and paprika. Shake the chicken breasts in the paper bag, two or three pieces at a time, to coat them with the flour mixture.

3. In a large skillet, heat 2 Tablespoons of butter and 2 Tablespoons of margarine until they are foaming. Brown the chicken breasts on both sides. As each batch of chicken breasts is browned, flame with 2 Tablespoons of cognac and arrange them in a large, at-

tractive, lightly greased round baking dish. Repeat until all of the chicken breasts are browned. Pour the sherry over the chicken breasts and set aside until one hour before serving. Do not wash the skillet.

4. Sauce: With a spatula, loosen the remaining glaze in the skillet, as this will give flavor to the sauce. Over low heat, melt 2 Tablespoons of butter, add the onion, garlic, and mushrooms and sauté until lightly browned. In a small bowl, dissolve the flour in ¼ cup of cold water, and pour into the mushrooms-and-onion mixture. Add the chicken stock and tomato paste and simmer, stirring constantly until the sauce is slightly thickened. Add the olives, chives, bay leaf, salt, and pepper. Stir well, and pour over the chicken breasts in the casserole.

5. Preheat the oven to 350 degrees. Just before baking, sprinkle the almonds and Parmesan cheese on top. Tent loosely with foil, and bake for 1 hour. Baste frequently. Remove the bay leaf.

6. Twenty minutes before serving, remove the chicken from the oven, and arrange the tomato quarters, and lobster or shrimp in an attractive pattern between the chicken breasts. Baste carefully with the sauce. Tent loosely with the foil and bake for 20 minutes. The lobster or shrimp will turn red when cooked.

Serve hot over rice.

May be prepared two days ahead through Step 4, covered, and refrigerated.

May be frozen after Step 4.

One of my favorite chicken dishes that can be made a day in advance.

POULET MAISON
(Chicken of the House)

8 8-ounce chicken breast halves, skinned, boned, and pounded
Flour
Salt and pepper
2 eggs, slightly beaten
2 teaspoons Triple Sec

COATING MIXTURE:
1½ cups breadcrumbs
2 cloves garlic, minced
2 Tablespoons paprika

½ cup Parmesan cheese, grated
1½ Tablespoons parsley, minced

* * *

½ cup butter, melted
2 onions, sliced
6 cups chicken stock, homemade or commercial
Cumberland Sauce (see page 96), or Sauce Béarnaise (see page 92), or Sauce aux Champignons (see page 90)

Serves 8

1. Dredge the chicken breasts with flour mixed with salt and pepper.

2. In a pieplate, combine the beaten eggs and Triple Sec. In another pieplate, prepare the coating mixture by combining breadcrumbs, garlic, paprika, Parmesan cheese, and parsley. Dip each chicken breast first into the eggs-and-Triple-Sec mixture, then into the coating mixture.

3. Roll each chicken breast into a paupiette (see page 157).

4. In a roasting pan, arrange the onion slices, and set the chicken breasts on top. Paint them generously with the melted butter.

5. Preheat the oven to 350 degrees, and bake for ½ hour.

6. Bring the chicken stock to a boil and add enough to the roasting pan to cover the chicken breasts halfway. Bake for 45 minutes more, basting frequently.

7. Prepare and heat either Sauce Cumberland, Sauce Béarnaise, or Sauce aux Champignons.

NOTE: *Leftover Sauce Béarnaise may be frozen and reused as a masking sauce to spoon over the chicken breasts. You should, however, make a fresh batch of Sauce Béarnaise to serve at the table.*

 TO SERVE Just before serving, spoon half of the sauce over the chicken breasts. Serve the other half in a separate bowl at the table.

 AHEAD May be prepared one day ahead through Step 5 and refrigerated.

 FREEZE May be frozen after Step 6. Thaw in refrigerator before reheating.

QUICK AND SIMPLE CHICKEN BREASTS ROSEMARY

8 8-ounce chicken breast halves
4 Tablespoons butter, at room temperature

1 Tablespoon fresh rosemary or
1½ teaspoons dried rosemary
salt and pepper
4 slices bacon, cut in half

1. Combine the softened butter with the rosemary, and rub onto both sides of the chicken breasts. Add salt and pepper.

2. Preheat the oven to 350 degrees. Bake the chicken breasts on a greased cookie sheet for 25 minutes. Preheat the broiler. Put a piece of bacon on top of each chicken breast, broil for 3 to 4 minutes, return to the oven for another 25 minutes.

SHORT AND SWEET
GINGERED CHICKEN BREASTS

8 8-ounce chicken breast halves
boned, skinned, and pounded
4 Tablespoons butter, melted
4 Tablespoons ginger marmalade

1 cup shredded coconut or 1 cup
chopped nuts (walnuts, pecans,
or almonds)

Serves 8

1. Put the melted butter and ginger marmalade in the blender, and blend for 10 seconds. Paint on both sides of the chicken breasts.

Paupiette

2. Dip the chicken breasts in the coconut or nuts, and shape into paupiettes.

3. Preheat the oven to 350 degrees. Bake the chicken breasts in a greased roasting pan for 45 minutes.

SPEEDY CHICKEN TARRAGON

2 3-pound broilers cut into
pieces, or 8 chicken breast
halves
¾ cup tarragon vinegar
¾ cup butter, melted

½ teaspoon Herbes Aromatiques
(see page 97)
or seasoned salt
1 teaspoon dried tarragon, or
2 teaspoons fresh tarragon

COATING MIXTURE:
2 cups Waverly or Ritz cracker
crumbs

Serves 8

1. Dip the chicken pieces in the tarragon vinegar. Next, drain and dip the chicken into the melted butter.

2. Dip each piece of chicken in the coating mixture, and place on a greased cookie sheet.

3. Preheat the oven to 350 degrees, and bake for one hour without turning.

TURKEY

Not only a perfect way to roast a turkey, but a carefree and easy one as well! The trick is marinating the turkey under the skin, as well as inside and out, for 1 to 2 days. There's no need to truss it, and once it's in the oven, you don't even open the door until the last hour or half hour before serving.

PERFECT ROAST TURKEY

1 turkey (any weight up to
  22 pounds)

2 Tablespoons butter, margarine
  or solid vegetable shortening

MARINADE:

1 cup oil
1½ Tablespoons Herbes Aromatiques or ½ teaspoon celery
   seed and ½ teaspoon beau
   monde
2 Tablespoons monosodium
  glutamate (MSG)
2 Tablespoons paprika
4 cloves garlic, minced, or 1 to 2
  Tablespoons dehydrated garlic,
  minced

UTENSILS:

Skewers or needle and thread
1 large heavy brown paper bag
3 paper clips or stapler
Large roasting pan with turkey
  turner, or rack

* * *

Perfect Roast Turkey Dressing
  (see page 166)

For the best flavor, marinate and refrigerate the turkey two days before roasting it. The turkey may be stuffed and refrigerated the day before cooking, *if you make certain both the dressing and the turkey are cold before stuffing.*

1. Clean the turkey well by rinsing it inside and out. Carefully remove any veins, arteries, or bits of lung which might be hidden
   in the cavity among the ribs. Dig out any pieces of kidney, often
   left on either side of the lower back bone, as they might affect
   the flavor. Pat the turkey dry inside and out with paper towels.

2. Marinade: In a bowl, combine the oil, Herbes Aromatiques,
   MSG, paprika, and garlic. Set aside ¼ cup for the last hour of
   basting the turkey.

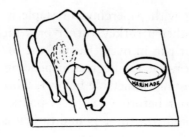

3. Marinating the Turkey: Remove any rings on your fingers!

   Starting at the keel bone, lift the skin above the breast, with your fingers, carefully pushing the skin away from the flesh. Try not to tear the skin . . . and don't use a knife. Once the skin is loosened, dip your fingers into the marinade and rub the breast meat under the skin generously with it.

4. Starting at the neck end, reach down under the skin with your fingers past the breast, and loosen the skin around the turkey legs. Again, rub the marinade between the skin and the meat. Rub the marinade inside the turkey cavity, then on the outside skin. Cover the turkey loosely with plastic, and refrigerate for a minimum of one day and two days would be best.

5. To stuff the turkey: Prepare the Perfect Roast Turkey Dressing. Refrigerate until chilled. *REMEMBER to always put cold dressing into a cold turkey and immediately refrigerate until 1 hour before roasting.*

   Fill the turkey cavity only three quarters full with dressing, and either close with skewers or sew closed with needle and thread. Fill the neck area only three quarters full, fold over the loose skin, and skewer or sew it closed. Do not pack the dressing in tightly, as it expands while the turkey is cooking and the dressing will become gummy. Wrap any extra dressing loosely in foil and roast for the last hour with the turkey.

6. Roasting the turkey: Preheat the oven to 325 degrees (or the proper temperature for your turkey's weight). Open the brown paper bag on a counter, seam side up. Spread the butter, margarine or solid vegetable shortening on the bottom of the inside of the bag. Put the turkey into the bag, breast side down and head first, with the tail and drumsticks at the open end.

Close the bag with paperclips, or staple it closed. Place the paper bag on either a turkey turner or a rack over a shallow roasting pan. Put pan in oven. Reduce the oven temperature to 300 degrees or leave at 325 degrees, depending on the size of the turkey (see Roasting Timetable below). Do not open the oven door until ½ hour before a 12- to 15-pound turkey is finished and 1 hour before a 16- to 22-pound turkey is finished.

7. Remove roasting pan from the oven. Slit the bag under the breast to allow the turkey juices to run into the roasting pan. Discard the paper bag. Set the turkey turner or rack and the turkey over another pan. Pour the turkey juices from the roasting pan into a bowl, and place in the freezer for 30 to 45 minutes to congeal the excess grease so it can be removed easily. Turn the turkey so that it is breast-side up. Place it on a rack over the roasting pan. Baste with the ¼-cup marinade set aside earlier.

For a 12- to 15-pound turkey, roast for ½ hour more, basting frequently. For a 16- to 22-pound turkey, roast for 1 hour more, basting frequently.

ROASTING TIMETABLE

TURKEY WEIGHT	DEGREES	MINUTES PER POUND
Whole Turkeys		
12 to 15 pounds, unstuffed	325°	20 to 25 minutes
12 to 15 pounds, stuffed	325°	25 to 30 minutes
16 to 22 pounds, stuffed or unstuffed	300°	20 minutes
Breasts		
under 6 pounds	325°	20 minutes
8 to 10 pounds	450°	1 hour total
10 to 12 pounds	450°	1½ hours total

NOTE: *Deduct 1 pound for giblets for 12- to 15-pound turkeys. Deduct 1½ pounds for giblets for 16- to 22-pound turkeys. Read any suggested roasting time of turkey growers, as varying feeds may affect the cooking time.*

Variation: Roast Breast of Turkey.

Select the largest turkey breast you can find, preferably between 10 to 12 pounds, because it will be juicier. Follow the instructions for marinating turkey. Place the turkey breast in a greased paper bag, breast-side down.

Remove turkey breast from the oven and reset the oven at 350 degrees. Slit the bag under the breast to allow the turkey juices to run into the roasting pan. Discard the paper bag. Defat the turkey juice (see page 160). Place turkey breast in the pan breast-side up, repaint with marinade and roast 20 to 30 minutes more.

Allow the turkey to rest for 15 to 20 minutes after it is removed from the oven before carving.

Remove the skewers used in stuffing. Using a long spoon, place turkey dressing in a serving dish. Remove the bowl of turkey juices from the freezer; discard the fat on top. Place in a saucepan along with any other juices or glaze from the roasting pan, and heat slowly.
Carve the turkey, and arrange on a heated serving platter. Spoon half of the heated juices over the dressing. Serve the other half in a bowl to be used for the sliced turkey.

Marinade: May be prepared one to two weeks ahead and refrigerated
Turkey: Should be marinated and refrigerated two days before roasting, or at least one day.
Dressing: May be prepared one day ahead and refrigerated but NOT stuffed in turkey. Chilled dressing may be stuffed in chilled turkey one day before roasting, and refrigerated.
Dressing only may be frozen.

ROCK CORNISH HENS

For a flamboyant and festive dinner! You may serve one Cornish Hen per person or half of a large hen. For flavor, soak the cherries in port overnight.

ROCK CORNISH HENS AUX CERISES FLAMBEES
(Rock Cornish Hens with Cherry Sauce)

1 16-ounce can pitted bing cherries, drained
½ cup Ruby port wine

* * *

3 22-ounce, or 6, 16- to 18-ounce Rock Cornish hens, cleaned thoroughly
½ teaspoon fresh ginger or dried ginger
1 teaspoon garlic, minced
1 teaspoon paprika

* * *

1 recipe Fruit Dressing (see page 168)

* * *

2 Tablespoons butter
1 Tablespoon margarine
3 Tablespoons cognac or brandy
¼ to ½ cup dry white wine

GLAZE:
¼ cup orange juice
¼ cup light corn syrup

SAUCE AUX CERISES:
2 Tablespoons butter
1 clove garlic, minced
12 mushrooms, washed thoroughly, sliced
1 teaspoon meat glaze, or Bovril
1½ cups beef stock, homemade or commercial
1 Tablespoon potato starch
½ cup of Ruby port wine (drained from cherries)
1 Tablespoon apple jelly
½ teaspoon fresh dill

GARNISH:
2 Tablespoons parsley, chopped
2 Tablespoons cognac or brandy

Serves 6

1. Drain the cherries. Soak them in the port overnight at room temperature.

2. Preparing the hens: Combine the ginger, garlic, and paprika. Rub this mixture inside the cavity of each hen. Set aside.

3. Prepare one recipe of Fruit Dressing.

4. Stuff each hen loosely with the Fruit Dressing. Close the opening of the cavity with skewers or sew together with a needle and heavy thread.

5. In a large skillet, heat 1 Tablespoon of butter and 1 Tablespoon margarine. Brown the hens over the high heat, until they are

golden brown on all sides. Turn off the heat. Discard any butter-margarine mixture left in the skillet.

6. In a small pan, warm the cognac slightly. Light a match to it, and pour the flaming cognac over the hens. Set the hens in a greased roasting pan. Do not wash the skillet.

7. Preheat the oven to 300 degrees. In a small saucepan melt the remaining Tablespoon of butter and add the dry white wine. Baste the hens frequently with this mixture. Roast hens for 1 hour and 15 minutes.

Combine the orange juice and light corn syrup for a glaze, and baste the hens with it. Bake an additional 15 minutes at 400 degrees, allowing the skin to crisp. Remove skewers or thread.

8. Sauce aux Cerises: Heat the butter in the unwashed skillet in which the hens were browned and flamed. Add garlic and mushrooms and toss for a minute. Stir in the meat glaze or Bovril and the beef stock, and mix carefully.

Drain the port wine from the cherries. In a small dish, dissolve the potato starch in the wine, and add to the skillet. Mix well, and continue to stir until the sauce thickens. Add the apple jelly, and stir until dissolved. Fifteen minutes before hens are to be served, add dill and cherries.

Variations: Cerises Suprêmes (Chicken Breast with Cherries): Sauce aux Cerises may be served over Poulet Maison (see page 155). Canard aux Cerises: The Sauce aux Cerises may be served over roast duck.

For large-size hens, cut in half lengthwise. Warm sauce over low heat. Set the hens on a platter, pour the sauce over and sprinkle with parsley. Flame with 2 Tablespoons cognac or brandy at the table.

Cornish Hens may be prepared one day ahead through Step 6 and refrigerated. Sauce aux Cerises may be prepared one day ahead and refrigerated.

May be frozen after Step 6. Defrost overnight in the refrigerator.

DUCK

This Chinese duckling recipe is simple to make and tastes as delectable as its name sounds because of the unusual combination and texture of the seasonings. It can be a main course, or an hors-d'oeuvre with the duckling cut into bite-size pieces. Five Powdered Spices is a commercial product available at Chinese or Japanese food stores and some supermarkets. If none is available, simply omit it.

PLUM BLOSSOM DUCK

2 5-pound ducklings, quartered
2 onions, grated
2 large cloves garlic, minced
4 Tablespoons Hoisin sauce
(available at Chinese markets)
Five Powdered Spices
Salt and pepper
4 oranges, cut in half

SAUCE:
1 17-ounce can purple plums,
pitted, with juice
1 large onion, cut in eighths

1 6-ounce can frozen lemonade
concentrate
⅓ cup chile sauce
¼ cup soy sauce
1 teaspoon Sauce Diable
1 Tablespoon grated fresh ginger
or dried ginger
2 teaspoons mustard
2 drops Tabasco

GARNISH:
Parsley sprigs
8 green onion "brushes"

Serves 6

1. Rinse off the duck, and pat dry with paper towels.

2. Make a paste of the grated onions, garlic and Hoisin sauce and coat both sides of the duck quarters with it. Sprinkle lightly with Five Powdered Spices, salt and pepper.

3. Cut the oranges in half and arrange on a rack in a roasting pan. Put a portion of duck on top of each orange. Preheat the oven to 350 degrees, and roast the duck for 1 hour. Prick the duck skin with a fork frequently to allow the fat to drain. The total roasting time is about 2 hours.

4. Sauce: In the blender, purée the plums, plum juice, and the onion

pieces. Remove to a saucepan, and add the concentrated lemonade, chile sauce, soy sauce, Sauce Diable, ginger, mustard, and Tabasco. Simmer for 15 to 20 minutes.

5. When the duck has roasted for 1 hour (or more if there still seems to be fat on the pieces), remove from the oven. Pour off the excess fat and wipe out the roasting pan. Put back the duck pieces side by side with the orange halves and brush all of them with the hot plum sauce. Return to the oven and continue to roast for another hour, basting frequently with the plum sauce, until the ducks are tender and the duck and oranges glazed. Reserve some of the plum sauce to serve at the table.

6. Garnish: For green onion brushes, cut the green onions into pieces 3 inches long. With a knife, make vertical cuts in the bulb end and place in a bowl of ice water for 1 hour.

TO SERVE Arrange duck and oranges on a heated platter. Garnish with sprigs of parsley, and the green onion brushes. Heat sauce and serve at table. Use the green scallion brushes to paint extra plum sauce on the duck.

AHEAD Ducklings may be prepared one day ahead through Step 5, and refrigerated. Brush on additional sauce before reheating. Sauce may be prepared two days ahead and refrigerated.

FREEZE Duck may be frozen after Step 5. Sauce may be frozen.

DRESSINGS

My family leaves the turkey to the guests and concentrates on this dressing. It can also be used to stuff a chicken, a crown roast of pork, or a boned leg of lamb. The dressing should look moist, but not have puddles of liquid or be soupy. You can test it by pressing a small amount against the palm of your hand; only a few droplets of liquid should be evident.

PERFECT ROAST TURKEY DRESSING

1 pound bulk sausage
½ pound ground beef
½ cup butter or margarine
1 cup onions, minced
2 cloves garlic, minced
1 cup celery with a few leaves, minced
½ cup green pepper, minced
½ pound mushrooms, sliced

1 cup chicken stock, homemade or commercial
2 eggs, lightly beaten
1 teaspoon sage, dried
1 8-ounce package corn bread stuffing mix
½ cup semi-dry white wine
Salt and pepper

Fills a 12 to 15 pound turkey

1. Slice sausage ½ inch thick. Place in a large skillet, cover with water, and simmer until water is almost evaporated and fat is rendered from sausage. Discard any liquid remaining in the skillet. Add beef and continue to sauté both meats until nicely browned. Drain meats on paper towels.

2. In the same skillet, melt the butter and sauté the onions and garlic until golden brown. Add celery, green pepper, and mushrooms. Cook an additional 5 minutes over a medium heat.

3. In a large bowl, combine the sausage and ground beef, chicken stock, sautéed vegetables, eggs, sage, and corn bread stuffing mix. Blend well. Add only enough wine to moisten the dressing. Add salt and pepper to taste. If the stuffing is not sufficiently moist add additional beaten eggs.

TO SERVE

Remove dressing from the turkey. Serve with turkey gravy.

AHEAD

May be prepared four days ahead and refrigerated.

FREEZE

May be frozen. Defrost 24 hours in the refrigerator.

Fruit dressing is delicious with roast duck, chicken breasts, Cornish hens, or baked in a casserole as a side dish.

FRUIT DRESSING

1 Tablespoon butter
1 onion, chopped
½ cup celery, without leaves, chopped
½ cup dried breadcrumbs
1 cup cooked rice
¼ teaspoon marjoram
¼ teaspoon thyme
Pinch of sage
Salt and pepper

1 7-ounce can pineapple tidbits, drained
½ cup fresh orange sections cut into pieces
¼ cup golden raisins
2 Tablespoons blanched, slivered almonds
¼ cup dry white wine

Makes 3 cups

In a large skillet, melt the butter, add the chopped onion and celery and sauté over low heat until golden. Add the breadcrumbs, cooked rice, marjoram, thyme, sage, salt and pepper, and stir through. Stir in the pineapple, orange, raisins, almonds, and wine.

NOTE: *If used as a side dish, add ½ cup chicken stock and bake covered for about half an hour, or until liquid is absorbed.*

May be prepared four days ahead and refrigerated.

Do not freeze.

CHAPTER 7

Meat

METHODS OF COOKING MEAT

There are several methods for cooking meat.

1. *Simmering:* This is a method for browning meat in fat and cooking in liquid over low heat for a long period of time. It is the most common way of stewing. Good cuts for simmering include: beef shoulder clod, beef round, rump, or chuck, lamb, or veal.

   Meat can be cooked in one piece, or in chunks with all fat removed. Lightly flour meat, sauté in butter and oil until browned. Pour off excess fat, and flame. Use any one or a combination of water, vegetable juice, stock, or wine to cover halfway. Simmer over low heat, tightly covered, on top of the stove, or in a 300 to 325-degree oven until the meat is tender.

   Potatoes and vegetables can be added for the last 45 minutes. I recommend wrapping them separately in cheesecloth bags, (potatoes in one bag, carrots in another, green beans in another and so forth) so they can be easily removed for attractive grouping on a serving platter.

   When the cover is lifted off the pot, never allow the condensation to drip into the pot, as it dilutes the liquid.

2. *Braising:* Same method as simmering, except that less liquid is used. Only enough is used to cover up to one quarter of the meat. Brisket of beef, with all the fat removed, can be used, as can eye of round, beef rump, round roast, veal, and lamb.

3. *Roasting:* This is a dry heat method. A meat thermometer should be used. Place it in the thickest part of the meat, avoiding the bone. Meat is placed fat side up on a rack over a roasting pan in the oven. No liquid is added as it would steam the meat. Roast tender cuts of meat in this manner, such as beef rib roast, rolled roast, sirloin roast, tenderloin, lamb, veal, and pork.

TEMPERATURE CHART FOR ROASTING			
	Rare	Medium	Well-Done
Beef	140 degrees	160 degrees	170 degrees
Lamb	130 to 135 degrees		160 degrees
Veal	---	160 degrees	---
Pork	---	---	180 degrees

For best results, remove roast from the oven 5 to 10 minutes before reaching the desired temperature. Allow it to "set" before carving until the thermometer does reach the desired temperature. It will continue to cook at room temperature because of its internal heat.

4. *Broiling:* This method is for cooking tender cuts of meat quickly under direct high heat. The broiler should be preheated and hot before meat is placed in it. The meat can be seasoned or marinated before broiling *except* for using salt which draws out the moisture and prevents proper broiling. Broil meat on a rack set over the broiling pan. For steaks and burgers up to one inch thick, broil two to three inches from heat. For steaks and burgers one and a half to two inches thick, broil three to five inches from heat.

Brown meat on first side, add salt to the cooked side, and turn over. Broil the second side until it is browned. Broiled meats should be brown on the outside and red or pink inside.

5. *Barbecuing:* This is the same process as broiling, except that meat is placed directly over high heat. The charcoal in the barbecue should be very hot, grey in color, before the meat is barbecued.

BEEF

Of all meats, beef seems to be the most distinctly American. Our national image includes the hamburger along with apple pie and the flag.

There is more to beef than the hamburger and the steak. There are a wide variety of cuts that range from the lowly chuck to the high-minded filet mignon. Actually some lean boneless cuts of beef that cost more per pound end up to be cheaper than the lower priced cuts when you realize how much weight in fat and bone is thrown away. A six-pound chuck roast can add up to more money per person than a boneless flank steak at twice the price. Try to estimate the cost of each serving before buying beef.

Devilled roast beef bones, which used to be considered a leftover dish, are now featured in some restaurants as a dish on their own. They're excellent for parties or family dinners because they are inexpensive and easily prepared ahead and frozen, except for the brief last minute roasting.

DEVILLED ROAST BEEF BONES

3 racks of roast beef bones, about 3 pounds each, not cut up (A roast beef rack contains seven bones. Count on two bones per serving.)

SEASONED FLOUR:

3 large cloves garlic, minced
2 Tablespoons paprika
Salt and pepper
1 cup flour

MUSTARD COATING:

1 cup brown mustard

1 Tablespoon brown sugar
1 cup breadcrumbs

OPTIONAL MUSTARD SAUCE:

1½ cups of Sauce Béchamel (see page 88)
1½ cups brown mustard
1¼ Tablespoons Worcestershire Sauce

GARNISH:

2 bunches of parsley

Serves 6 to 8

1. Seasoned flour: Combine garlic, paprika, salt and pepper. Blend into one cup of flour. Rub the beef bones with the seasoned flour, coating them carefully.

2. Preheat the oven to 325 degrees. Place the bones on a rack over a roasting pan, with the meaty side up, and roast 1½ to 2 hours, or until the meat is tender. Remove from the oven and allow to cool enough to be handled.

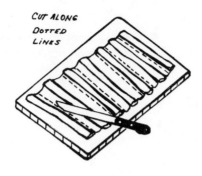

CUT ALONG
DOTTED
LINES

3. The bones should be cut so that a piece of meat remains on each side.

4. Mustard Coating: In a bowl, combine 1 cup of brown mustard with 1 Tablespoon of brown sugar. With a brush, lightly coat the meat. Then roll in breadcrumbs to coat thoroughly. Arrange on a lightly greased roasting pan or on a cookie sheet.

5. Preheat the oven to 425 degrees. Roast the bones for 20 minutes, or until golden brown.

6. Optional Mustard Sauce: Prepare 2½ cups of Béchamel Sauce. Add brown mustard with Worcestershire Sauce. Heat over low flame and do *not* allow to boil.

NOTE: *If you serve a standing rib roast, save the bones for "devilling." Since the bones are already roasted, start with Step 4. If you have leftover roast beef gravy, add 1 Tablespoon of mustard to it, and heat.*

TO SERVE

Arrange the bones on a platter of parsley. Heat optional sauce and serve at the table.

AHEAD

Bones may be prepared one day ahead through Step 4 and refrigerated. Sauce may be prepared two days ahead and refrigerated.

FREEZE

Bones may be prepared through Step 4 and frozen. Defrost for 3 to 4 hours before roasting.

A tenderloin of beef, properly cooked, is one of the most elegant of party dishes. It is expensive, and there's a lot of fat on it, but there is no bone nor gristle, and it is the tenderest, most flavorful cut of beef. It can be served alone or with any of a variety of sauces. A tenderloin weighs from six to eight pounds untrimmed, but by the time the fat is trimmed off, half the original weight may be lost. Count on ½ pound of trimmed tenderloin per person.

PERFECT BEEF TENDERLOIN

1 tenderloin of beef
½ cup butter
4 Tablespoons shallots, minced, or 2 cloves garlic, minced
1 Tablespoon Kitchen Bouquet

OPTIONAL:
Sauce Poivre Vert (Green Pepper Sauce) (see page 87)
Sauce Béarnaise (see page 92)

GARNISH:
Sprigs of watercress

UTENSILS:
String
Meat Thermometer

Serves 6 to 8

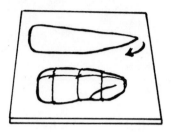

1. Trim the tenderloin of all fat.

2. Tuck the tail end under so the filet has an even thickness.

3. Tie the meat around at three or four places, then tie it lengthwise. Insert the meat thermometer at the thickest part.

4. Melt the butter, stir in the shallots or garlic, and Kitchen Bouquet. Baste the meat before roasting.

5. Preheat the oven to 450 degrees. While roasting, baste with the melted butter mixture. Roast meat for 30 to 40 minutes, or until the thermometer registers 120 degrees for rare, 125 degrees for less rare, or 135 degrees for medium.

NOTE: *If you are fortunate enough to have any of the roasted tenderloin left over, refrigerate it, if possible, in one piece rather than in slices.*

Do not reheat the meat. Use the following restaurant technique instead. Slice the meat cold, when you take it out of the refrigerator and allow it to come to room temperature. Bring Bordelaise, mushroom, or any other stock-based sauce to a boil. Arrange the meat slices on hot plates, and spoon the hot sauce over it. (Do not use an egg-yolk sauce such as Hollandaise or Béarnaise, as high heat will curdle it.)

Set on a heated platter, and garnish with watercress.
Serve with heated sauce.

May be prepared ahead through Step 3.

Do not freeze.

This is the only recipe for rare beef that I know of that can be prepared a day ahead.

FILETS DE BOEUF AUX CHAMPIGNONS
(Filet Mignon with Mushrooms)

1 1-inch thick slice of filet
mignon per person
2 to 3 cloves garlic, minced
1 teaspoon Lemon-Pepper
Marinade

      *   *   *

3 Tablespoons butter
3 Tablespoons cognac

      *   *   *

½ cup butter
2 Tablespoons flour
1 cup Sauce Brune (see page 83)
or beef stock
A few drops of Tabasco
1 Tablespoon Sauce Diable
1 Tablespoon Kitchen Bouquet

¼ cup dry sherry
Salt and pepper
¾ pound mushrooms, sliced

OPTIONAL:
Lemon juice to taste

GARNISH:
Chives, minced
Parsley sprigs

UTENSILS:
Au gratin pan or
three-quart rectangular pyrex dish

Serves 8 to 10

1. Trim all fat from the filets. Make a paste of the minced garlic and Lemon Pepper Marinade. Rub the paste on both sides of each filet.

2. In a skillet heat 3 Tablespoons of butter until it is sizzling. Add the filets and brown quickly over moderately high heat so the outside is crusty, and the inside is raw. *Do not crowd the pan or the meat will turn grey and be overcooked.* Flame with the cognac. Remove the beef to an ovenproof platter or an au gratin pan.

3. In the same skillet, melt the butter, and stir in the flour. Remove from the heat, and add the Sauce Brune or beef stock. Return to the heat, and stir constantly until thickened. Add the Tabasco, Sauce Diable, Kitchen Bouquet, and dry sherry. Blend, and simmer for 1 minute. Add salt and pepper to taste, and lemon juice if needed. Allow the sauce to cool.

4. Arrange the sliced mushrooms over the meat, and spoon the *cool* sauce over the meat and mushrooms.

5. Preheat the oven. Bake until heated through and the sauce is bubbling, approximately 15 to 20 minutes.

Variation: Burger aux Champignons
For less festive occasions, it can also be made with very lean one-inch thick hamburgers.

 Garnish with minced chives and sprigs of parsley.

 May be prepared one day ahead through Step 4 and refrigerated. Bring to room temperature before baking.

 Do not freeze.

This "Chicken-in-the-Basket" is made with filet mignon! It's a showstopper—a culinary work of art that almost looks too good to eat!

CHICKEN IN THE BASKET
(With Filet Mignon)

8 filet mignon steaks, 1-inch thick
Butter, enough to sauté
  2 Tablespoons cognac
  8 Potato Baskets (see pages 218 to 220)

DECORATIVE CHICKEN HEADS:

½ pound chicken liver pâté, divided into 8 one-inch balls
Beaks are 8 carrot triangles about ½ inch long
Eyes are 16 currants
Cockscomb is 8 pimiento slices or tomato slices

DECORATIVE TAIL-FEATHERS:

  4 Tablespoons butter
  1 pound mushrooms, sliced thin
Salt and pepper

DECORATIVE CHICKEN WINGS:

16 large crinkled potato chips
  8 artichoke bottoms
  2 cups Sauce Béarnaise (see page 92)
  2 bunches fresh parsley

UTENSILS:

Wide-neck pint-sized thermos to keep Sauce Béarnaise warm

Serves 8

1. Prepare the potato baskets.

2. Decorative Chicken Heads: Divide the pâté into eight portions, and form into small balls for the head. Attach a carrot triangle for the beak. Use a currant for each eye. Cut the tomatoes or pimientos into slivers for the cockscomb. Set on a dish, cover with plastic, and refrigerate.

3. Decorative Tail-Feathers: In a large skillet, melt the butter, and sauté the mushrooms over medium heat for 2 minutes. Add salt and pepper to taste. Set aside.

4. In another skillet, briefly sauté the artichoke bottoms in butter on both sides. Set aside.

5. Sauce Béarnaise: Prepare 1 hour before serving, and put into thermos jar to keep warm.

[178]

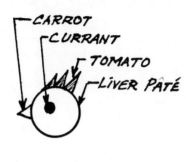

CARROT
CURRANT
TOMATO
LIVER PÂTÉ

Step 2

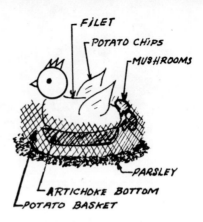

FILET
POTATO CHIPS
MUSHROOMS
PARSLEY
ARTICHOKE BOTTOM
POTATO BASKET

Step 6

6. Assembling the Chickens: In a 12-inch skillet, melt the butter over high heat, and sauté the filet mignons, browning them quickly on both sides. Cook to desired rareness. Flame with cognac. Reheat the artichoke bottoms and mushrooms.

On each dinner plate, arrange a bed of parsley. Set a potato basket on it. Put a heated artichoke bottom in the bottom of the basket, then the filet mignon. Place 1 Tablespoon of Sauce Béarnaise over each filet mignon. Arrange the heated mushrooms for the tail-feathers. Place potato chips as wings. Set the "chicken head" on top.

Serve remaining Sauce Béarnaise separately in a bowl.

Potato Baskets may be made one day ahead and kept at room temperature. "Chicken Heads" may be assembled one day ahead and refrigerated. Mushrooms may be sautéed one day ahead and refrigerated. Artichoke bottoms may be sautéed one day ahead and refrigerated.

Potato Baskets may be frozen and defrosted at room temperature. Pâté may be frozen and defrosted overnight in the refrigerator.

---

[179]

This is an excellent main-course steak; or it can be used at a cocktail party where you'd like to serve something more filling than canapés and hors-d'oeuvres. It should be assembled a day ahead to allow the sauce to marinate. It is baked instead of broiled, making it an ideal, no-fuss dish. Steak will go further if served on sliced, hot garlic bread.

SIRLOIN PANCHO

Approximately 4 pounds of sirloin
   steak, 2½-inches thick, with all
   fat trimmed off
2 cloves garlic, minced
1 large onion, sliced very thin
1 pound mushrooms, sliced
2 12-ounce bottles of chili sauce
6 to 9 ounces of beef stock, homemade or commercial
6 to 9 ounces of dry red wine

OPTIONAL:
Sliced, hot garlic bread

UTENSIL:
Small roasting pan, just slightly
   larger than steak

Serves 8

1. Place the steak in a small roasting pan. Spread the minced garlic evenly over the surface of the steak. Cover with sliced onions and mushrooms.

2. In a bowl, combine the chili sauce, 6 ounces of the beef stock, and 6 ounces of the wine. Spoon carefully over the steak, being careful not to disturb the mushrooms and onions.

3. Preheat oven to 425 degrees. Bake the steak for 1 hour, adding a little more beef stock and wine if amount of sauce seems skimpy.

Slice the steak on an angle across the grain of the meat.
Serve extra sauce at the table.
If served on garlic bread, spoon extra sauce on top.

May be made one day in advance through Step 2 and refrigerated.

Do not freeze.

A festive and economical family or company dish from South America.

CARNE DE NARANJA
(Mexican Beef with Oranges)

2½ pounds lean beef shoulder clod,
  cut into 1½-inch cubes
½ cup flour
2 cloves garlic, minced
  Salt and pepper

* * *

3 to 4 Tablespoons oil
3 Tablespoons cognac or
  brandy

* * *

3 Tablespoons fresh lemon juice
¾ cup fresh orange juice
2/3 cup dry white wine
2 Tablespoons brown sugar
1 cup golden raisins
1 medium onion, sliced
2 green peppers, cut into
  large pieces
¼ teaspoon cinnamon
¼ teaspoon nutmeg

GARNISH:
  1 large orange, unpeeled, cut
    into half-cartwheels
  4 Tablespoons parsley, minced

SERVE WITH:
Riz San Joaquin (see page 223)
  or 3 cups cooked rice

UTENSIL:
Large oval or round platter

Serves 6

1. Dredge the meat in mixture of the flour, garlic, salt and pepper.

2. In a large saucepan, heat the oil and sauté the floured meat slowly, browning it well on all sides. Flame with 3 Tablespoons of cognac or brandy. Add the lemon and orange juices, wine, and brown sugar. Cover tightly, and simmer gently for 1 hour.

3. Add the raisins, onion, green pepper, cinammon and nutmeg, and simmer covered for another 30 minutes, or until the meat is tender.

Heat the beef over low heat until hot. On a large oval or round platter, place the beef in the center. Spoon rice in a ring around the meat. Arrange the orange cartwheels on the rice so that they touch each other.
Sprinkle beef with minced parsley.

May be prepared one day ahead through Step 3.

May be frozen after Step 3. Defrost overnight in the refrigerator.

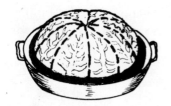

An excellent meal-in-one for your family or a dinner party that can be frozen and ready to heat. I usually make two or three at a time. I serve one and freeze the others. It improves the flavor if you prepare the Chou Farci one day ahead, and then reheat it before serving.

CHOU FARCI À L'ALSACIENNE
(Alsatian Stuffed Cabbage)

1 large head of cabbage
(Savoy cabbage if available)

BEEF FILLING:

2 heaping teaspoons Sour Salt or citric acid (available at most markets)
½ cup cold water
1 large onion, peeled and quartered
3 eggs
3 pounds lean ground beef
¼ cup long-grain white rice, uncooked
¾ cup red wine
3 teaspoons salt
½ teaspoon white pepper

SAUCE:

1 1-pound and 13-ounce can of sauerkraut with juice

2 large carrots, peeled, sliced thinly on an angle
1 1-pound can tomatoes, with juice
1 10¾-ounce can tomato soup
1 cup dark-brown sugar, packed firm
½ cup red wine
1 cup yellow raisins
10 to 12 gingersnaps, crushed

UTENSILS:

Cheesecloth, a 24-inch square
String
A Dutch Oven or an eight-quart stock pot
An au gratin pan or a large oval or round ovenproof serving dish.

Serves 6 to 8

1. Preparing cabbage: Using a paring knife, make cuts around the stem of the cabbage. Steam in a colander over two to three inches of boiling water for 10 to 12 minutes. Allow the cabbage to soften so the leaves can be shaped properly. Drain the cabbage by turning it upside down. Separate the leaves and scrape the heavy vein from each leaf to make it lie flat.

2. Beef filling: Soak the sour salt in ½ cup of cold water until it dissolves. Put the onion and eggs in the blender and purée. In a large bowl, combine the ground beef, rice, wine, 2 to 3 Table-

spoons of the dissolved sour salt, salt and pepper. The beef filling should be strongly seasoned and have a tart taste, or the flavor will be lost in the sauce.

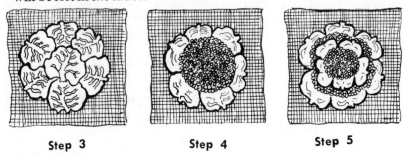

Step 3   **Step 4**   **Step 5**

3. Spread out the cheesecloth on a counter. Take six or seven large cabbage leaves, and place them with the stem ends facing so that they overlap on the cheesecloth. Put another large cabbage leaf in the center.

4. Divide the meat mixture into thirds. Spoon one third of it onto the center of the leaves, using a large wooden spoon, and gently spread the meat mixture toward the outer edges, leaving about a two-inch border of cabbage leaves.

5. Make a second circle of cabbage leaves, again overlapping them. Spread one third of the remaining meat mixture over this layer.

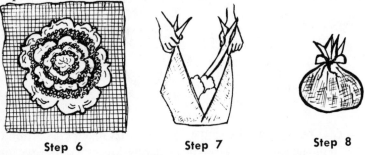

Step 6   **Step 7**   **Step 8**

6. Make two more layers of cabbage leaves, so that there are four in all. Make the third layer smaller than the second; fill it with half the remaining mixture. Make the fourth layer of cabbage leaves the smallest; fill it with the rest of the meat mixture.

7. With each hand, take two corners of the cheesecloth. Bring the edges together, and reshape the leaves so that they form the shape of a whole cabbage.

8. Tie the four corners of the cheesecloth together with string. With scissors, cut off excess cheesecloth above the tied string.

9. Sauce: In a large bowl, combine the sauerkraut with juice, carrots, tomatoes with juice, tomato soup, brown sugar, wine, raisins, and the remaining dissolved sour salt. Mix well.

10. Cooking the Chou Farci: The total cooking time is 2¼ hours. Break the remaining cabbage into small pieces and arrange on the bottom of a Dutch Oven or a stock pot. On top of it, place the cabbage, tied-side down. Pour the sauce over it, bring to a simmer, and cook slowly for 1½ hours, basting occasionally.

   Remove the cabbage and cut off the cheesecloth. Set it on a large, round ovenproof serving dish, and cut into eight wedges. Remove and discard the cabbage pieces from the bottom of the pan. Add the crushed gingersnaps to the remaining sauce, and heat until the gingersnaps are dissolved. Spread over and between the cabbage wedges.

   Preheat the oven to 350 degrees.

   Bake covered or tented with foil for 20 minutes. Discard the foil, baste with sauce, and bake another 25 minutes, basting once or twice.

 Baste just before serving.

 May be prepared two days ahead through Step 9 and refrigerated.

 May be frozen. Remove cheesecloth, and thaw in the sauce. Defrost for 24 hours in the refrigerator.

BURGERS EN CROÛTE
(Hamburgers in Pastry)

1 recipe of cream cheese pastry (see page 241) or 2 packages of frozen unbaked patty shells (12)
3 pounds ground beef, as lean as possible
Herbes Aromatiques (see page 97) or seasoned salt
1 Tablespoon grated onion

* * *

2 Tablespoons butter
2 Tablespoons margarine
2 medium onions, chopped fine
2 cloves garlic, minced
1 pound mushrooms, sliced thin
2 green peppers, chopped fine
Salt and pepper

EGG WASH:

2 egg yolks
2 teaspoons water

MUSHROOM SAUCE:

2 Tablespoons butter
¼ to ½ pound mushrooms, sliced thin
3 Tablespoons cognac or brandy

UTENSIL:

Roasting pan with rack that will fit into refrigerator

Serves 6

1. Pastry: Prepare one recipe of cream cheese pastry. Pat into an eight-inch circle. Wrap in foil or plastic and refrigerate for several hours. For commercial frozen patty shells, allow two per eight-ounce burger. Thaw them out several hours before using.

2. Burgers: Season the ground beef with Herbes Aromatiques or seasoned salt, pepper and grated onion. Form into six eight-ounce burger patties four inches in diameter and one inch thick.

3. Partially broil the burgers over a very hot barbecue grill, or sauté them quickly in a hot skillet so that both sides are a crusty brown and the insides are raw. Set on a rack over a roasting pan, cover with plastic, and refrigerate for at least two hours until chilled.

4. Sautéed Vegetables: In a large skillet, melt the butter and margarine and sauté the onion, garlic, mushrooms and green peppers until they are soft. Add salt and pepper to taste. Remove to a bowl, cover and refrigerate for at least 2 hours until chilled.

5. To Assemble: On a floured surface, roll out the chilled cream cheese pastry to one-eighth inch thickness.

[186]

Step 6

Step 7

Step 8

6. Cut into six rectangles about 8 inches by 10 inches, or large enough to encase a burger. (For commercial patty shells, combine two and roll out to a rectangle 8 inches by 10 inches.) Spoon an equal amount of the sautéed vegetables in the middle of each square of pastry. Put a burger on top of the vegetables. Paint the egg wash on the outside edges of the pastry.

7. Fold the dough over, and seal the edges. Be sure the burger is completely covered. Trim away any excess dough, but save it for decoration.

8. Turn the patties over, so the seam is on the bottom. With the extra pieces of pastry, make decorations or initials on top of each patty. Paint the top of the pastry with egg wash. Place on a greased cookie sheet.

9. Mushroom Sauce: In a skillet, melt the butter, and sauté the mushrooms until golden. Salt and pepper to taste.

10. Preheat the oven to 400 degrees. Bake the burgers for 15 to 20 minutes or until the pastry is golden brown.

TO SERVE

Heat the mushroom sauce and flame with 3 Tablespoons cognac or brandy. Spoon an equal amount over each burger.

AHEAD

The burgers may be prepared a day ahead through Step 4 and refrigerated.
The mushroom sauce may be prepared a day ahead and refrigerated.

FREEZE

Do not freeze.

VEAL

Most veal in this country is no longer milk-fed veal, but baby beef, and it tends to be very expensive. At this time, the best value is the frozen New Zealand boned leg of veal roast which costs about one third the price of domestic veal. It can be roasted whole, cut into chunks for simmering or stewing, or into one-quarter-inch slices for scallopini.

Marinate baby beef or New Zealand veal in equal parts of dry white wine and lemon juice for one hour before cooking.

Veal scallopini can be substituted for any recipes calling for chicken breasts.

TOUR DE VEAU WELLINGTON
(Veal Towers in Pastry)

8 slices veal cut from leg, approximately three inches in diameter and ¾ inch thick
⅓ cup lemon juice
⅓ cup white wine

SEASONED FLOUR:

1 cup flour
1 teaspoon sage
2 teaspoons oregano
2 cloves garlic, minced
1 Tablespoon paprika
Salt and pepper

* * *

3 to 4 Tablespoons olive oil
3 to 4 Tablespoons butter or margarine
Aubergines Frites Au Gratin (Baked Eggplant, see page 217), ½ inch thick, 8 slices

Tomates Gratinees à la Bonne Femme (Broiled Tomatoes, see page 218), 8 slices
8 large mushrooms
2 cans crescent dinner rolls

EGG WASH:

2 egg yolks
2 Tablespoons cream or milk

GARNISH:

3 Tablespoons Parmesan cheese, grated
24 pitted black olives
2 bunches fresh parsley

Serves 8

1. Veal: Trim any fat from the veal. Marinate for 1 hour in lemon juice and wine. In a pieplate, combine the flour, sage, oregano, garlic, paprika, salt and pepper. Coat the veal slices on both sides with the seasoned flour, and refrigerate for at least a half hour.

2. Heat 2 Tablespoons oil and 2 Tablespoons of butter in a large skillet, and sauté the floured veal slices on both sides until they are golden brown. Don't crowd the veal. Brown only four slices at a time, using more oil and butter if needed. Set aside.

3. Prepare the Aubergines Frites Au Gratin and bake for 15 minutes.

4. Prepare the Tomates Gratinees à la Bonne Femme, but do *not* broil.

5. Assembling Each Tower: On an ungreased cookie sheet or baking pan, place a slice of veal on the bottom; next, a slice of baked eggplant; then the tomato; and top with the uncooked mushroom.

6. Crescent Roll Dough: Open one can at a time of the crescent rolls, and unroll the dough. Separate the eight triangles along the perforated lines. Cut off 1½ to 2 inches of dough from the base of each triangle and save it for decorating. Cut each triangle in half vertically. Each tower uses three strips of dough.

   Place the point of each strip on top of the mushroom, drape it down over the tower, and press the dough against the veal at the bottom.

7. Egg Wash: Paint egg wash on the dough strips so that they will brown.

8. Decoration: Use the extra scraps of dough for decoration on the towers. Paint over them with egg wash.

9. Sprinkle each tower with a little Parmesan cheese and refrigerate until ready to bake.

10. Preheat the oven to 350 degrees. Bake for 15 to 20 minutes or until the pastry is golden brown.

When veal towers are golden brown, attach three black olives with toothpicks to the top of each. Serve on a bed of fresh parsley.

May be prepared one day ahead through Step 5, covered with plastic, and refrigerated. Bring to room temperature before baking.

Do not freeze.

ESCALOPE DE VEAU VIENNOISE
(Scalloped Veal Viennese Style)

1½ to 2 pounds veal from the leg, cut into eight slices, ¼ inch thick

MARINADE:

⅓ cup lemon juice
⅓ cup dry white wine
Flour
2 eggs, beaten

COATING MIXTURE:

1 cup breadcrumbs
3 Tablespoons Parmesan cheese, grated
1 teaspoon parsley, minced
½ teaspoon salt
¼ teaspoon pepper, freshly ground
¼ teaspoon nutmeg
2 to 4 Tablespoons butter

SAUCE:

1 2½-ounce can rolled anchovies with capers (set aside eight for garnish)
4 Tablespoons butter
⅛ teaspoon paprika
3 Tablespoons parsley, minced

GARNISH:

1 15-ounce jar of dill pickle slices
1 15-ounce jar of pickled beets
Bottle of capers
13 thin lemon slices
8 rolled anchovies
2 hard-cooked egg yolks, minced
2 hard-cooked egg whites, minced
2 Tablespoons parsley, minced

Serves 8

1. Trim and pound the veal slices into ⅛ inch thickness. Marinate them for one hour in the lemon juice and wine.

2. Remove the veal slices and flour them lightly on both sides.

3. In a pie plate, combine two eggs and add 2 Tablespoons of the marinade. Dip the veal slices in this mixture. (Save the remaining marinade for the sauce.)

4. Coating mixture: In another pie plate, combine the breadcrumbs, Parmesan cheese, parsley, salt, pepper and nutmeg. Dredge the veal slices in the coating, and allow them to stand at least 15 to 20 minutes before cooking.

5. In a large skillet, heat 2 Tablespoons of the butter and sauté four veal slices over low heat until they are golden brown and tender. Drain them on paper towels. Arrange on an ovenproof platter and keep warm in a low oven. Repeat the process with the other four veal slices, using more butter if necessary.

6. Sauce: Mince three of the anchovies. In a small pan, heat 4 Tablespoons of butter, and stir in 3 Tablespoons of the remaining marinade, paprika, minced anchovies and parsley.

Variation: Scalloped Chicken Viennoise may be prepared with boned, skinned, and pounded chicken breasts instead of veal.

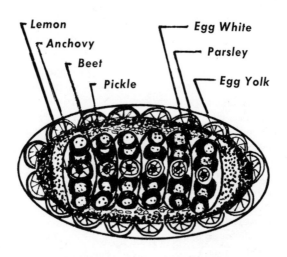

- Lemon
- Anchovy
- Beet
- Pickle
- Egg White
- Parsley
- Egg Yolk

TO SERVE

Arrange the veal slices slightly overlapping on an oval platter. Spoon hot sauce over the veal. Garnish each slice with overlapping slices of pickles and beets. Place a lemon slice in the center, and top with a rolled anchovy. At either end of the platter, arrange minced egg yolk. On either side of the platter, arrange the minced egg whites. Make an outer edge of parsley. Cut the remaining lemon slices in half, and arrange in a scallop around the outside edge.

AHEAD

May be prepared early in the day through Step 3.

Do not freeze.

I recommend this classic veal for a spring or summer buffet. You can spend the day on the beach or tennis court, and serve an elegant dinner you've prepared the day before.

VITELLO TONNATO
(Cold Roast Veal with Tuna Sauce)

3½ pounds boned leg of veal, rolled and tied
1 2-ounce can anchovies. Cut 2 anchovy fillets into 12 small pieces. Reserve the remaining anchovies and oil for the sauce.
2 Tablespoons olive oil
1 large onion, with skin, sliced
2 stalks celery, with leaves, coarsely chopped
2 carrots, coarsely chopped
2 cloves garlic, unpeeled, split in half
1 Tablespoon parsley, chopped
¼ teaspoon thyme
⅛ teaspoon sage
6 peppercorns
2 bay leaves
Grated rind of 1 lemon
Grated rind of 1 orange
1 medium sour, or dill, pickle
2 cups dry white wine

Chicken stock, homemade or commercial, to cover veal

SAUCE:
1 cup cold veal broth (liquid from cooked veal)
Anchovy fillets
6 to 8 Tablespoons mayonnaise
1 7-ounce can tuna, drained, rinsed, minced
¼ teaspoon oregano
2 to 3 Tablespoons lemon juice
Salt and pepper

*　　*　　*

½ cup cold cooked rice per person

*　　*　　*

1 bunch parsley, minced
capers, well-drained and rinsed

Serves 6

1. Cut twelve slits in the veal, and insert a piece of anchovy into each slit.

2. In a large heavy saucepan, heat the olive oil and brown the veal on all sides. Cover with cold water, and bring to a boil. Simmer for about 3 minutes. Remove the veal to a colander. Discard the grey veal water and wash out the pan. Wash off the veal with cold water, and return to the pan.

3. To the veal, add the onion, celery, carrots, garlic, parsley, thyme, sage, peppercorns, bay leaves, lemon and orange rinds, pickle,

and wine. Add enough chicken stock to cover the meat. Bring to a boil, reduce the heat, and simmer covered for an hour, or until the meat is tender and a fork pierces it easily. Do not overcook or the meat will be stringy.

Cool and place the entire saucepan in the refrigerator overnight.

4. The next day, lift off and discard the fat from the veal broth. Remove the veal, wrap in plastic or foil, and refrigerate. Heat the broth over medium-high heat, and cook until the amount of liquid is reduced to about three cups.

Strain the veal broth, and allow to cool. Discard the vegetables.

5. In the blender, put 1 cup of the cool veal broth. Add the oil from the anchovies. Wash off the remaining anchovy fillets and add to blender. Add 6 Tablespoons mayonnaise, the minced tuna, oregano, lemon juice and pepper, and blend. More veal broth, mayonnaise, and lemon juice may be necessary for taste and consistency. Add salt and pepper to taste.

6. Cold rice: Combine the cooked rice with the minced parsley.

7. To assemble: Slice the veal thin. On a large platter, mound the cold cooked rice and parsley. Arrange overlapping veal slices on top, leaving the ring of rice outside. Spoon only half of the sauce over the meat, and sprinkle with parsley and capers.

Cover loosely with foil and refrigerate at least 3 to 5 hours.

TO SERVE

Garnish rice with lemon wedges or slices. Serve remaining sauce in a bowl at the table.

AHEAD

Veal must be prepared at least one day ahead. It can be cooked two days ahead. Platter may be assembled and refrigerated one day ahead. Cover with plastic.

FREEZE

Do not freeze.

LAMB

The time and the place to eat lamb is springtime in France, when any dish made with their succulent young milk-fed lamb is superb.

Second best is our own domestic high-quality lamb . . . when it is cooked properly. Americans have tended to treat lamb as a poor relative, and to underseason and overcook it. In France, it is always served pink. It can be as delicate and tender as beef. It is a versatile meat, high in flavor, and very low in calories and cholesterol.

In the old days, young lamb was available only in the spring, and we had to settle for the stronger tasting mutton the rest of the time. Now high production makes tender young lamb available throughout the year.

There are two rules to remember about lamb: first, don't overcook it, and second, always remove all excess fat before cooking it.

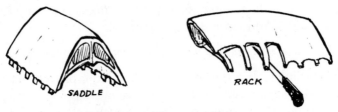

TERMS AND TYPES OF LAMB

1. *Saddle of Lamb:* Weighs about 5 pounds and is the most prized cut of lamb. It serves four.

   It must be specially ordered from the butcher. Concave in shape, it is the entire rib-cage.

   Season it with salt, pepper, garlic, and rosemary. Roast 12 to 15 minutes per pound in a 350-degree oven. Slice vertically. A slice of saddle of lamb should look like a slice of brisket.

2. *Rack of Lamb:* Weighing about 2½ pounds, it is one side of the ribs. It may be roasted whole, barbecued, cut into chops, or three or four racks may be made into a Crown Roast of Lamb. (see page 202). It serves two.

   If rack of lamb is cooked whole, "french" the rib bones, or remove 1½ inches of meat from the bone ends.

   To roast a rack of lamb cook it 12 to 15 minutes per pound in a 450-degree oven. Slice it into individual chops with bone attached, or bone out the filet or eye of the rack, and slice into noisettes, one-half-inch round slices.

3. *Leg of Lamb:* It weighs 6 to 8 pounds and may be: roasted whole; boned and rolled into a roast; or butterflied and boned and then broiled or barbecued. (see Perfect Roast Leg of Lamb, page 196, and Barbecued and Butterflied Leg of Lamb, page 198). It serves four to six.

4. *Loin Chops:* These are very expensive and delicious. Season with salt, pepper, garlic and rosemary. Broil on both sides until browned, and pink inside. Serve one or two per person.

5. *Shoulder Chops:* Very economical, they're usually cut ¾- to 1-inch thick. Sprinkle with meat tenderizer and seasonings. Barbecue over hot coals, or under the broiler, until browned on each side. They should be served pink inside. Serve one or two per person.

6. *Lamb Shanks:* Economical, this cut is excellent for lamb stew. Allow one per person.

BONING A LEG OF LAMB

A boned, butterflied leg of lamb can be barbecued like a steak, or stuffed and rolled. Your butcher may bone it for you, but very often, he will charge you extra per pound for doing it.

1. Starting with a 6 to 7 pound leg of lamb, remove excess fat and the membrane from the leg of lamb.

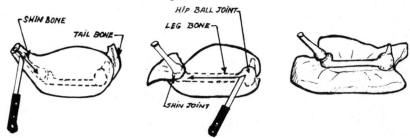

2. Cut off the tail bone. With a sharp boning knife, cut down along the shin bones, and scrape the flesh away from the bone.

3. Find the ball joint in the thick part of the leg. Cut in and around it to loosen the meat. Make a cut into the meat down the leg bone toward the shin joint. Scrape and pull the flesh away from the bone.

4. Carefully cut away any sinew or tendons around the joints. It may be necessary to twist and break the joint to release the bone from the meat.

A leg of lamb, when prepared right, is an elegant dinner! Lamb tastes best when it is served medium rare and has a faint pink color.

BONED STUFFED LEG OF LAMB

6 to 7 pound leg of lamb
Perfect Roast Turkey Dressing
  (see page 166)
String

Salt and Pepper
Garlic
Rosemary

Serves 6 to 8

Stuff the boned and butterflied leg of lamb with Perfect Roast Turkey Dressing. Tie with a string. Season with salt, pepper, garlic and rosemary, and roast 15 to 20 minutes per pound in a 325-degree oven for pink meat, or 30 to 35 minutes per pound for well-done lamb.

If a meat thermometer is used, roast until the indicator reaches 130 to 135 degrees for pink, and 160 degrees for well done.

PERFECT ROAST LEG OF LAMB

1 leg of lamb, 6 to 7 pounds,
  all fat removed
2 cloves garlic, minced
1 Tablespoon paprika
1 Tablespoon fresh rosemary, or
  1½ teaspoons dried rosemary
2 teaspoons salt
½ teaspoon pepper

ORANGE BASTING SAUCE:
1 6-ounce can frozen orange
  juice concentrate
¼ cup dry red wine
¼ cup butter

UTENSIL:
Meat thermometer

Serves 6 to 8

1. Make twelve small slits in the leg of lamb, underneath and on top. Combine the garlic, paprika, rosemary, salt and pepper, and press a little of this mixture into each slit.

2. Orange Basting Sauce: In a small pan, melt the butter and add the orange juice concentrate and wine. Stir well, and simmer for 15 minutes.

3. Preheat the oven to 350 degrees. Insert the meat thermometer into the thickest part of the lamb, not touching the bone.

4. Roasting Timetable: For medium-rare meat, cook for 12 to 15 minutes per pound, or until the thermometer is at 130 or 135 degrees. For well-done meat, cook for 30 to 35 minutes per pound, or until the thermometer is at 160 degrees.

   Roast the lamb for one hour then baste with Orange Basting Sauce, and continue to baste every half hour until the meat thermometer registers 10 degrees *below* the desired temperature. Remove the lamb from the oven, and let it stand. It will continue cooking because of the internal heat. Allow the thermometer to reach the desired temperature before carving.

Variation: Rock Cornish Hen à l'Orange
Orange Basting Sauce may be used when roasting or barbecuing Rock Cornish game hens.

To carve, set the lamb on its side and slice across the wide end towards the shank. This will avoid the bone, and enable you to cut large slices of meat.

May be prepared one day ahead through Step 2.

Leftover lamb may be cut into cubes, with fat removed, and frozen.

The first time I tasted this, I thought it was an excellent steak!

BARBECUED BUTTERFLIED LEG OF LAMB

6 to 7-pound leg of lamb, boned,
    trimmed of fat, and butterflied

SAUCE:
  1 cup ketchup
  1 cup water
  ¼ cup Worcestershire Sauce
  ¼ cup vinegar

Few drops Tabasco
¼ cup brown sugar, packed firm
  1 teaspoon celery salt
  1 teaspoon chile powder
  1 teaspoon salt

Serves 6

1. In a saucepan, warm the ketchup, water, Worcestershire Sauce, vinegar, Tabasco, brown sugar, celery salt, chile powder and salt. Do not boil it.

2. Pour the sauce over the lamb and marinate it overnight in the refrigerator.

3. Barbecue the lamb 8 to 10 inches from the hot coals for about 50 minutes. Turn it often, basting every 10 to 15 minutes. Do not overcook the lamb. It should be crisp on the outside and pink inside.

Variation: Lamb chops and rack of lamb may also be used.

 Slice on the diagonal. Serve additional sauce at the table.

 May be made two days ahead through Step 2.

 Do not freeze.

This is a treasured recipe of the Leone family of Detroit.

ABBACCHIO ALLA CACCIATORA
(Lamb Hunters' Style)

3 pounds spring lamb, boned, and cut into 1½-inch cubes, with all fat removed
1½ Tablespoons olive oil
1¼ Tablespoons butter
½ teaspoon rosemary
Pinch of sage
2 cloves garlic, minced
Salt and pepper
1 Tablespoon flour
¾ cup red wine

1 cup of chicken stock, homemade or commercial
4 anchovy fillets, drained

GARNISH:
2 Tablespoons parsley, minced

* * *

Serve with Riso all' Uovo-Limone
(Lemon Rice, see page 223)

Serves 6

1. In a large saucepan, heat the oil and butter, and brown the lamb cubes on all sides. Add the rosemary, sage, garlic, salt and pepper, and stir for 2 to 3 minutes.

2. Blend in the flour, and gradually add the red wine and the chicken stock, stirring constantly until the sauce is slightly thickened.

3. Cover the pan and simmer slowly for about 40 minutes, or until the lamb is tender.

Heat the lamb. In a small bowl, blend the anchovies with a little of the sauce, add to the lamb and simmer for 5 minutes. Sprinkle with parsley and serve with Riso all' Uovo-Limone.

May be prepared without anchovies one day ahead and refrigerated.

May be frozen, without anchovies.

PERSILLADE CARRÉ D'AGNEAU
(Parslied Lamb Rack)

2 racks of lamb, 2½ pounds each

PERSILLADE:

1 cup breadcrumbs
6 Tablespoons fresh parsley, minced
2 shallots, minced
2 teaspoons paprika
6 Tablespoons of any 1 of the following: drippings from roast-ed rack of lamb, butter, margarine or chicken stock (lowest in calories)

GARNISH:
Parsley sprigs

UTENSIL:
Roasting pan with rack

Serves 4

1. Trim all fat from the lamb racks, and french the bone ends (see page 194).

2. Preheat the oven to 450 degrees. Set the lamb racks on a rack in a roasting pan, and roast for 12 to 15 minutes, or until browned outside and pink inside.

3. Persillade: In a bowl, combine the breadcrumbs, parsley, garlic, shallots, paprika, and either drippings, butter, margarine or stock. Spread this mixture on the meaty side of the lamb racks.

4. Preheat the broiler, and place the racks under the broiler briefly until the persillade is lightly browned. Check often to be sure it is not burning.

Cut into single chops, or noisettes.
Garnish with parsley.

Persillade may be prepared one or two days ahead using butter or chicken stock.

Do not freeze.

PORK

Pork can be prepared in an almost endless variety of ways. The choice roasts are rib, tenderloin, or leg of pork, which can be roasted whole, boned, or stuffed and rolled. The important thing to remember about pork is that its unique and distinctive flavor is brought out best when it is cooked at a low temperature. Fast cooking and high heat makes pork tough and dry.

Pork must be cooked thoroughly until it is grey or white in color. If it is pink, it needs more cooking time. Since pork is a rich meat, it should be balanced by lighter accompanying dishes.

CROWN ROAST OF PORK TIVOLI

1 5-pound crown pork roast, with
   fat removed
   Lemon juice
   Salt and pepper
1 recipe of Fruit Dressing (see
   page 168) or Perfect Roast
   Turkey Dressing (see page 166)

MUSTARD MIXTURE:

½ cup Dijon mustard
2 Tablespoons soy sauce
2 cloves garlic, minced
1 teaspoon sage
¼ teaspoon ground ginger
1 teaspoon marjoram

GARNISH:

Paper frill to cover rib bones or
   kumquats, fresh or preserved
Raw cranberries or grapes strung
   on heavy white thread

UTENSILS:

Roasting pan with rack
Foil
Meat thermometer

Serves 6

1. Preheat the oven to 325 degrees. (Total roasting time is approximately 3 to 3 ½ hours.) Dampen a paper towel with lemon juice and wipe the pork roast with it. Insert meat thermometer. Place the pork in a roasting pan on a rack. Sprinkle with salt and pepper. Cover the rib bones with foil so they don't burn. Crumple some foil and set it in the center of the roast so that it keeps its shape during roasting. Roast for 1 hour uncovered.

2. Baste with the mustard mixture, and roast another 1 ½ hours, basting every half hour.

3. Prepare the Fruit Dressing or Perfect Roast Turkey Dressing.

4. When the roast has been in the oven for about 2 ½ hours, remove the crumpled foil from the center. Paint the inside of the roast with mustard mixture, and fill it with the dressing. Cover with foil, and continue roasting until the dressing is cooked, or the meat thermometer reaches 185 degrees.

Variation: Crown Roast of Lamb may be used. Use 2 teaspoons fresh rosemary or 1 teaspoon dried rosemary instead of sage in the mustard mixture. Roast until thermometer reaches 120 degrees and then remove the foil. Paint the inside of the roast with mustard mixture, and fill with the dressing. Roast until the thermometer reaches 130 to 135 degrees. May be roasted without dressing. When serving, fill the center with mushrooms and peas or brussel sprouts.

TO SERVE — Remove the foil from the rib bones and cover each bone with a paper frill or kumquat. Decorate with a string of raw cranberries or grapes.

AHEAD — May be prepared early in the day through Step 3, and if dressing is prepared ahead, it should be refrigerated.

FREEZE — Do not freeze.

This technique of making a Chinese oven within your own gas or electric oven works well for roasting tenderloins, spareribs, barbecued pork, and quartered chickens. For the best flavor, the meat should be marinated overnight. It can be served cold as an hors-d'oeuvre or hot as a main course.

CHINESE RED ROAST PORK

6 strips boneless lean pork, each 2 inches by 6 inches, cut from tenderloin or butt (approximately 6 pounds)

MARINADE:

6 Tablespoons canned Hoisin Sauce, or honey
¼ cup dry sherry
2 Tablespoons soy sauce
1 teaspoon fresh ginger, grated
3 cloves garlic, minced
¾ teaspoon Chinese Five Spices
3 green onions, minced

¼ cup sugar
¼ teaspoon pepper
¼ teaspoon red food coloring

SERVE WITH:

Indonesian Rice (see page 224)
Apricot Sambal (see page 204)

UTENSILS:

6 large size paper clips, or drapery hooks
Large roasting pan lined with foil

Serves 8 to 10

1. Trim all fat from the pork.

2. Marinade: In a baking dish, combine the Hoisin Sauce, sherry, soy sauce, ginger, garlic, Chinese Five Spices, green onions, sugar, pepper and food coloring. Place the pork strips into the marinade, turning them so they are well coated. Cover the dish and refrigerate overnight.

3. To make a Chinese Oven in your own oven: Place one oven rack in the highest slot in the oven. Place the other one in the lowest position. Fill the foil-lined roasting pan with hot water ½-inch deep, and set it on the lower rack. (The water will prevent the meat from becoming dry, and will also catch the drippings.)

   Bend each paper clip into an S shape. Fifteen minutes before roasting, take the pork out of the refrigerator. Set one end of the paper clip into each strip of pork, 1 inch from the heaviest end. Hang the other end of the paper clip over the upper oven rack. The pork should hang *above* the water in the roasting pan. Space the strips far enough apart so they are not touching.

4. When the pork strips are hung from the top rack, turn on the oven to 425 degrees. The pork should start to cook in a cold oven. Roast for 15 minutes at 425 degrees. Reduce the heat to 325 degrees, and continue roasting for 1 hour and 15 minutes, or until tender. Baste often with the marinade. (Total roasting time is one hour and 30 minutes.) Remove from the oven, slip out the paper clips and cut diagonally into ⅛-inch thin slices.

Serve the remaining marinade hot in a separate bowl.

Pork may be marinated two days ahead and refrigerated.

Pork may be frozen for two to three months.

APRICOT SAMBAL
(Hot Apricot Purée)

2 cups dried apricots
1 12-ounce can apricot nectar
1½ teaspoons curry powder
3 Tablespoons honey
1 teaspoon almond extract
2 Tablespoons dry mustard

1 Tablespoon fresh ginger, grated
2 to 3 Tablespoons dry sherry

UTENSIL:
2-quart saucepan

1. Place the apricots in a 2-quart saucepan, barely covering with apricot nectar. Bring to a simmer and cook until the apricots are tender, 20 to 30 minutes.

2. Purée the cooked apricots in the blender.

3. Return to the saucepan. Add the curry powder, honey, almond extract, mustard, ginger, and sherry to taste. Stir thoroughly. Cook over very low heat until hot. Be careful the mixture does not scorch on the bottom.

CHAPTER 8

Vegetables

Good as a first course or a vegetable. With the addition of shrimp, it is a delectable main course for lunch or supper.

ARTICHOKES GROTTO AZUR
(Stuffed Artichokes)

4 large artichokes
Lemon juice
½ cup olive oil
½ cup water
½ cup dry white wine

FILLING:
2 Tablespoons onion, minced
2 Tablespoons Parmesan cheese, grated
1 clove garlic, minced
1 Tablespoon capers, drained and rinsed
1 Tablespoon parsley, minced

½ teaspoon salt
¼ teaspoon pepper
1 cup fine breadcrumbs

OPTIONAL:
¾-pound bay shrimp, or cooked shrimp cut into ½-inch pieces

* * *

1 cup chicken stock, homemade or commercial
½ cup dry white wine

Serves 4

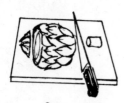

Step 1

Step 2

Step 3

1. Wash the artichokes. Remove the two bottom layers of leaves. Place each artichoke on its side, cut off the top leaves, and the bottom of the stem.

2. With scissors, cut the tip off each leaf to eliminate the sharp thorns.

3. Spread the leaves apart. Use a small spoon to reach inside and scrape out the fuzzy inedible part of the artichoke. Brush the inside and the bottom with lemon juice to prevent discoloration.

4. In a 4- or 5-quart saucepan, set the artichokes upright and cover with boiling water. Parboil, covered, for 25 to 30 minutes depending on their size. Drain upside down.

5. Put the partially cooked artichokes rightside up in a roasting pan, and spoon 2 Tablespoons of the olive oil, 2 Tablespoons of the water, and 2 Tablespoons of the wine over each artichoke.

6. Filling: In a bowl, combine the minced onion, cheese, garlic, capers, parsley, salt, pepper, breadcrumbs, and shrimp.

7. Assembling: Spoon the filling into the center of each artichoke, reserving some to put in between the leaves.

8. Baking: Preheat the oven to 375 degrees. Spoon an additional ¼ cup chicken stock, and 2 Tablespoons of wine over each artichoke to moisten the filling. Cover with foil, and bake for 45 minutes. Uncover, baste, and bake for 15 minutes more. Total baking time is 1 hour. Baste before removing from the pan.

 Serve hot. Spoon any remaining pan juices over each artichoke.

 May be prepared one day ahead through Step 7.

 Do not freeze.

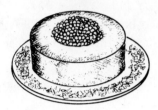

Even people who say they don't like carrots ask for this recipe!

BORDURE DE CAROTTES
(Carrot Ring)

1½ cups butter, at room
    temperature
1 cup brown sugar, firmly
    packed
4 eggs, separated
3 cups raw carrots, finely grated
    (approximately 1 pound)
2 Tablespoons cold water
2 Tablespoons lemon juice
2 cups flour
1 teaspoon baking soda
2 teaspoons baking powder
1 teaspoon salt

      *   *   *

¼ cup breadcrumbs

UTENSILS:
3-quart ring mold, lightly greased
Round serving platter

SERVE WITH:
Petits Pois à la Française
    (see page 211)

Serves 8 to 10

1. In the electric mixer, cream the butter with the brown sugar. Add the egg yolks, and beat until thick. Add the grated carrots, water, lemon juice, flour, baking soda, baking powder, and salt. Mix well on low speed.

2. In a separate bowl, beat the egg whites until stiff. Fold the beaten egg whites into the carrot mixture.

3. Dust the greased ring mold with breadcrumbs. Place carrot mixture in the mold.

4. Preheat the oven to 350 degrees. Bake for 1 hour. Remove from the oven and allow to cool for 3 minutes. With a dull knife, loosen the edges and center of the ring.

Turn carrot ring out onto a heated, round serving platter. Fill the center with carefully drained Petits Pois à la Française.

May be prepared one day ahead through Step 1.

Grated carrots may be frozen. Defrost before using.

A beautiful way of serving cauliflower filled with peas cooked in the classic French style. While the cauliflower is cooking, prepare the cheese sauce and the peas.

ROSETTE DE CHOU-FLEUR À LA FRANÇAISE
(Rosette of Cauliflower with Peas)

1 large head cauliflower
1 teaspoon salt

CHEESE SAUCE:
1 cup cheddar cheese, grated
1 cup sour cream
1 teaspoon dried basil

PETITS POIS À LA FRANÇAISE:
6 Tablespoons butter
¾ cup lettuce, chopped fine
3 pounds fresh peas
¼ cup shallots, minced
   or 12 pearl onions
1 sprig parsley
2 to 4 teaspoons sugar

1 teaspoon salt
⅛ teaspoon white pepper

BUTTERED BREADCRUMBS:
4 Tablespoons butter
1 cup breadcrumbs

GARNISH:
Pimiento strips

UTENSILS:
Steamer or colander
Round serving platter
2-quart saucepan

Serves 6

1. Cauliflower: Trim the heavy outside leaves from the cauliflower. Cook the cauliflower in a steamer or colander placed over boiling water in a large covered saucepan. Depending on the size of the cauliflower, it will take from 15 to 20 minutes. Drain the cauliflower, and turn it flower-side down on a heated serving platter. Hollow out the core. Keep warm until ready to serve.

2. Cheese Sauce: Melt the cheese in the top of a double-boiler. Add the sour cream and the basil, and keep warm until ready to serve.

3. Petits Pois à la Française: In a 2-quart saucepan, melt the butter. Set the lettuce on top of the melted butter. Add the peas, shallots or pearl onions, parsley, sugar, salt and pepper, and simmer, covered, until the peas are tender, about 10 or 15 minutes. No water is necessary. Stir occasionally. Remove parsley before serving.

4. Buttered Breadcrumbs: In a small skillet, melt 4 Tablespoons of butter, add the breadcrumbs and toss until they are well coated. Sauté until lightly browned.

5. Assembling: Fill the hollow of the cauliflower with the cheese sauce. Put a third of the peas on top of the cheese sauce. Arrange the remaining peas in a circle around the cauliflower. Decorate the outer rim of the cauliflower with the buttered breadcrumbs.

Garnish with pimiento strips.

Cauliflower with the cheese sauce may be prepared 30 minutes ahead and kept warm in a 200-degree oven.

Do not freeze.

This is a concentrated mushroom essence, almost like a mushroom butter. It is excellent to have on hand because of the many ways you can use it. Add it to omelettes, crêpes, scrambled eggs, mashed potatoes, vegetables or chicken dishes. Spoon it over hamburgers or steaks. Use duxelles to enhance sauces like Sauce Béchamel or Sauce Brune. You can no doubt find other ways to use it. I freeze it in small amounts for easy use.

DUXELLES
(Mushroom Concentrate)

2 pounds fresh mushrooms washed thoroughly and dried
½ cup butter
3 Tablespoons olive oil
½ cup minced shallots, or white part of green onions

BOUQUET GARNI:
1 bay leaf

½ teaspoon thyme
Few sprigs parsley

* * *

½ cup Madeira wine, or ¼ cup brown stock, homemade or commercial
Salt and pepper

Makes 2 cups.

1. Mince the mushrooms in a food chopper or vegetable grater.

2. In a 10-inch or 12-inch skillet, heat the butter and olive oil; add the shallots or green onions and the mushrooms. Stir well. Add the bouquet garni, tied in cheesecloth. Cook uncovered over low heat until most of the moisture has evaporated, approximately 40 to 45 minutes. The mushrooms will become dark in color and

begin to separate into small individual pieces. Stir every 10 or 15 minutes to prevent the mushrooms from sticking to the bottom of the pan.

3. Add the wine or brown stock, and continue to cook until all of the liquid is evaporated, approximately 2 hours. The mushrooms will be almost black in color.

4. Remove the bouquet garni; add the salt and pepper to taste.

Variations: Hot Mushroom Hors-d'Oeuvres:
Combine an equal amount of duxelles with either grated cheese or Perfect Pâté (see page 22). Spread on toast rounds, and broil until hot.

Artichoke Bottoms with Duxelles (Hors-d'Oeuvres or Vegetable):
Spoon 1 Tablespoon of duxelles onto each of 8 artichoke bottoms. In a small bowl, combine 4 Tablespoons mayonnaise, 4 Tablespoons grated Parmesan cheese and 2 Tablespoons of minced onion. Place a spoonful of this mixture on top of the duxelles. Bake for 10 to 15 minutes in a 375 degree oven.

May be prepared two weeks ahead and refrigerated.

May be frozen.

These stuffed onions are not only a vegetable course, but a handsome garnish on a meat platter. They could also be served in an au gratin dish.

OIGNONS À LA GRÈQUE
(Stuffed Greek Onions)

10 large oval-shaped onions
Chicken stock to cover onions in
   pan

FILLING:
1 Tablespoon butter
2 cloves garlic, minced
1 pound lean ground beef
   Leftover pieces of onion,
   minced
2 Tablespoons sour cream
¼ teaspoon Sauce Diable
   (available at most markets)
2 Tablespoons fresh dill, minced
1 teaspoon salt
¼ teaspoon pepper
2 hard-cooked eggs, minced
¼ cup cooked rice, or ⅓ cup
   toasted pine nuts

       * * *

2 to 4 Tablespoons olive oil
2 to 4 Tablespoons butter
2 to 3 Tablespoons brown sugar

      * * *

Paprika

GARNISH:
Minced parsley

UTENSILS:
Large skillet
Ovenproof serving platter or au
   gratin dish, lightly greased

Serves 10

1. Peel off the outer layer of each onion, and cut off the stem and root ends. Make one vertical slit cutting half way through to the center.

2. In a saucepan, bring the chicken stock to a boil, then add the onions. Be sure there is enough stock to cover them. Simmer for 15 to 20 minutes, or until the onions are soft enough to separate easily into layers. Allow to cool enough so that they can be handled.

[214]

3. Peel away three to four layers of the onions. Save the inside pieces to mince and add to the filling. You will have between 30 and 40 onion skins, or three to four per person.

4. Filling: In a skillet, heat the butter; add the garlic and sauté the ground beef until it is slightly browned. Remove from the heat; drain off any excess fat. Add the minced onions, sour cream, Sauce Diable, dill, salt, pepper, hard-cooked eggs, and the rice or pine nuts.

5. Assembling: Place 1 Tablespoon or more of the filling into each onion skin and roll it closed.

6. Sauté the onions in two or three batches. In a large skillet, heat approximately half of the olive oil and butter. Add half of the brown sugar, and stir over a low flame until the sugar begins to bubble. Add the first batch of onions, seamside down. Sauté them slowly over low heat, until they are browned evenly. Turn them when necessary, and baste with glaze on the bottom of the skillet. Remove the browned onions and any pan juices or glaze that can be lifted from the skillet to an ovenproof platter or au gratin dish. Repeat, using more olive oil, butter and brown sugar, as necessary, until all of the onions are browned. Sprinkle with paprika.

7. Preheat the oven to 375 degrees. Bake the onions for about 20 minutes until heated through. Baste once or twice while baking with juices in the pan.

 Sprinkle the onions with minced parsley.

 Onions may be prepared one day ahead through Step 6 and refrigerated. Allow them to come to room temperature, and bake until heated through.

 May be frozen after Step 6.

This is the French technique for puréeing peas as well as other vegetables such as carrots, broccoli, mushrooms, asparagus and others.

PURÉE DE POIS FRAIS AUX CHAMPIGNONS
(Purée of Fresh Peas in Mushrooms)

3 10-ounce packages of frozen peas, cooked and drained
4 Tablespoons butter
2 Tablespoons flour
2 Tablespoons cream
¼ teaspoon salt
⅛ teaspoon pepper

* * *

½ cup butter
24 large mushroom caps, stems removed, washed thoroughly

GARNISH:
Parsley sprigs

UTENSILS:
Blender and strainer, food mill or ricer
2-quart sauce pan

Serves 6 to 8

1. Purée the cooked peas in blender, food mill, or ricer. (If a blender is used, the peas must then be strained to remove the hulls.)

2. In a 2-quart saucepan, melt the 4 Tablespoons of butter; stir in the flour. Cook until lightly browned, stirring constantly. Remove from the heat, and stir in the cream. Add the puréed peas, salt, and pepper. Blend well.

3. In a small pan, melt the ½ cup of butter; brush it on the inside and outside of the mushroom caps. Place them on a greased cookie sheet. Spoon some of the puréed peas into each mushroom cap.

4. Preheat the oven to 400 degrees. Bake for 10 minutes.

Garnish with sprigs of parsley.

May be prepared two days ahead through Step 3, and refrigerated.

Puréed peas may be frozen.

The remarkable thing about eggplant is that it takes on totally different flavors, depending on how it is prepared. Be sure to buy an eggplant that is firm and smooth, so that it is not dehydrated or bitter. It will keep for up to a week in the refrigerator if you store it in a tightly sealed plastic bag. For this fast-and-easy baked eggplant, you don't even need to peel it. Bake it only until the covering is a light brown.

AUBERGINES FRITES AU GRATIN
(Baked Eggplant with Cheese)

1 2-pound eggplant, cut in ⅛- to ¼-inch slices
½ cup mayonnaise
¾ cup crushed saltine crackers

¾ cup Parmesan cheese or Gruyère-type cheese, grated fine

Serves 4

1. Peel and slice the eggplant into ⅛- to ¼-inch slices. Coat both sides of the eggplant slices with a little mayonnaise. In a pie plate, combine the crushed saltines and grated cheese, and dip the eggplant slices into it. Place them on a greased cookie sheet.

2. Preheat the oven to 425 degrees, and bake for 15 minutes, until golden brown, and remove from oven.

 Serve hot.

 May be prepared early in the day through Step 1 and refrigerated.

 Do not freeze.

TOMATES GRATINEES À LA BONNE FEMME
(Broiled Tomatoes with Cheese)

2 large tomatoes, cut into 3
½-inch thick slices, or 3
tomatoes halved
4 Tablespoons mayonnaise
4 Tablespoons Parmesan or
Gruyère cheese, grated

4 Tablespoons shallots,
minced, sautéed
2 Tablespoons parsley, minced

Serves 4

In a small dish, combine the mayonnaise, grated cheese, shallots, and parsley. Spread this mixture on the tomatoes. Preheat the broiler and broil for 2 or 3 minutes, or until lightly browned.

Potato baskets are elegant and versatile. Fill them with an entrée like filet mignon, stroganoff, escargot, creamed seafood or poultry, or a curry. Or fill them with a variety of vegetables such as fresh asparagus tips with hollandaise sauce, baby carrots, or whole or puréed peas. Here are two recipes for potato baskets. The first requires a Bird's Nest Fryer Set; the second needs no special equipment.

NIDS DE POMMES DE TERRE, NUMBER ONE
(Potato Baskets)

2 pounds potatoes, peeled
3 pounds solid vegetable
shortening

UTENSILS:
1 Bird's Nest Fryer Set
Scissors

Serves 6

1. Shred the potatoes on a medium grater, and put them in a bowl of cold water to prevent discoloration. As needed, drain them on a paper towel and pat them dry.

| Step 2 | Step 3 | Step 4 |

2. Heat the shortening to 375 degrees. Dip the larger metal basket into the hot fat. Remove it and line it so the potatoes are about ¼ inch thick and come up 2 inches on the sides of the basket. Now, dip the smaller basket into the hot fat, remove it, and set it into the potato-lined larger basket. Hold the handles firmly together, and with scissors cut away any pieces of potato sticking out of the basket.

3. Holding the handles together, plunge the baskets into the hot fat, and fry until crisp and golden brown, approximately 6 or 7 minutes.

4. Carefully remove the smaller basket. With a knife, loosen the potato nest in the larger basket, or strike the top edge of the basket sharply to loosen it. Set the basket on a paper towel to drain. Repeat the process with the other baskets.

Fill the baskets just before serving.

May be prepared one day ahead and kept at room temperature.

May be frozen. Bring to room temperature before filling.

NIDS DE POMMES DE TERRE, NUMBER TWO
(Potato Baskets)

1 1-pound package of frozen
   shoestring potatoes
3 eggs, slightly beaten
4 ounces cheddar cheese,
   shredded

1½ teaspoons salt

UTENSIL:
   1 cupcake pan (4½ inches by
     1¼ inches), well greased

1. Thaw the potatoes and cut into 1-inch pieces.

2. In a bowl, combine the eggs, cheese, and salt. Add the potatoes and toss until they are evenly coated. Allow to stand for about 10 minutes.

3. Divide the mixture into six portions. Press each portion into the cupcake pan, ¼ inch thick on the bottom and sides.

4. Preheat the oven to 375 degrees, and bake until the baskets are delicately browned, approximately 15 to 20 minutes.

5. Carefully loosen the baskets and remove.

 TO SERVE   Fill the baskets just before serving.

 AHEAD   May be prepared one day ahead and kept at room temperature. Reheat in a 200-degree oven.

 FREEZE   May be frozen. Bring to room temperature before filling. Reheat in a 200-degree oven.

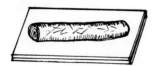

You can make incredibly good strudels that combine proteins, starches and vegetables. Use commercial phylo pastry leaves.

SPINACH STRUDEL

SPINACH STRUDEL FILLING:
(for one strudel)
- 3 bunches fresh spinach
- 1 pound mozzarella cheese, coarsely chopped
- 1 cup Parmesan cheese, grated
- ½ cup green onions, minced
- 6 Tablespoons butter, chilled, coarsely diced
- 1 teaspoon cinnamon
- Salt and pepper

PHYLO PASTRY:
For two strudel rolls, use twelve leaves, or six per roll

GARNISH:
Parsley, minced

Two strudel rolls serve 6 to 8

1. Spinach Strudel Filling: Remove the stems and wash the spinach leaves thoroughly. Pat dry with paper towels. Chop the spinach very fine.

2. In a bowl, combine the chopped spinach, cheese, green onions, coarsely diced butter, cinnamon, salt and pepper.

3. Follow the directions in the Pastry Chapter for Strudel Roll (see page 254).

Serve hot. Sprinkle with minced parsley.

May be assembled one day ahead and refrigerated. Bring to room temperature before baking.

May be frozen. Allow to defost for 30 minutes before baking. Increase baking time as necessary.

This is a no-worry, foolproof technique for boiling rice so that each grain will be perfectly cooked and separated.

PERFECT BOILED RICE

2½ quarts water
1 Tablespoon salt
1 to 2 cups long-grain converted rice

UTENSILS:

5- or 6-quart saucepan
colander or strainer

Makes 3 to 4 cups rice

1. Bring the water to a boil; add the salt and rice. Boil covered or uncovered for 13 minutes.

2. Pour the water and the rice into a colander or strainer. Rinse with cool water.

NOTE: *1 cup uncooked rice serves 4 to 5.*

15 minutes before serving, pour 2 inches of water into a pan and bring to a boil. Set the colander with the rice over the pan but not touching the water. Cover with lid or foil, reduce the heat, and simmer for 15 minutes.

May be prepared through Step 2 early in the day.

Do not freeze.

This recipe is elegant and quick.

RISO ALL' UOVO-LIMONE
(Italian Lemon Rice)

3 cups cooked rice

    *   *   *

3 eggs, lightly beaten
2 Tablespoons lemon juice
¾ cup Parmesan cheese,
    grated

Salt and pepper

GARNISH:
  2 Tablespoons parsley, minced

Serves 4 to 6

1. In a small bowl, combine the beaten eggs with the lemon juice, Parmesan cheese, salt and pepper.

2. Add the egg-lemon-Parmesan mixture to the hot rice five minutes before serving, and keep warm. Sprinkle with parsley.

Another speedy rice dish.

RIZ SAN JOAQUIN
(Mexican Black Olive Rice)

3 cups cooked rice

    *   *   *

¾ cup pitted black olives, rinsed,
    drained, and cut in quarters

Salt
Pinch of cayenne
½ cup parsley, minced

Serves 4 to 6

Add the olives, salt, cayenne, and parsley to the hot rice and stir through. Keep warm.

A good versatile rice dish that is particularly good with Chinese Red Roast Pork.

INDONESIAN RICE

½ cup butter
1 large onion, minced
1 clove garlic, minced
2/3 cup pine nuts, oven-roasted
¾ teaspoon nutmeg
2 teaspoons turmeric
¼ cup currants, soaked
   in sherry

2 cups uncooked rice
4 cups chicken stock, homemade
   or commercial

GARNISH:
Green onions, minced

Serves 8

1. In a skillet, melt the butter and sauté the onion and garlic until golden brown. Add the pine nuts, nutmeg, turmeric, and currants, and blend well.

2. Put the chicken stock and rice in a large pan. Bring to a boil, reduce heat, and simmer covered for 20 to 25 minutes or until the liquid is absorbed and the rice is tender.

3. Combine the hot rice with the sautéed ingredients.

Variation: Rice Ring Indienne
Add ¼ cup finely chopped chutney to the Indonesian Rice. Grease a 1½-quart ring mold; pack the rice into the mold. Set in a bain-marie (water bath) and cover loosely with foil. When ready to serve, unmold the rice ring onto a round platter. Lamb or chicken curry may be served in the center.

 Garnish with minced green onions.

 May be prepared one day ahead through Step 1.

 Do not freeze.

CHAPTER 9

Salads

Here is a technique for making a tossed green salad eight hours in advance right in the salad bowl with the dressing. There's nothing to do before serving except toss it. It can be a green salad or a whole meal. The dressing can be made separately, of course, and stored in a jar in the refrigerator.

PERFECT TOSSED GREEN SALAD

SALAD DRESSING:

½ teaspoon salt, or 2 anchovies, minced
1 clove of garlic, split
2 Tablespoons lemon juice
1 teaspoon Dijon mustard
6 Tablespoons oil (salad oil, olive oil, or walnut oil—or a combination of oils)
⅛ teaspoon pepper
1 uncooked egg, parboiled 10 seconds
1 Tablespoon capers, drained and rinsed

* * *

1 large head lettuce, washed, drained, and dried
1 small red onion, sliced thin, or 5 green onions, minced

OPTIONAL:

2 tomatoes, peeled and quartered
½ green pepper, cut into julienne matchsticks
½ cucumber, sliced
1 stalk celery, sliced
½ cup celery root, uncooked, peeled, cut into julienne matchsticks
6 artichoke hearts, quartered
Cooked chicken, beef, ham, or Swiss cheese, cut into julienne matchsticks

* * *

3 Tablespoons Parmesan cheese, grated
½ cup croûtons

Serves 6 to 8

NOTE: *If you use the anchovies, do not use salt at the bottom of the salad bowl.*

1. Salad Dressing: Put the salt at the bottom of a large salad bowl. Rub the salt with the garlic clove to flavor it. Either mince the garlic and add to the dressing, or discard it, as you prefer. Add the lemon juice, mustard, oil, and pepper, and blend thoroughly with a whisk. If you are using anchovies, blend them in. Add the egg, and whisk until the mixture looks creamy. Stir in the capers.

2. Assembling: Tear the lettuce into bite-sized pieces, and set in the salad bowl on top of the dressing. *Do not toss.* Arrange the onion slices and any of the optional ingredients on top. Cover with plastic and refrigerate.

Sprinkle the salad with Parmesan cheese, add the croûtons, and toss until the lettuce is well coated. Serve with Pumpernickel à la Perino's.

May be prepared eight hours ahead and refrigerated.

PUMPERNICKEL À LA PERINO'S

Thin-sliced pumpernickel
Parmesan cheese, grated

Sweet butter, at room
temperature

1. Spread the pumpernickel with the butter, and sprinkle lightly with the freshly grated Parmesan cheese.

2. Preheat the oven to 300 degrees and toast until crisp and slightly curled. May be stored with butter and cheese for 6 months in a tightly covered plastic container.

A nourishing and very good winter salad that is a meal-in-one. You put the finishing touches on it at the table to be sure the dressing is hot.

SALADE D'EPINARDS CHAUDS
(Hot Spinach and Mushroom Salad)

1½ pounds fresh, young spinach leaves
½ pound mushrooms, sliced
1 bunch green onions, white and green part, minced

SALAD DRESSING:
Fat from 4 slices of bacon
¼ cup vinegar
½ teaspoon salt
¼ teaspoon pepper
2 cloves garlic, minced
⅛ teaspoon mustard
¼ teaspoon oregano
¼ teaspoon basil

1 teaspoon sugar
2 Tablespoons cognac

GARNISH:
4 slices bacon, fried, drained, crumbled
2 hard-cooked eggs, minced
6 small balls of bleu cheese rolled in chopped nuts

OPTIONAL:
1 avocado, sliced

Serves 6

1. Tear the stems off the spinach leaves and wash thoroughly. Dry them on paper towels. Put the spinach in the salad bowl. Add the sliced mushrooms and green onions.

2. Salad Dressing: Fry the bacon until it is crisp. Drain and crumble coarsely. Reserve for garnish. The bacon fat in the skillet is for the dressing. In a bowl, combine the vinegar, salt, pepper, garlic, mustard, oregano, basil, sugar, and cognac. Heat the bacon fat, add the vinegar mixture, and stir well.

TO SERVE

At the table, pour the hot dressing over the spinach, mushrooms, and green onions; toss well. Sprinkle with crumbled bacon and minced hard-cooked eggs. Garnish with bleu cheese balls (and sliced avocado).

AHEAD

May be prepared early in the day through Step 2.

When fresh mushrooms are available, this is one of the best of all salads. It can be served as a first course before the entrée or after it.

SALADE DE CHAMPIGNONS ET NOIX
(Mushroom and Walnut Salad)

½ pound mushrooms, washed and
   dried, sliced thin
1 teaspoon lemon juice
2 Tablespoons red wine vinegar
5 Tablespoons walnut oil (available at gourmet food shops)
4 Tablespoons parsley, chopped
½ teaspoon salt
⅛ teaspoon freshly ground pepper

½ cup walnuts, coarsely chopped
   and toasted

GARNISH:

Cherry tomatoes or 1 tomato cut
   in sixths
Lettuce leaves

Serves 2

1. Sprinkle the mushrooms with lemon juice to keep them from turning dark.

2. In a 2-quart bowl combine the vinegar, walnut oil, parsley, salt and pepper. Whisk until thoroughly blended. Add the mushrooms and the walnuts. Toss until the mushrooms and nuts are well coated. Serve immediately on a bed of lettuce.

Serve on chilled salad plates.
Garnish with tomatoes.

May be prepared 2 hours ahead through Step 1.

A refreshing salad to serve after the entrée anytime you can get your hands on fresh mint. Other vegetables may be added to make it a meal-in-one salad.

SALADE DE MENTHE
(Minted Green Salad)

SALAD DRESSING DE MENTHE:

6 Tablespoons olive oil
Salt
1 clove garlic, halved
6 Tablespoons lemon juice
½ teaspoon pepper
2 teaspoons fresh mint, minced
¼ teaspoon oregano
1 egg

* * *

2 heads romaine lettuce, washed, dried, broken into pieces

2 tomatoes, peeled and quartered
½ cup green onions, chopped
½ cup Parmesan cheese, grated
1 pound bacon, fried until crisp, drained, chopped fine

GARNISH:

1 cup croûtons

UTENSIL:

Large wooden salad bowl

Serves 12

1. Salad Dressing De Menthe: Pour 2 Tablespoons of the olive oil into the salad bowl. Sprinkle with salt, and rub the salt with the cut clove of garlic. Add the other 4 Tablespoons of olive oil, lemon juice, pepper, mint, oregano, and egg. Beat thoroughly with a whisk.

2. Assembling: Put the lettuce broken into pieces on top of the dressing. Do not toss. Arrange tomatoes around the outer edge. Sprinkle with the green onions, cheese, and bacon.

Just before serving, toss the salad and add the croûtons.

May be made early in the day and refrigerated.

The four colors of this spectacular salad come from the four garnishes: the black olives, the pale green cucumbers, the dark green parsley, and the yellow chopped egg. It's perfect for a hot-weather luncheon or dinner, or for a buffet.

POULET CHIN CHIN GARNI QUATRE COULEURS
(Four-Colored Chicken Salad)

8 cups chicken stock, homemade or commercial
14 chicken breast halves

CHIN CHIN ITALIAN DRESSING:
½ cup commercial Italian dressing
3 Tablespoons vinegar
½ teaspoon caraway seeds
⅛ teaspoon oregano
⅛ teaspoon basil
⅛ teaspoon salt

ITALIAN MAYONNAISE:
½ cup Chin Chin Italian dressing
1 cup mayonnaise
1 Tablespoon vinegar
3 Tablespoons sugar
1½ teaspoons celery seed
⅛ teaspoon salt
Dash of paprika

* * *

½ cup sour cream
1 Tablespoon honey
2 8-ounce cans water chestnuts, drained and sliced
1 cup walnut or pecan halves, coarsely chopped

* * *

1 large head iceberg lettuce, rinsed and drained

* * *

8 waxed paper triangles

GARNISH:
1 bunch parsley, minced fine
1 3-ounce can minced black olives, drained
8 hard-cooked eggs, minced
1 large cucumber, sliced thin
1 3-ounce jar, or can, sliced pimientos
1 cherry tomato

Serves 8

1. Poaching Chicken Breasts: Prepare chicken stock. The last 15 minutes of cooking time, add the chicken breasts and cook at a gentle simmer, with the pan covered. Remove from heat; allow to cool; refrigerate the chicken in the stock overnight.

2. Take the chicken breasts from the stock, and scrape off any jellied broth on them. Remove and discard the chicken skin. Set aside four of the chicken breast halves. Cut the ten chicken breasts into 1-inch pieces, and put in a large bowl.

3. Chin Chin Italian Dressing: Combine the commercial Italian dressing, vinegar, caraway seeds, oregano, basil, and salt.

4. Italian Mayonnaise: In a bowl, blend the Chin Chin dressing from Step 3 with the mayonnaise, vinegar, sugar, celery seed, salt, and dash of paprika. Set aside ½ cup to use in Step 6 to coat the chicken breasts set aside in Step 2. Add the sour cream and honey to the remainder of the Italian mayonnaise and mix well. Add the chicken chunks and toss carefully. Refrigerate. Just before assembling the salad, stir in the water chestnuts and nuts.

5. Assembling: On a large platter, arrange the lettuce leaves. Mound the chicken-and-Italian-mayonnaise mixture evenly on the lettuce.

Step 6   **Step 7**

6. Bone the four chicken breast halves set aside previously, and cut each in half, lengthwise. Set in a circle on top of the mounded chicken. Lightly coat the eight portions of chicken with the Italian mayonnaise reserved from Step 4.

7. Divide the salad into eight sections by putting a triangle of the waxed paper between each chicken breast. Decorate each of the sections with one of the four different garnishes. Sprinkle the first section with minced parsley, the second section with minced eggs, the third section with minced black olives, and the fourth section with sliced cucumbers. Then repeat the pattern. Remove the waxed paper triangles, and replace them with the red pimiento strips. Place the cherry tomato on top.

Chicken breasts can be poached two days ahead and refrigerated. Italian mayonnaise can be made two days ahead and refrigerated. The salad can be assembled early in the day, draped with plastic, and refrigerated.

An easy, inexpensive, and filling meal-in-one salad that is a great favorite with children and adults alike. Without the beans, tortilla chips and guacamole, it is even a tasty diet salad.

ENSALADA DE FRANCA
(Mexican Salad)

1 pound very lean ground beef
1 teaspoon butter
1 teaspoon oil
1 7-ounce can Taco Sauce
¾ cup red kidney beans, cooked and drained (may use canned)
1 head iceberg lettuce, washed and shredded

OPTIONAL:

½ to 1 cup Tortilla Chips

GARNISH:

1½ cups cheddar cheese, grated
1 8-ounce can black olives, pitted

1½ cups Perfect Guacamole (see page 234)
Sour cream
2 large tomatoes, quartered, or one box of cherry tomatoes

UTENSIL:

Large round or oblong platter, or large salad bowl

SERVE WITH:

Tortillas, heated
7-ounce can Taco Sauce

Serves 6

1. In a skillet, heat the butter and oil and brown the meat. Drain off any excess fat. Stir in the can of Taco Sauce, and allow to cool.

2. Combine the meat mixture, kidney beans, lettuce, and tortilla chips.

3. Assembling: Mound the meat mixture on the large platter. Around the edge of the meat mixture, make a 2-inch border of the grated cheese. Arrange a row of black olives along the inside edge of the cheese, reserving a few. Cover inside the circle of black olives with the guacamole. Put a dollop of sour cream in the center of the guacamole. Garnish with the remaining black

olives, either whole or cut in strips and formed into a flower. Arrange the tomato quarters or cherry tomatoes around the base of the cheese-covered meat mixture.

Variation: Leftover meat loaf (chopped fine) or leftover pot roast (trimmed of all fat and ground) may be used instead of the ground beef.

Serve with tortillas and additional sauce.

Ground beef may be browned one day ahead and refrigerated. Salad may be assembled 2 to 3 hours ahead and refrigerated.

PERFECT GUACAMOLE

3 avocados, ripe
1 jalapeño chile, seeds removed, chopped
1 tomato, chopped
1 onion, minced
2 cloves garlic, minced

2 Tablespoons lime or lemon juice
1½ Tablespoons olive oil

Makes 1½ cups

Peel and mash the avocados, reserving one pit. Stir in the chile, tomato, onion, garlic and lime or lemon juice. Peel the pit and set in the center of the bowl. Float olive oil on top, cover with plastic, and refrigerate. (The oil and pit will keep the guacamole from turning dark). Just before serving, remove the pit and stir in the oil.

This Mexican salad is a festive arrangement of fruits and vegetables that could also serve as a 4th of July centerpiece.

ENSALADA DE NOCHE BUENA
(Christmas Eve Salad)

4 oranges, peeled
1 pineapple, peeled, cored, and sliced
3 limes, peeled and sliced
4 red apples, unpeeled and cored
4 bananas, peeled
1 jicama, peeled and sliced (Mexican root available in many markets)
3 Tablespoons lemon juice
1 8-ounce can beets, sliced and drained

     *   *   *

4 or 5 clumps of endive, or 1 bunch chicory

GARNISH:
Seeds of 1 pomegranate

1 cup peanuts, chopped

OPTIONAL:
1 stick sugarcane, peeled and chopped (available at Latin-American markets)
¼ cup sugar

DRESSING:
Juices of the sliced oranges, pineapple, and limes
1 cup mayonnaise

UTENSIL:
12- to 15-inch round ceramic platter

Serves 12

1. Slice the oranges, pineapple, and limes over a bowl to catch the juices and save them for the salad dressing.

2. Thinly slice the apples and bananas; cut the jicama into crescent slices. Sprinkle with lemon juice.

3. Wash and pull apart the endive or the chicory. Shred half of it, and place in the center of the platter. Arrange the leaves around the edge.

4. Assembling: Around the outer edge, overlap alternate sections of orange and banana slices. Next place a circle of crescent slices of jicama. Arrange the lime slices on top. Then alternate overlapping slices of apple and pineapple. Set the remaining orange slices on top of these. Shape the beets to resemble petals of a flower in the center of the platter.

5. Garnish: Sprinkle pomegranate seeds and peanuts (and, if you like, sugar cane and sugar) over the entire salad.

6. Dressing: Thin the mayonnaise with the reserved fruit juices.

Variation: For a 4th of July salad, when pomegranates are not available, substitute grapes or sliced strawberries.

TO SERVE

Serve the dressing over the salad, or separately in a bowl.

AHEAD

Fruits may be sliced 1 hour ahead. If you make layers of apple, oranges, bananas, then limes, this will help to keep the bananas and apples from turning dark.

SALAD DRESSINGS

Well worth the trouble if you are planning to use straight mayonnaise to mask something. If you are going to combine it with other seasonings, use the commercial mayonnaise.

CLASSIC MAYONNAISE

2 egg yolks
1 teaspoon Dijon mustard
1 Tablespoon tarragon or wine
  vinegar, or lemon juice
2 small cloves garlic, minced
  (optional)

1 cup peanut oil, vegetable oil,
  or olive oil (or half vegetable
  oil and half olive oil)
Salt and white pepper

Makes 1½ cups

1. Place the yolks, mustard, half the vinegar (or lemon juice), and garlic in a large bowl. Beat for one minute with a wire whisk or an electric mixer.

2. Add the oil slowly, drop-by-drop, whipping vigorously and constantly. When half the oil has been used, the remainder may be added, by Tablespoons, beating constantly. Add salt and pepper to taste. If the finished mayonnaise seems too thick, beat in the remainder of the vinegar.

May be prepared two weeks ahead.

*A good dressing to serve with poached fish,
shellfish, and raw vegetables.*

SAUCE VERTE
(Green Mayonnaise)

1 cup loosely packed spinach
leaves or ½ package frozen
spinach, thawed
3 sprigs parsley
¼ cup watercress, leaves only
2 Tablespoons lemon juice
2 Tablespoons green onions
¼ teaspoon dry mustard
1 teaspoon dried basil or
tarragon

2 anchovy fillets
1 cup mayonnaise, commercial

OPTIONAL:
Tabasco Sauce

* * *

2 Tablespoons capers, rinsed
and drained

Makes 2 cups

1. Remove stems from spinach, wash thoroughly, and dry. If frozen
   spinach is used, press out excess moisture with paper towels.

2. Place the spinach, parsley, watercress, lemon juice, green onions,
   mustard, dried basil or tarragon, anchovies, and mayonnaise (and
   Tabasco) in the blender for 10 or 15 seconds.

3. Fold in the capers, taste for seasoning, and refrigerate until
   chilled.

May be kept in the refrigerator for one month.

CHAPTER 10

Pastries and Desserts

PASTRY DOUGHS

All pastry shells should be waterproofed before filling, whether savory or sweet. For a quiche, paint with lightly beaten egg white. For dessert pies, paint with Apricot Glaze. Fruit and custard pies should always be baked in the lower third of the oven.

APRICOT GLAZE

1 11-ounce jar apricot preserves
4 Tablespoons apricot brandy,
  or Galliano liqueur

UTENSIL:

Blender or strainer

1. Loosen the top of the jar, and place the jar in a pan of hot water over low heat until the preserves are liquified.

2. In a blender, combine the apricot preserves, apricot brandy or Galliano liqueur, or press these ingredients through a strainer. Refrigerate. It will keep indefinitely.

This is an easy-to-make tender pastry dough that makes delicious pie crusts or tarts for hors-d'oeuvres and desserts. Cream cheese pastry should be rolled out when it is chilled. Take out of the refrigerator only the amount that you need.

CREAM CHEESE PASTRY

1 cup butter (½ pound) at room temperature
8 ounces cream cheese, at room temperature
¼ cup heavy cream

2½ cups flour
1 teaspoon salt

Makes 2 pie shells

In a mixer, cream the butter and cream cheese. Beat in the cream. Blend in the flour and salt. Wrap the dough in waxed paper and chill in the refrigerator for at least 1 hour before using.

May be prepared four days ahead and refrigerated.

May be frozen.

You can't fail with this pie crust recipe. For a two-crust pie, double the recipe.

PERFECT PIE CRUST

1½ cups flour
¼ cup butter
¼ cup solid vegetable shortening
¼ teapsoon salt
¼ cup cold liquid: water or
   orange or lemon juice
   combined with water

UTENSILS:

9-inch pie pan, greased
Rolling pin
Waxed paper
Rice or lima beans

Makes one 9- or 10-inch pastry shell

OPTIONAL:
Rind of lemon or small orange

1. In a mixer, blend the flour, butter, shortening, and salt until the mixture is crumbly, and in pieces the size of peas. Add the liquid, and mix until the dough comes clean from the bowl and forms a ball. Flatten into an 8-inch round circle, wrap in plastic, and refrigerate for 30 minutes.

2. Place the dough on a well-floured surface; marble or formica is preferred. Roll the dough into a 12-inch circle.

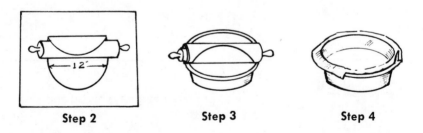

Step 2   Step 3   Step 4

3. Starting at the edge of the circle, roll the dough over the rolling pin.

4. Gently unroll the dough onto the pie pan.

5. Without forcing or stretching the dough, press it into the pie pan. Be careful that the dough is not too thick where the bottom and sides meet. Allow 1 inch of dough to hang over the edge of the pan. Trim off the excess. Turn the 1 inch of overhanging dough under to form a narrow rolled rim.

Step 6   **Step 7**   **Step 8**

6. For a fluted edge, place the index finger of one hand on the rim; with the index finger and thumb of the other hand, squeeze the dough.

7. For a rope edge, using the index finger and thumb of each hand, pinch the dough in opposite directions.

8. To bake, preheat the oven to 400 degrees. With a fork, prick the sides and bottom of the pie shell. Set a piece of waxed paper on the dough; cover it with rice or lima beans to prevent shrinking. Bake for 25 minutes. Remove the paper and rice or lima beans (save to use for other pie crusts). Return the pie crust to the oven until it is lightly browned, approximately 5 minutes.

NOTE: *If the recipe calls for an unbaked shell, which will be filled before baking, do not prick the dough.*

May be prepared one or two days ahead and refrigerated. May be baked one day ahead, loosely wrapped in wax paper, and kept at room temperature.

May be frozen after Step 7. Defrost for 10 minutes at room temperature before baking.

You can fill this pastry shell with any fruit or dessert custard and garnish with whipped cream.

PÂTE SABLÉE
(Sweet Pastry Dough)

2 egg yolks
¼ cup sugar
⅓ cup butter, at room temperature
½ teaspoon grated lemon rind
2 teaspoons sherry
1 cup, plus 2 Tablespoons flour
⅛ teaspoon salt

UTENSILS:

A 10- or 11-inch flan pan with removable bottom, greased, or a 9- or 10-inch pie plate, greased
Rolling pin
Waxed paper
Rice or lima beans

*   *   *

Apricot Glaze (see page 240)

1. In a mixer, blend the yolks, sugar, butter, lemon rind, and sherry. Stir in 2 Tablespoons of the flour and the salt. Carefully work in the rest of the flour. Turn the pastry out on waxed paper; flatten into an 8-inch circle. Wrap in waxed paper and chill for 1 hour or overnight.

2. Pat the chilled dough evenly onto the bottom and sides of a greased flan pan or pie plate. Be careful that the dough is not too thick where the bottom and sides meet. Cut out a piece of waxed paper to fit over the dough, and press it in firmly. Cover with rice or lima beans to weight down the pastry; make sure they are scattered carefully around the outer edge.

3. Preheat the oven to 350 degrees. Bake the pastry shell for 15 minutes, or until lightly browned. Turn the oven down to 300 degrees; remove the waxed paper and lima beans or rice (save for other pie crusts). Return the pastry shell to the oven until it is medium brown, approximately 5 minutes. Cool, paint with Apricot Glaze, and fill as directed.

May be prepared one or two days ahead and refrigerated.

May be frozen after Step 3. Defrost for 10 minutes at room temperature.

In the Burgundian region of France, fresh-baked hot gougère is served at the end of the day with a glass of Burgundy, a custom we could borrow with profit! Gougère is actually the classic cream puff pastry (pâte à choux) with cheeses, mustards, and pepper added. Serve it midday as an hors-d'oeuvre or as a bread with dinner.

You follow exactly the same technique to make dessert cream puffs, then pipe out 1- to 2-inch rounds with a pastry bag onto a greased pan. Bake 25 minutes, or until puffed and golden brown, and fill as desired with chocolate mousse, whipped cream, or ice cream.

GOUGÈRE DE BOURGOGNE
(Burgundy Cheese Bread with Technique for Puff Pastry)

PÂTE À CHOUX:
(Cream Puff Pastry)

1 cup milk
4 Tablespoons butter
1 scant teaspoon salt
⅛ teaspoon pepper
1 cup flour
4 eggs

    *   *   *

1 teaspoon Dijon Mustard
½ teaspoon dry mustard
1 cup Swiss or Gruyère
  cheese, grated

GARNISH:

2½ Tablespoons mayonnaise
2 Tablespoons Parmesan cheese,
  grated
1 teaspoon paprika

UTENSILS:

9-inch cake pan, lightly greased
Pastry bag

Serves 6 to 8

1. Pâte à Choux: In a 2-quart saucepan, heat the milk, butter, salt, and pepper, and bring to a rolling boil. Add the flour, all at once, stirring vigorously until the mixture forms a ball and leaves the sides of the pan clean. (If the batter does not come away from the sides of the pan, throw it away, and start over again!)

    Remove the pan from the heat. Add the 4 eggs, one at a time, using an electric hand mixer, if possible, to incorporate each egg thoroughly before adding the next one. Keep beating until the dough is shiny and smooth.

2. Add all of the mustards and grated Swiss or Gruyère cheese, and blend well.

3. Assembling: Fill the pastry bag with dough until it is three-fourths full.

Pipe two rings of dough 1-inch wide around the outer edges of the cake pan, side by side. Then pipe overlapping circles on top of the first two rings. The circles should abut the sides of the pan. (They should be hollow in the center.) Refrigerate at least 1 hour or overnight.

If you do not have a pastry bag, drop rounded *Tablespoons* of the dough next to and touching each other, on the outer edge of the pan. They should abut the sides of the pan. On top of these, drop rounded *teaspoons* of the dough between the larger spoonfuls.

4. Baking: Preheat the oven to 400 degrees. Pâte à choux pastry is best if slightly chilled before baking, and if it goes from the refrigerator directly into a hot oven. Bake 40 to 45 minutes, or until it is puffed up and golden brown.

Variation: Individual Hors-d'Oeuvre Cream Puffs
If any dough is left over, pipe out 1- or 2-inch rounds with a pastry bag onto a greased pan. Bake for 25 minutes, or until puffed and golden brown. Brush with a little mayonnaise, dust with grated Parmesan cheese and paprika. Serve warm.

 Brush with mayonnaise and dust with Parmesan cheese and paprika. Serve hot or cold.

 May be prepared one day ahead through Step 3.

 May be frozen after Step 4. Remove from the freezer directly to a preheated 375-degree oven until heated through.

I would rather eat a 1-inch square of home-made puff pastry than a whole box of imported chocolates! To me, it's the most exquisite of all the French pastries, the one that literally melts in your mouth. There are dozens of ways to use puff pastry: hors-d'oeuvres, patty shells, vol-au-vent, turn-overs, meat "en croûte," napoleons, as well as other dessert pastries and cookies. Never throw away puff pastry scraps; they can be rerolled with cheese for hors-d'oeuvres, or with sugar for small pastries (see page 250).

PÂTE FEUILLETÉE
(Puff Pastry)

4 cups Wondra flour, or 1¼ cups unbleached all-purpose flour and 2¾ cups unbleached pastry (not cake) flour

1 pound sweet butter, left at room temperature for 30 minutes

1 cup cold water, approximately
1 Tablespoon lemon juice
1 teaspoon salt

Makes approximately 3 pounds

Prepare puff pastry only in cool weather and freeze it for any time of the year.

There are a few special tricks to this pastry. The basic technique is encasing and rolling a pound of butter in the détrempe, the flour-and-water mixture. The butter and the détrempe must have the same consistency before you begin to enclose the butter. As a general rule, unless otherwise noted, puff pastry should be chilled before baking. Remove from the refrigerator directly to a hot oven.

1. Détrempe: Set aside 3 Tablespoons of the flour; place the remaining flour in a large bowl. Cut ½ cup (¼ pound) of the butter into ¼-inch pieces. Combine the flour and buttter with a pastry blender or in the mixer until it is crumbly.

2. Blend in three-quarters of a cup of water, the lemon juice, and the salt. Press the dough together to make it firm and pliable.

If necessary, work in a few more drops of water. Knead for a few minutes. Flatten the dough into an 8-inch circle, wrap it in plastic, and refrigerate for 25 minutes.

3. To prepare the butter, sprinkle an 8-inch by 10-inch piece of foil with 1½ Tablespoons of the flour. Place the remaining ¾ pound of butter on it; sprinkle the remaining 1½ Tablespoons of flour on top of the butter. Fold the foil loosely over the butter, and shape the butter into a "brick" 3 inches by 5 inches by 1½ inches thick. Refrigerate with the détrempe.

Step 4

Step 5

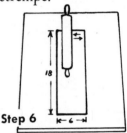

Step 6

4. Rolling, Folding, and Turning: Place the dough on a well-floured surface, and sprinkle lightly with flour.

Leaving the center of the dough the same size as the brick of butter and ⅓ inch thick, roll out the dough into a four-leaf clover shape. Make the four "petals" ¼ inch thick.

5. Place the butter brick in the center of the dough. Stretch each "petal" over the butter. Overlap the petals, and seal so that the butter is completely enclosed. (If the butter is not completely enclosed, it will break out of the dough.) Lightly flour.

6. When rolling, use a firm and constant motion, and be very careful not to push the butter out through the ends. Roll the dough into a rectangle three times longer than it is wide, approximately 6 inches by 18 inches. Sprinkle lightly with flour as necessary to prevent sticking. Turn the rolling pin sideways, and gently flatten the ends, so the dough is uniform in thickness.

Step 7

Step 8

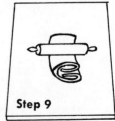

Step 9

7. Fold each end of the rectangle to meet in the center. Roll so that it is slightly flattened.

8. Now, fold the top over.

9. Turn the dough a quarter turn to the right, so that it is like a book. Flatten it slightly with the rolling pin. Going back to Step 6, repeat the procedure. You have now completed the first of three "turns." For each turn, you roll and fold the dough twice. To keep track of the turns, make one fingerprint on the "book." Wrap the dough in plastic, then in a dampened dishtowel, and refrigerate for 30 to 45 minutes.

Step 10

10. For the second turn, roll and fold twice more, going back to Step 6. Mark the corner of the "book" with two fingerprints.

11. For the third and final turn, roll and fold twice more, again going back to Step 6. Mark the book with three fingerprints.

12. Wrap and refrigerate for 1 to 3 hours before using. At this point, your pastry contains 700 layers of butter!

 Follow directions called for in a recipe using puff pastry.

 May be prepared three days ahead and refrigerated.

 May be frozen if wrapped carefully. Allow to defrost overnight in the refrigerator.

PALMIERS AU FROMAGE
(Puff Pastry Cheese Leaves)

½ recipe Pâte Feuilletée
   (see page 247)
1½ cups grated cheese: cheddar,
   Gruyère, or Parmesan, or
   a combination of cheeses

Makes 48

PALMIERS AU SUCRE
(Puff Pastry Cookies)

¼ recipe Pâte Feuilletée
   (see page 247)
1 cup sugar

Makes 24

| Step 1 | Step 2 | Step 3 |

1. Sprinkle a board with half of the cheese, or the sugar. Roll out the puff pastry into a rectangle 6 inches by 14 inches, and ⅛ inch thick. Sprinkle with remaining half of the cheese or sugar.

2. Fold along the length of the dough, 1 inch on both sides. Repeat and keep folding both sides toward the center 1 inch at a time until they meet. Flatten slightly with a rolling pin.

3. Turn roll onto its side. Cut into ¼-inch slices, dip into additional cheese or sugar, and place them on an ungreased cookie sheet. Flatten each one slightly with the heel of your hand, so that it resembles a palm leaf. Refrigerate for 30 minutes before baking.

4. Baking: Preheat the oven to 375 degrees. Bake for 10 minutes, and as the palmiers brown, turn them over and bake until the other side is lightly browned, approximately 10 minutes. Those on the outside will bake more quickly.

TO SERVE — Cheese palmiers may be served hot or cold.

AHEAD — May be prepared one week ahead. Store in tightly covered container between sheets of waxed paper.

FREEZE — May be frozen before or after baking.

---

[250]

There is a great sense of accomplishment in making your own brioche, to say nothing of the superb taste. Besides bread, brioche dough is used to prepare lamb, ham, or other meats "en croûte." If used with meat, use only 2 tablespoons of sugar.

BRIOCHE
(French Yeast Dough)

1 cup milk
1½ cups butter (¾ pound)
5 packages dry yeast
7 cups flour mixture (3½ cups Wondra flour, 3½ cups all-purpose flour)
¾ cup sugar
1 Tablespoon salt
7 eggs, at room temperature
⅛ teaspoon vanilla

EGG WASH:

1 egg

1 teaspoon water

UTENSILS:

Deep-fat thermometer
4-quart bowl, lightly greased
Large brioche pan, or 2-quart glass casserole, lightly greased, or 24 individual brioche pans or cupcake pans

Makes one large or twenty-four individual brioches

1. In a saucepan, heat the milk and butter until the mixture reaches 120 degrees to 130 degrees on the thermometer.

2. In a mixer, combine the yeast, 2½ cups of the flour, sugar, and salt. Add the heated milk and butter. Beat 2 minutes at medium speed, scraping the sides of the bowl occasionally with a spatula. Add ½ cup more of the flour, all 7 eggs and the vanilla. Beat 2 minutes at high speed. Add the remaining 4 cups of flour, and beat until blended well.

3. Place the dough on a lightly floured surface. Knead by hand until the dough is smooth and elastic, approximately 15 minutes. Or, if you have a mixer with a dough-hook attachment, lightly flour the bowl and knead until the dough is smooth and elastic, approximately 8 minutes.

4. Place the dough in the 4-quart bowl. Mark the height of the

[251]

dough on the outside of the bowl with tape or marking pencil. Cover with plastic and a warm, damp towel. Allow to rise until doubled in bulk, approximately 1 hour at room temperature, or overnight in the refrigerator. When the dough has doubled, punch it down to its original size (to the mark on the outside of the bowl). Cover again with plastic and a warm, damp towel. Allow to double in bulk for a second time, approximately 1½ to 2 hours at room temperature.

5. To shape a large brioche, dust the inside of the greased brioche pan or glass casserole with flour and shake out the excess. Take three quarters of the dough and form it into a smooth ball by kneading lightly and rolling it between the palms of your hands. Place the ball in the bottom of the pan. Dampen your fingers, and make a funnel-shaped hole in the center of it, about 2½ inches wide by 2 inches deep. Lightly flour your hands and roll the remaining quarter of the dough into a tear-drop shape. Set the pointed end into the funnel-shaped hole. Cover with plastic and a warm, damp towel. Allow to double in bulk for the third and final time, approximately 1 to 2 hours at room temperature.

6. To bake a large brioche, preheat the oven to 400 degrees. Lightly beat 1 egg with a teaspoon of water for the egg wash. Remove the plastic and cloth from the brioche. Gently paint the surface with the egg wash, but do not paint the area where the top and bottom balls join. Allow to dry for 1 minute. Repaint with egg wash. With scissors, make four slanting cuts into the large ball where the top ball joins it. Bake for 35 minutes on the middle shelf of the oven.

7. To form individual brioches, dust the greased cupcake pans with flour, and shake out the excess. Set one quarter of the dough aside. Divide the remaining three quarters of the dough into four long rolls, and cut each roll into six pieces. Shape each piece into a small ball and place in the bottom of the cupcake pan. With the

point of the scissors, make a small hole in each ball. With the quarter of the dough set aside, make four rolls, and cut each roll into six pieces. Form tiny teardrops to fit into the holes in the large balls. Cover with plastic and a warm, damp towel and allow to double in bulk.

8. To bake individual brioches, preheat the oven to 400 degrees. Brush each brioche with egg wash. Allow to dry for 1 minute. Repaint with egg wash. With scissors, make four slanting cuts into each large ball where the top ball joins it. Bake for 15 minutes on the middle shelf of the oven.

Variation: Hollow out and fill a large brioche with crab filling (see page 142), or another lightly sauced mixture. Hollow out individual brioches and fill each with an artichoke bottom and a poached egg; cover with Sauce Hollandaise. Warm in a preheated oven. (Save the dough from the centers for bread crumbs.)

Serve warm with butter.

May be baked one day ahead. To reheat, place in a brown paper bag for about 15 minutes in a preheated 350-degree oven.

May be frozen before or after baking. Defrost 30 minutes before baking or reheating.

Strudels can be made with vegetable filling to serve as a main course, or with the traditional dessert fillings, like apple, cheese, or apricot.

TECHNIQUE FOR STRUDEL ROLL
WITH PHYLO PASTRY

Phylo leaves (use number called
    for in recipe)
½ cup butter, melted (¼ pound)
1 cup breadcrumbs

Waxed paper
2-inch white-bristle paint brush
Baking pan
Serrated-blade knife
Long serving platter

UTENSILS:

Dish towel, dampened

NOTE: *Always buy unfrozen phylo pastry leaves at Greek, Lebanese, or Italian markets.*

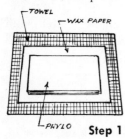
Step 1

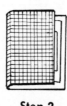
Step 2

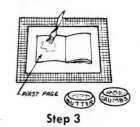
Step 3

1. Dampen a dish towel, spread it on the counter, and cover it with waxed paper. Unfold the phylo leaves and set them on top of the waxed paper. Fold the towel, waxed paper, and phylo leaves in half like a book.

2. Consider the towel the book cover, the waxed paper the inside cover, and the phylo leaves the pages of a book.

3. Start opening the "book." Turn to the first "page" (the first phylo leaf) and brush it with melted butter, then sprinkle with breadcrumbs.

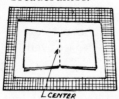
Step 4

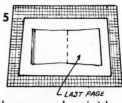
Step 5

4. Turn to the next "page" of phylo, brush with butter, and sprinkle with breadcrumbs; repeat this procedure on each "page" until you get to the center of the book. Close the "book."

Topping: In a small bowl, combine the brown sugar, butter, whipping cream, salt, and chopped pecans. Spread on top of the pumpkin mixture. Decorate with pecan halves.

4. Topping: In a small bowl, combine the brown sugar, butter, whipping cream, salt, and chopped pecans. Spread on top of the pumpkin mixture. Decorate with pecan halves.

5. Preheat the broiler. Broil the pie 3 inches from a low flame, until the surface begins to bubble. Watch carefully so the topping does not burn.

6. Bourbon-Flavored Whipped Cream: Whip the cream and fold in the bourbon. Refrigerate until ready to serve.

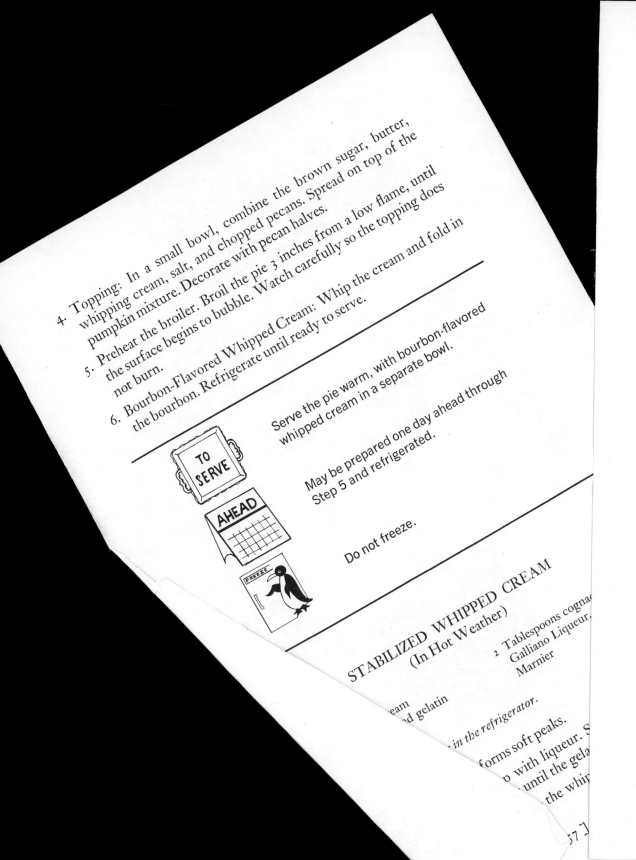

TO SERVE
Serve the pie warm, with bourbon-flavored whipped cream in a separate bowl.

AHEAD
May be prepared one day ahead through Step 5 and refrigerated.

FREEZE
Do not freeze.

STABILIZED WHIPPED CREAM
(In Hot Weather)

2 Tablespoons cognac, Galliano Liqueur, Marnier

...eam
...d gelatin

...in the refrigerator.

...forms soft peaks.
...p with liqueur. S...
...until the gela...
...the whi...

57]

---

5. Starting from the "back cover" of the book, repeat the process going backwards to the center, brushing each "page" with butter and sprinkling with breadcrumbs.

6. The "book" is now open at the center fold. Spread a strudel filling on this center area, being careful to arrange it on the lower third of the "page" so the strudel can be easily rolled.

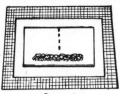

Step 6   Step 7   Step 8

7. Tuck in the ends at the left and right ends of the "book."

8. Roll the strudel jelly-roll fashion, using the towel and waxed paper to help you roll it. Place the strudel seamside down on an ungreased baking sheet. Brush the top with melted butter.

9. Baking: Preheat the oven to 400 degrees. Bake for 10 minutes, then remove from the oven, and brush again with melted butter. It is important to slice the strudel roll at this point, when it is partially baked.

    With the serrated-blade knife, carefully cut on the diagonal into 1½-inch slices. Use a see-saw motion, so that the strudel does not fall apart. Press the slices back together so it looks like one long roll. Return to oven, and bake for an additional 15 minutes. (25 minutes total baking time).

TO SERVE
Brush with melted butter. Arrange the sliced strudel roll on a long platter.

AHEAD
May be assembled one day ahead through Step 8 and refrigerated. Bring to room temperature before baking.

FREEZE
May be frozen after Step 8. Allow to defrost for 30 minutes before baking. Increase baking time as necessary.

This pie comes with a guarantee—it is delicious.

TOASTED COCONUT CREAM PIE

10-inch pastry shell, prebaked
  (see page 242)
4 eggs, separated
½ cup sugar
⅓ cup milk
1 package unflavored gelatin
2 teaspoons vanilla
⅛ teaspoon cream of tartar
⅛ teaspoon salt

2 cups whipping cream
4 Tablespoons cognac

* * *

Apricot Glaze (see page 240)

GARNISH:
1¾ cups shredded coconut, toasted

Serves 8

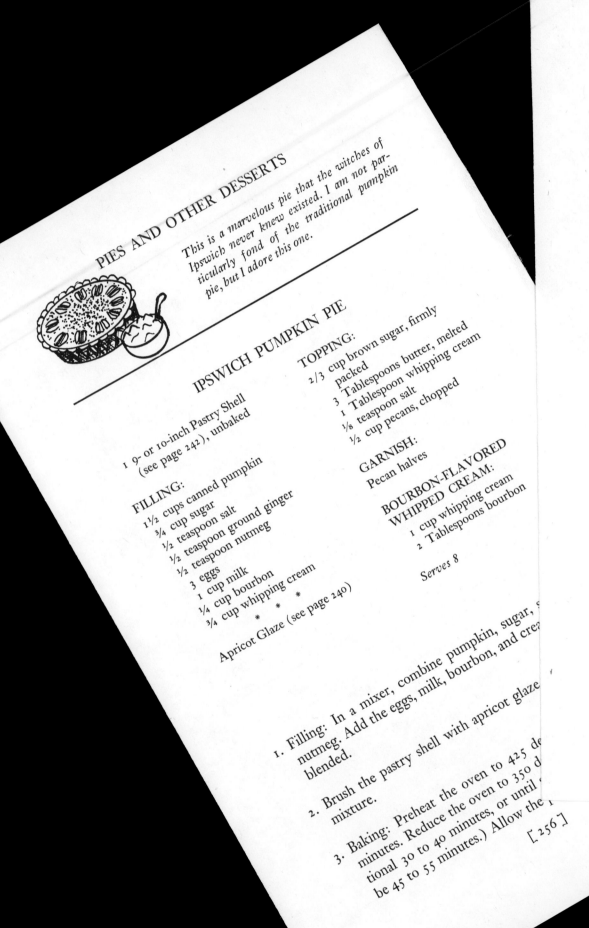

PIES AND OTHER DESSERTS

This is a marvelous pie that the witches of Ipswich never knew existed. I am not particularly fond of the traditional pumpkin pie, but I adore this one.

IPSWICH PUMPKIN PIE

1 9- or 10-inch Pastry Shell
  (see page 242), unbaked

FILLING:
1½ cups canned pumpkin
¾ cup sugar
½ teaspoon salt
½ teaspoon ground ginger
½ teaspoon nutmeg
3 eggs
1 cup milk
¼ cup bourbon
¾ cup whipping cream

TOPPING:
2/3 cup brown sugar, firmly
  packed
3 Tablespoons butter, melted
1 Tablespoon whipping cream
⅛ teaspoon salt
½ cup pecans, chopped

GARNISH:
Pecan halves

BOURBON-FLAVORED
WHIPPED CREAM:
1 cup whipping cream
2 Tablespoons bourbon

Serves 8

* * *

Apricot Glaze (see page 240)

1. Filling: In a mixer, combine pumpkin, sugar, s...
nutmeg. Add the eggs, milk, bourbon, and crea...
blended.

2. Brush the pastry shell with apricot glaze...
mixture.

3. Baking: Preheat the oven to 425 de...
minutes. Reduce the oven to 350 d...
tional 30 to 40 minutes, or until e...
be 45 to 55 minutes.) Allow the ...

4. Topping: In a small bowl, combine the brown sugar, butter, whipping cream, salt, and chopped pecans. Spread on top of the pumpkin mixture. Decorate with pecan halves.

5. Preheat the broiler. Broil the pie 3 inches from a low flame, until the surface begins to bubble. Watch carefully so the topping does not burn.

6. Bourbon-Flavored Whipped Cream: Whip the cream and fold in the bourbon. Refrigerate until ready to serve.

Serve the pie warm, with bourbon-flavored whipped cream in a separate bowl.

May be prepared one day ahead through Step 5 and refrigerated.

Do not freeze.

STABILIZED WHIPPED CREAM
(In Hot Weather)

1 cup whipping cream
½ teaspoon unflavored gelatin

2 Tablespoons cognac, rum, Galliano Liqueur, or Grand Marnier

NOTE: *Keeps for 1 or 2 days in the refrigerator.*

1. Whip the cream until it forms soft peaks.

2. Soften the gelatin in a cup with liqueur. Set the cup in a pan of boiling water over low heat until the gelatin is dissolved.

3. Beat the dissolved gelatin into the whipped cream until it reaches the desired thickness.

This pie comes with a guarantee—it is delicious.

TOASTED COCONUT CREAM PIE

10-inch pastry shell, prebaked
   (see page 242)
4 eggs, separated
½ cup sugar
⅓ cup milk
1 package unflavored gelatin
2 teaspoons vanilla
⅛ teaspoon cream of tartar
⅛ teaspoon salt

2 cups whipping cream
4 Tablespoons cognac

*   *   *

Apricot Glaze (see page 240)

GARNISH:
1¾ cups shredded coconut, toasted

Serves 8

5. Starting from the "back cover" of the book, repeat the process going backwards to the center, brushing each "page" with butter and sprinkling with breadcrumbs.

6. The "book" is now open at the center fold. Spread a strudel filling on this center area, being careful to arrange it on the lower third of the "page" so the strudel can be easily rolled.

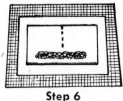
Step 6

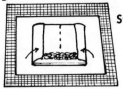

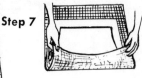
Step 7

Step 8

7. Tuck in the ends at the left and right ends of the "book."

8. Roll the strudel jelly-roll fashion, using the towel and waxed paper to help you roll it. Place the strudel seamside down on an ungreased baking sheet. Brush the top with melted butter.

9. Baking: Preheat the oven to 400 degrees. Bake for 10 minutes, then remove from the oven, and brush again with melted butter. It is important to slice the strudel roll at this point, when it is partially baked.

   With the serrated-blade knife, carefully cut on the diagonal into 1½-inch slices. Use a see-saw motion, so that the strudel does not fall apart. Press the slices back together so it looks like one long roll. Return to oven, and bake for an additional 15 minutes. (25 minutes total baking time).

TO SERVE — Brush with melted butter. Arrange the sliced strudel roll on a long platter.

AHEAD — May be assembled one day ahead through Step 8 and refrigerated. Bring to room temperature before baking.

FREEZE — May be frozen after Step 8. Allow to defrost for 30 minutes before baking. Increase baking time as necessary.

This is a marvelous pie that the witches of Ipswich never knew existed. I am not particularly fond of the traditional pumpkin pie, but I adore this one.

IPSWICH PUMPKIN PIE

1 9- or 10-inch Pastry Shell
(see page 242), unbaked

FILLING:
1½ cups canned pumpkin
¾ cup sugar
½ teaspoon salt
½ teaspoon ground ginger
½ teaspoon nutmeg
3 eggs
1 cup milk
¼ cup bourbon
¾ cup whipping cream

*   *   *

Apricot Glaze (see page 240)

TOPPING:
2/3 cup brown sugar, firmly
packed
3 Tablespoons butter, melted
1 Tablespoon whipping cream
⅛ teaspoon salt
½ cup pecans, chopped

GARNISH:
Pecan halves

BOURBON-FLAVORED
WHIPPED CREAM:
1 cup whipping cream
2 Tablespoons bourbon

Serves 8

1. Filling: In a mixer, combine pumpkin, sugar, salt, ginger, and nutmeg. Add the eggs, milk, bourbon, and cream. Mix until well blended.

2. Brush the pastry shell with apricot glaze. Pour in the pumpkin mixture.

3. Baking: Preheat the oven to 425 degrees. Bake the pie for 15 minutes. Reduce the oven to 350 degrees, and bake for an additional 30 to 40 minutes, or until set. (Total baking time should be 45 to 55 minutes.) Allow the pie to cool until it is lukewarm.

1. Put the egg yolks in the top of a double-boiler, and beat with a whisk until they are lemon colored. The bottom of the double-boiler should have a small amount of water that is simmering, not boiling. The water should not touch the top pan containing the eggs, or the eggs will curdle. Add 5 Tablespoons of the sugar and all of the milk to the yolks, and stir constantly for 5 minutes. Add gelatin and stir until it is completely dissolved. Remove from heat and stir in the vanilla. Pour into a large bowl and allow to cool.

2. Beat the egg whites until foamy, and add the cream of tartar and salt. Continue beating until soft peaks form. Add the remaining sugar, 1 Tablespoon at a time, and continue beating until the peaks are stiff and shiny. Fold into egg yolk and gelatin mixture.

3. In a mixer, whip the cream until soft peaks form. Add the cognac and beat until stiff. Fold the whipped cream into the mixture above.

4. Paint the pastry shell with Apricot Glaze, and spoon the pie filling over it. Refrigerate.

5. To prepare toasted coconut, preheat the oven to 350 degrees. Spread the coconut on a cookie sheet, and bake for 5 to 6 minutes, or until lightly browned. Stir often to prevent burning.

TO SERVE

Set the pie plate on a serving platter.
Sprinkle generously with the toasted coconut.

AHEAD

May be prepared one day ahead.

Do not freeze.

EASTER DUCK YEAST CAKE

¼ cup yellow raisins
½ cup sherry

DOUGH:

 1 package dry yeast
¼ teaspoon salt
¼ teaspoon ground cardamom
⅓ cup sugar
 3 cups all-purpose flour
 6 Tablespoons evaporated milk
½ cup butter (¼ pound), diced
½ cup, plus 2 Tablespoons hot
    water
 3 egg yolks

 1 11-ounce jar raspberry
    preserves

FILLING:

½ cup sugar
¼ cup flour
 3 Tablespoons butter, at room
    temperature
 1 teaspoon cinnamon
 2 teaspoons unsweetened cocoa
¾ cup toasted nuts, chopped

GLAZE:

 1 cup confectioners' sugar
½ teaspoon vanilla
 2 Tablespoons Grand Marnier
    or cognac
 2 Tablespoons milk

UTENSILS:

Deep-fat thermometer
Large bowl, lightly greased
Large cookie sheet, greased

Serves 12

1. Soak the raisins in sherry overnight; allow to remain at room temperature.

2. In a mixer, combine the yeast, salt, cardamom, sugar, and 1¼ cups of the flour.

3. In a small bowl, heat the milk, butter, and hot water until it is 120 degrees to 130 degrees. Be sure the butter is dissolved. Add to the yeast mixture and beat for 3 minutes. Add the egg yolks and another ½ cup of the flour. Beat an additional 3 minutes. Blend in the remaining flour to make a soft dough.

4. Place the dough on a lightly floured surface. Knead by hand until smooth, approximately 6 to 8 minutes. If you have a mixer with a dough-hook attachment, lightly flour the bowl, and knead the dough until smooth, approximately 4 minutes.

5. Set the dough in a large greased bowl; turn it over so that the dough is greased all over. Cover with plastic and a warm, damp towel. Allow to rise until doubled in bulk, approximately 1½ to 2 hours at room temperature, or overnight in the refrigerator.

6. Filling: Drain the raisins, and save the sherry for plumping other fruits. In a bowl, combine the sugar, flour, butter, cinnamon, cocoa, nuts, and raisins, and mix until crumbly.

7. Turn the dough out on an unfloured surface. Roll and stretch it into a rectangle 40 inches by 8 inches by 1/4 inch thick. (If the surface is too small, roll the dough in two pieces and pinch together afterwards.) Spread the dough lightly with the raspberry preserves. Sprinkle the filling over the dough to within 1 inch of the edges. Roll up jelly-roll fashion into a narrow roll 2 inches in diameter and 40 inches long.

8. Shaping the duck: Seal one end of the roll, and twist it a few times. Cut off a 3-inch length from each end of the roll and set aside. Shape the roll into a large "S" on the greased cookie sheet. Use about one-third of the roll for the head and neck, and the other two-thirds for the body. Shape the duck loosely with the coils close together, but not touching. With the two pieces set aside, shape the beak, tail, and feet, and put into place. Moisten the dough slightly to attach them. Cover with plastic and a warm damp towel, and allow to rise in a warm place until double in bulk, approximately 50 minutes.

9. Baking: Preheat the oven to 325 degrees. Bake for 35 to 45 minutes, or until golden brown. Turn the pan to insure even browning.

10. Glaze: While the cake is baking, combine the confectioners' sugar and vanilla in a small bowl. Add the liqueur and enough milk to make the mixture smooth and creamy for easy spreading.

11. Remove the "duck" from the oven and, while it is still warm, paint with the glaze.

TO SERVE — Place in brown paper bag in a 200-degree oven until warm. Cut into slices.

AHEAD — May be prepared one day ahead.

FREEZE — May be frozen. Reheat in brown paper bag in 200-degree oven.

*These are ambrosia. The raisins should be
soaked overnight so they plump up, and the
dough should be made one day before baking.*

MINIATURE STRUDEL PINWHEELS

2 cups yellow raisins
¾ cup orange juice

DOUGH:
1 1-pound can solid vegetable
    shortening
4 Tablespoons sugar
3 egg yolks
5 cups flour, sifted
1 teaspoon baking powder
⅛ teaspoon salt
1 cup orange juice

        *   *   *

1 7-ounce jar marshmallow cream

        *   *   *

1 11-ounce jar strawberry, rasp-
    berry, or apricot preserves
Cinnamon sugar (½ cup sugar and
    4½ teaspoons cinnamon)
2 cups walnuts, toasted and
    chopped
2 cups coconut, flaked or shredded
3 egg whites
⅛ teaspoon cream of tartar
⅛ teaspoon salt

GARNISH:
Confectioners' sugar

Makes 5 dozen

1. Soak the raisins in orange juice overnight. Allow to remain at room temperature. Drain and save the liquid for Step 3.

2. Dough: In a mixer, cream the shortening and sugar. Add the egg yolks and blend well. Sift the flour, baking powder, and salt together. Alternate adding the flour and the orange juice to the creamed mixture; blend well. Wrap the dough in plastic, and refrigerate overnight.

3. In a bowl, dilute the marshmallow cream with the orange juice from Step 1 so that it will spread easily.

4. Assembling: The strudel is prepared in four rolls. Divide the dough in four parts, and refrigerate three of them. Roll one part of the dough into a rectangle 1/8 inch thick, and about 6 inches by 16 inches. Spread a quarter of the marshmallow and orange juice mixture on top of the dough. Spoon two narrow strips of

the preserves on top of the marshmallow layer. Sprinkle with 2 Tablespoons of cinnamon sugar, and ¼ each of the nuts, raisins, and coconut. Roll lengthwise, jelly-roll fashion, and place on a greased cookie sheet. Repeat the procedure with the remaining three parts of dough, placing two on each cookie sheet. Beat the egg whites until foamy, and add the cream of tartar, salt, and 2 Tablespoons of the cinnamon sugar. Paint the four strudel rolls with this mixture.

5. Baking: Preheat the oven to 350 degrees. Bake for 18 minutes. Remove from the oven. With scissors, cut part way through into 1-inch slices, to make it easier to slice when it has finished baking. Return to the oven, and bake for an additional 12 minutes, or until browned. Total baking time is approximately 30 minutes. Finish cutting through each slice with a knife. With a spatula, remove the slices to a wire rack to cool.

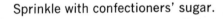

 Sprinkle with confectioners' sugar.

 May be prepared one week ahead. Store in a tightly covered container, between sheets of waxed paper.

 May be frozen.

TOURTE AUX POMMES
(Apple Tart)

PASTRY SHELL:
- ½ cup sweet butter (¼ pound), at room temperature
- ½ cup sugar
- 2 eggs
- 1½ cups flour
- 1½ teaspoons baking powder
- 1 teaspoon vanilla

FILLING:
- 4 pounds green apples, coarsely grated or sliced thin
- ¾ cup sugar
- 3 Tablespoons lemon juice
- 1 Tablespoon grated lemon rind

* * *

- 1½ cups almonds, coarsely chopped

TOPPING:
- ¾ cup dark brown sugar, firmly packed
- 2 Tablespoons flour
- 1 Tablespoon butter
- 2 Tablespoons Grand Marnier, or cognac

SERVE WITH:
Crème Fraîche or
Crème Chantilly

UTENSIL:
10-inch spring-form baking pan, lightly greased

Serves 8

NOTE: *The pastry shell should be prepared a day ahead.*

1. Pastry Shell: In a mixer, cream the butter and sugar. Beat in the eggs, one at a time. Add the flour, baking powder, and vanilla, and blend well. Press the dough onto the bottom, and up the sides of the pan. Cover with plastic and refrigerate overnight.

2. Filling: Combine the apples, sugar, lemon juice to taste, and the lemon rind. Spoon the apple mixture into the pastry shell.

3. Baking: Preheat the oven to 450 degrees. Bake 10 to 15 minutes. Reduce the heat to 350 degrees, and bake for another 15 minutes. Remove the tourte from the oven, and spread the chopped nuts on top of it. The topping can be prepared during this first half hour of baking.

4. Topping: Mix the brown sugar, flour, butter, and liqueur until it is crumbly. Spread over the chopped nuts.

5. Bake an additional hour. (Total baking time is 1½ hours.) Remove from the oven, and allow to cool.

Remove sides of springform pan. Serve with Crème Fraîche or Crème Chantilly.

Tourte may be prepared one day ahead and refrigerated. Topping may be prepared three days ahead.

Do not freeze.

CRÈME CHANTILLY
(Flavored Whipped Cream)

1 cup whipping cream
2 Tablespoons cognac, rum, or
  Grand Marnier

Whip the cream until it forms soft peaks. Add the liqueur or spirit, and continue whipping until it reaches the desired thickness.

CRÈME FRAÎCHE
(French Cream)

1 part sour cream
2 parts whipping cream

UTENSILS:

Thermometer
Crock or bowl

NOTE: *An excellent culture of creams to keep on hand for recipes calling for whipped or sour cream. It won't curdle when cooked, and is a delicious topping for soups, fruits and desserts.*

1. Combine creams in a saucepan. Heat to 110 degrees.

2. Place in a bowl or crock, allow to sit at room temperature over-'night, or until it thickens. Refrigerate.

3. To start a new batch, place ⅓ cup of the old batch in a glass measuring cup. Add whipping cream to fill the cup. Repeat Steps 1 and 2. It will keep for 2 weeks.

PETITS ROULEAUX DE NOIX AU CHOCOLAT
(Miniature Chocolate-Coated Nutrolls)

NUTROLL:

6 eggs, separated
1 cup sugar
1 cup nuts, finely ground
2 teaspoons baking powder
¼ teaspoon cream of tartar
¼ teaspoon salt

FLAVORED WHIPPED CREAM:

2 cups whipping cream
4 Tablespoons rum or cognac

CRÈME DE BEURRE AU CHOCOLAT:

(Chocolate Butter Cream)

1 cup unsalted butter (½ pound), at room temperature
1 egg yolk
½ cup confectioners' sugar
3 Tablespoons unsweetened cocoa

½ teaspoon vanilla
3 Tablespoons rum or cognac
1 teaspoon instant coffee granules

* * *

Additional confectioners' sugar for assembling

GARNISH:

2 cups nuts, coarsely chopped and toasted

UTENSILS:

11-inch by 16-inch jelly-roll pan
Waxed paper
Damp dishtowel
Small decorative paper cupcake liners

Serves 8 to 10

1. Nutroll: In a mixer, cream the egg yolks and 3/4 of a cup of the sugar until lemon-colored. Add the ground nuts and baking powder, and blend thoroughly.

   In a separate bowl, beat the egg whites until foamy, and add the cream of tartar and salt. Continue beating until soft peaks form. Add the remaining ¼ cup sugar, 1 Tablespoon at a time, and continue beating until the peaks are stiff and shiny. Fold into the batter. Grease the jelly-roll pan, and line it with waxed paper, allowing 3 inches extra to overlap at each end. Grease the waxed paper. Spread the mixture in the pan evenly.

2. Baking: Preheat the oven to 350 degrees. Bake 20 minutes. Remove from the oven, and cover the pan immediately with the damp dishtowel. Allow to cool. Refrigerate with the dishtowel

until ready to assemble. Prepare Crème de Beurre au Chocolat and Flavored Whipped Cream while the nutroll is baking.

3. Crème de Beurre au Chocolat: In a mixer, cream the butter and egg yolk. Add the ½ cup of confectioners' sugar gradually, and blend thoroughly. Add the cocoa, vanilla, rum or cognac, and instant coffee granules. Mix well. Add enough cream so the mixture can be spread easily. Refrigerate.

4. Flavored Whipped Cream: Whip the cream until it is in soft peaks. Add the rum or cognac and continue beating until stiff. Refrigerate.

5. Assembling: To remove the nutroll from the pan, take off the towel, and sieve confectioners' sugar generously over the cake. Loosen the edges of the nutroll with a spatula, and turn it out onto fresh waxed paper. Carefully peel off the cooked waxed paper. Cut the cake lengthwise into two long strips, and set one aside. Spread one strip with half the flavored whipped cream. Roll jelly-roll fashion, using the waxed paper at the side to steady and guide it. Repeat with the second strip. Chill 1 to 2 hours.

6. Cover both nutrolls with the chocolate butter cream, and sprinkle generously with the nuts. Refrigerate for 1 to 2 hours.

Variation: Large Nutroll
Do not cut the cake in half lengthwise. Fill with the flavored whipped cream and fresh strawberries. With a pastry bag, pipe eight rosettes of whipped cream down the center of the nutroll and top each one with a strawberry, a crystallized violet, or a toasted nut half.

Cut each roll diagonally in ¾-inch slices.
Stand each slice in a paper cupcake liner.

May be prepared unsliced two days ahead through Step 6 and refrigerated.
The nutroll may be prepared one week ahead, and refrigerated in the pan covered by the damp dishtowel.

May be frozen after Step 6 and carefully wrapped in freezer paper. Slice while frozen.

Perfect for Thanksgiving, Christmas, New Year's or any festive winter night! The raisins should be soaked overnight before making the pudding.

PERFECT PLUM PUDDING

1 cup cream sherry
1 cup raisins

* * *

1 cup carrots, uncooked
 (approximately 2 carrots,
 uncooked, cut into chunks)
1 cup dates, pitted
1 cup flour
1 teaspoon salt
1 teaspoon baking soda
1 teaspoon cinnamon
¼ teaspoon ground cloves
½ teaspoon nutmeg
1 cup margarine or suet, at
 room temperature
1 cup sugar
1 cup breadcrumbs
1 cup milk
2 Tablespoons cognac

GARNISH:
 2 Tablespoons cognac, for
  flaming
Holly leaves

UTENSILS:
Grinder
2-quart steam pudding mold with
 lid, or 2-quart ovenproof baking
 dish, greased
Steamer, or, if steamer is not available, a 5- to 6-quart saucepan
 and 1 small pyrex custard dish

BRANDY SAUCE:
½ cup butter or margarine,
 at room temperature
1 cup confectioners' sugar,
 sifted
½ teaspoon salt
1 to 2 ounces cognac

Serves 8

NOTE: *The total cooking time is 4 hours.*

1. Soak the raisins in sherry overnight. Allow to remain at room temperature. Drain and save the sherry for plumping other fruits.

2. In a food grinder, finely grind the raisins, carrots, and dates.

3. Combine the flour, salt, baking soda, cinnamon, ground cloves, and nutmeg.

4. In a mixer, cream the margarine or suet and sugar. Blend in the flour and spice mixture. Add the ground raisins, carrots, dates, breadcrumbs, milk, and cognac, and mix well. Pour into the greased mold, and cover with a lid or seal with heavy duty foil.

5. Set the mold in the steamer. If a steamer is not available, set the small Pyrex custard dish upside down in the center of a large sauce-pan, and balance the mold on top of it. Carefully fill the pan with water until it reaches the bottom of the mold. Steam for 1 hour. Remove from heat, cool, and refrigerate if it is not to be served that day.

6. Steam for an additional 3 hours.

7. Brandy Sauce: In a mixer, cream the butter, sugar, and salt, and beat until light and fluffy. Beat in the cognac.

 Serve warm, with Brandy Sauce in a separate bowl. Set the mold on a platter, and garnish with holly leaves. Flame with cognac at the table.

 May be prepared one year ahead through Step 5 and refrigerated.
Brandy Sauce may be prepared three days ahead.

 May be frozen. Defrost for 30 minutes, then steam for 3 hours.

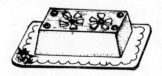

I was never a fan of fruitcake, until a student shared this family recipe. Fruitcake is made in batches to give as Christmas presents, and this one is enough for sixteen friends, plus one for yourself. Make it at least two weeks in advance so it "ages." Soak the dried fruits overnight before you start making the fruit-cake.

PERFECT FRUIT CAKE

1 24-ounce bottle of dry sherry
2 pounds yellow raisins
1 pound currants
½ pound dried apricots, cut into julienne strips
2 pounds dates, pitted
1½ pounds candied cherries, halved
1½ pounds candied pineapple, cut into wedges
1½ pounds walnut halves, toasted
1½ pounds pecan halves, toasted
1 cup flour

BATTER:

1 1/6 cups butter, at room temperature
3½ cups sugar
7 eggs, at room temperature
2½ cups flour
1½ teaspoons baking soda
1 teaspoon cinnamon
1 teaspoon nutmeg

½ teaspoon ground cloves
½ teaspoon ground allspice
1 Tablespoon vanilla
⅓ cup bourbon
1⅛ cups semi-dry white wine
1 Tablespoon grated orange peel
1 Tablespoon grated lemon peel

* * *

1 to 2 Tablespoons solid vegetable shortening
Brown paper

GARNISH:

Red and green candied cherries
Candied pineapple wedges
Nuts

UTENSILS:

17 1-pound foil loaf pans, or cupcake pans, greased
Roasting pan

Makes 17 1-pound loaves, or 170 miniatures

1. Place the sherry in a large bowl, and add the raisins, currants, apricots, and dates. Allow to plump up at room temperature overnight

2. Drain the fruits, and save the sherry for plumping other fruits. Using your hands, mix the fruits carefully, and be sure they are all separated from each other. Add the walnuts and pecans, and mix thoroughly. Add the flour, and mix with your hands until fruits and nuts are evenly coated. Set aside.

3. Batter: In a mixer, cream the butter and sugar. Add the eggs, one at a time, beating well after each one. Add the flour, baking soda, cinnamon, nutmeg, cloves, allspice, vanilla, bourbon, and wine. Blend well. Add the orange and lemon peels, and mix thoroughly. Pour the batter over fruit-nut mixture, and mix carefully with your hands.

4. Cut pieces of brown paper to fit the bottom of each baking pan. Grease both sides of the brown paper, and place in greased loaf pans. Pour the batter into the pans, filling them to the top.

5. Baking: Preheat the oven to 250 degrees. Place the loaf pans on a rack in the upper third of the oven. Fill the roasting pan with hot water, and place it on the lowest rack of the oven. Keep refilling it with hot water, if necessary, while the fruit cake is baking so it does not dry out. Bake eight loaves at a time for 2½ to 3 hours or until a toothpick comes out clean.

6. Allow the fruit cakes to cool in their pans on a rack, then loosen and turn out. Remove the brown paper, and put the cakes back into the pans.

7. Garnish the cakes with cherries, pineapple wedges, and nuts. Wrap in colored plastic for gifts.

Variation: Miniature Fruit Cakes
Line greased cupcake pans with greased paper cup liners and bake twenty-four at a time in a 240-degree oven for 1 hour; or bake in an 8-inch greased tube pan, lined with greased brown paper, for 2½ to 3 hours.

 Cut into thin slices; overlap on a serving platter.

 Must be made two weeks ahead, and kept at room temperature to age. Will keep three months in the refrigerator.

 Wrap in heavy foil. May be frozen for one year.

One of the marvelous frozen custards from Italy. It should be made several days ahead.

CRÈME GLACÉE À L'ITALIENNE
(Italian Frozen Custard with Chocolate Sauce)

4 egg whites
⅛ teaspoon cream of tartar
⅛ teaspoon salt
4 Tablespoons sugar

* * *

2 cups whipping cream
2 teaspoons sugar
1 Tablespoon vanilla
2 Tablespoons Galliano liqueur

* * *

1 cup chocolate chips
½ cup toasted slivered almonds

CHOCOLATE SAUCE:
9 ounces milk or dark chocolate
¼ to ½ cup whipping cream
2 Tablespoons Galliano liqueur

GARNISH:
Maraschino cherries with stems

UTENSILS:
Freezer-proof serving bowl or individual goblets

Serves 6 to 8

1. In a mixer, beat the egg whites until foamy and add the cream of tartar and salt. Continue beating until soft peaks form. Add the 4 Tablespoons of sugar, 1 Tablespoon at a time, and continue beating until the peaks are stiff and shiny.

2. Beat the whipping cream until it thickens. Add the 2 teaspoons of sugar, vanilla, and Galliano liqueur and continue beating until stiff. Fold into the meringue mixture, and pour into the freezer-proof bowl. Freeze only until icy crystals form.

3. In the top of a double boiler, melt the chocolate chips over hot water. Add the almonds. While the chocolate mixture is hot, fold it into the icy meringue mixture. Blend thoroughly and carefully. (Small chunks of chocolate will form.) Place in a bowl, cover, and freeze.

4. Chocolate Sauce: In a small saucepan, heat the chocolate and 1 Tablespoon of the cream over low heat until melted, stirring constantly. Remove from the heat and add Galliano liqueur, and more cream if a thinner consistency is desired. Serve warm over Crème Glacée à l'Italienne.

Serve in a glass bowl or individual goblets and garnish with cherries.

Should be made through Step 3 several days ahead and allowed to mellow.

May be frozen after Step 3 for two months.

A versatile lemon soufflé that can be a filling for chocolate cups, hollowed-out lemons, or a pastry shell. It can even be served on its own as a soufflé!

SOUFFLÉ AU CITRON GLACÉ
(Cold Lemon Soufflé)

1 Tablespoon, plus 1 teaspoon
  unflavored gelatin
2 Tablespoons cold water
Grated rind of 4 lemons
½ cup fresh lemon juice, strained
1 cup sugar

*   *   *

1 cup egg whites (approximately
  8), at room temperature
⅛ teaspoon cream of tartar
⅛ teaspoon salt
2 Tablespoons Galliano liqueur

1 cup cream, whipped
1 recipe Coulettes au Chocolat
  (see page 276), or 6 lemon shells,
  or a 10-inch pastry shell,
  prebaked

GARNISH:

Candied violets
Mint leaves
Whipped cream

Serves 4 to 6

1. In a small saucepan, dissolve the gelatin in cold water. Add the lemon rind, lemon juice, and ¾ of a cup of the sugar. Stir over low heat until the gelatin is dissolved. Transfer to a 3-quart bowl. Allow to cool and then chill until the mixture thickens.
2. In the mixer, beat the egg whites until foamy, and add the cream of tartar and salt. Continue beating until soft peaks form. Add the remaining ¼ cup of sugar gradually, and continue beating until the peaks are stiff and shiny. Fold in the lemon mixture, Galliano, and whipped cream.
3. Fill the chocolate cups, hollowed-out lemons, or pastry shell, chill.

Decorate with whipped cream rosettes, candied violets, and mint leaves.

May be prepared one day ahead through Step 2.

May be frozen in chocolate cups or lemons. Defrost 30 minutes before serving.

*Not hard to make, but hard to keep around
once they are made.*

VIENNESE SANDWICH COOKIES

1 cup butter (½ pound), at
  room temperature
1 cup sugar
1 egg yolk
1 teaspoon vanilla
2 cups flour

     *   *   *

Sugar for dipping

FILLING:
2 cups confectioners' sugar
½ cup butter (¼ pound), at
  room temperature

2 to 4 Tablespoons lemon juice

GLAZE:
2 squares semi-sweet chocolate
1 Tablespoon butter

GARNISH:
Finely chopped nuts or coconut or
  colored cake decorations

Makes 3 dozen

1. In a mixer, cream together the butter and sugar. Add the egg yolk and vanilla, blend in the flour, and mix thoroughly. Cover the bowl and refrigerate for at least 2 hours.
2. Make 72 balls of dough about the size of a small walnut, and place them 2 inches apart on cookie sheets. Dip the bottom of a small glass in granulated sugar, and use it to flatten each ball of dough to a thickness of 1/8 inch.
3. Baking: Preheat the oven to 325 degrees. Bake 10 to 12 minutes. Use a spatula to remove the cookies to a wire rack to cool.
4. Filling: In a small bowl, cream the confectioners' sugar and butter, and add lemon juice to taste. Spread a spoonful on half of the cookies. Cover each one with another cookie.
5. Glaze: In a small saucepan, melt the butter and chocolate over low heat just until melted. Dip an edge of each double-cookie into the melted glaze, then into any of the garnishes desired.

May be prepared one week ahead, and stored in a tightly covered container in layers (between sheets of waxed paper).

May be frozen.

Fast, easy, and fantastic, and they don't have to be baked! Fill them with Soufflé Au Citron Glacé, ice cream, or mousse.

COULETTES AU CHOCOLAT
(Chocolate Cups)

9 ounces milk or semi-sweet chocolate
1 Tablespoon butter
1 Tablespoon Galliano or Grand Marnier liqueur

UTENSILS:
Paper cupcake pan liners
2-inch or larger cupcake pan to fit paper liners.

Makes 24 to 36, depending on the size of cupcake pan used

1. In a small saucepan, heat the chocolate and butter over low heat until almost melted. Remove from the heat and add the liqueur. Stir until the chocolate is completely melted.

2. Set the pan liners in the cupcake pan. Spoon heated chocolate into the bottom of each paper cup. With the back of the spoon, paint the chocolate up the sides so the paper cup is completely coated.

3. Place in the freezer until the chocolate has hardened.

4. Carefully pull away the paper cups. Fill with Citron Glacé, mousse, or other filling and refrigerate. If using ice cream, freeze until ready to serve.

Set chocolate cups into fresh paper cupcake liners.

May be frozen.

*A modest step into home distilling for pro-
ducing a dessert sauce that is potent and perfect for pouring over Bombe Al Zabaglione,
ice cream, sponge cake, or poached fruits. It
must be made two weeks ahead. The alcohol
can be purchased at the local drug store with
a prescription.*

ADVOCKAAT LIQUEUR
(Egg Nog Liqueur)

   8 large egg yolks
1½ cups sugar, minus 1 teaspoon
     (superfine sugar, if possible)
   1 vanilla bean, split
2⅓ cups evaporated milk
   ¾ cup 190-proof alcohol

UTENSIL:

Large bottle with top

Makes 2 cups

1. In a mixer, beat the yolks, sugar, and pulp scraped from the inside
   of the vanilla bean until it is lemon colored and the sugar granules
   are completely dissolved. Save the hull of the vanilla bean.

2. Slowly add the milk, and stir well. Pour into a pan, and cook over
   low heat until it is slightly thickened, stirring constantly with a
   whisk.

3. Remove from the heat and add the alcohol. Stir well. Pour into
   a large bottle, insert the hull of the vanilla bean, close tightly.
   Age for two weeks at room temperature, shaking bottle every
   four days.

Pour over desserts.

Must be made two weeks ahead. Keeps
indefinitely.

A superb chocolate shell that can be kept in the freezer, ready to be thawed on a half-hour's notice. It must be made one day ahead.

BOMBE AL ZABAGLIONE
(Chocolate Shell Filled with Zabaglione)

¼ pound unsweetened chocolate
2 eggs, separated
¼ cup sugar, plus 5 Tablespoons
4 Tablespoons sweet butter, melted
⅛ teaspoon cream of tartar
⅛ teaspoon salt
¼ teaspoon vanilla
1½ cups cream, whipped

ZABAGLIONE:
8 egg yolks
½ cup Galliano liqueur
½ cup whipping cream, not whipped

SERVE WITH:
Advockaat Liqueur (see page 277)

UTENSILS:
1½ quart mold, with cover if possible, melon mold, or metal bowl, lightly greased
Plastic wrap
2-inch paint brush
Bowl with ice cubes

Serves 8

1. Bombe: In a double-boiler, heat the chocolate until melted. In a mixer, beat 2 egg yolks with ¼ cup of the sugar until it is thickened and lemon colored. Add the melted chocolate and butter, and stir well. Beat the egg whites, adding the cream of tartar and salt. When frothy, stir into the chocolate mixture. Add the vanilla, and fold in ½ cup of whipped cream. Line the greased mold with plastic wrap. Using the paint brush, coat the mold with the mixture, leaving the center hollow. Freeze. (The bombe should be hardened before filling it.)

2. Zabaglione: Put 8 yolks in a mixing bowl. Beat lightly. Place bowl over a pan of simmering water. Beat rapidly with a whisk or electric hand beater, and add the Galliano liqueur and cream. When it is thick and foamy, remove the bowl from the pan of boiling water, and continue to beat over ice until it is cool and thick. Fold in the remaining cup of whipped cream, and refrigerate.

3. Assembling: When the bombe has hardened, spoon the zabaglione into the hollow of the mold, and freeze, preferably overnight.

Variations: The Bombe may be filled with any flavor of sherbert, ice cream or mousse. Individual bombes may be served in small pyrex custard cups. The Zabaglione may be served over fresh strawberries, or in a hollowed-out pineapple shell with pineapple chunks.

Place a hot towel briefly on the outside of the mold, and pull the plastic wrap gently until the bombe can be unmolded onto a cold platter. May be returned to the freezer until ready to serve. Pour Advockaat Liqueur (see page 277) over the bombe. Slice at the table.

Must be prepared one day ahead through Step 3.

May be frozen for several months.

Like the Taj Mahal, baking ice cream still makes for a dessert that many people consider a wonder. These should be assembled and frozen at least one day before serving.

INDIVIDUAL BAKED ALASKAS

GRASSHOPPER CAKE:

1½ cups flour
2 cups sugar
¾ cup sweetened cocoa
1½ teaspoons salt
1 teaspoon baking powder
1⅓ cups butter, at room
   temperature
4 eggs
2 teaspoons vanilla
2 Tablespoons corn syrup
2 cups nuts, chopped coarsely,
   toasted

ICE CREAM:

1 pint chocolate ice cream
1 pint coffee ice cream
1 pint cherry-vanilla ice cream

MERINGUE:

6 to 7 egg whites (2/3 cup)
¼ teaspoon cream of tartar
¼ teaspoon salt
2/3 cup sugar
½ teaspoon vanilla

GARNISH:

8 sugar cubes
8 maraschino cherries
Lemon extract

UTENSILS:

9-inch by 13-inch baking pan, lightly greased
Cupcake pan
8 paper cupcake liners

Serves 8

1. Grasshopper Cake: Sift the flour, sugar, cocoa, salt, and baking powder into a mixing bowl. Add the butter, eggs, vanilla, and corn syrup. Mix the ingredients thoroughly for about 2 minutes on the lowest mixing speed. Fold in the nuts. Spread the mixture into the baking pan.

2. Baking: Preheat the oven to 350 degrees. Bake for 40 or 45 minutes. Cake should look moist. (Do not overbake.) Remove from the oven and allow to cool. Cut into 3-inch rounds using a cup or glass. Set aside.

3. Ice Cream: Set the paper cupcake liners into the cupcake pan. Fill each cup ⅓ full with chocolate ice cream, and freeze thor-

oughly. Add a layer of coffee ice cream, and freeze thoroughly. Add the final layer of cherry-vanilla ice cream, and cover the cups with plastic to protect them from ice crystals. Freeze thoroughly.

4. Meringue: Beat the egg whites until foamy, and add the cream of tartar and salt. Continue beating until soft peaks form. Add the sugar, 1 Tablespoon at a time, and continue beating until the peaks are stiff and shiny. Add vanilla toward the end of beating.

5. Assembling: Set the 3-inch rounds of cake onto a cookie sheet. Peel off the cupcake liners from the frozen ice cream, and set each ice cream mold onto the center of a cake round. Quickly cover the cake and ice cream with meringue, carefully masking where the cake and ice cream meet. Swirl the meringue into peaks. Set the cookie sheet in the freezer.

TO SERVE

Preheat the oven to 500 degrees. Take the Alaskas directly from the freezer to the oven, and bake for 1 minute, or until the meringue is lightly browned. Insert a sugar cube into the hollow of each maraschino cherry. Drizzle lemon extract over the sugar, and set the cherry on top of the Baked Alaska. Ignite sugar with a lighted match.

AHEAD

Alaskas may be browned and frozen one day before serving.

FREEZE

Grasshopper cake and ice cream may be frozen for two months.

GRASSHOPPER STICKS

Prepare and bake a Grasshopper Cake.
(see page 280)

MINT FROSTING:
  2 cups confectioners' sugar, sifted
  4 Tablespoons butter, at room
    temperature
  2 Tablespoons milk
  1 to 2 teaspoons mint extract
Few drops green food coloring

MELTED CHOCOLATE
MIXTURE:
  1½ squares unsweetened
     chocolate
  1½ Tablespoons butter

Makes 40

1. Mint Frosting: Combine the sugar, butter, milk, mint extract, and food coloring, and beat well. Frosting should be pale green. Spread over the cake. When the frosting is set, cut partially through into 40 bars.

2. Melt the chocolate and butter. With a pastry brush, paint the mixture over the mint frosting. When the chocolate is hardened, follow the indentations and cut through into bars.

May be prepared one week ahead and stored in tightly covered container between sheets of wax paper.

May be frozen.

INDEX